If you're wondering why you need this new edition of *The Basics of American Politics* here are 10 good reasons!

1. Chapter 3, The Executive Branch: The Presidency and Bureaucracy, has been completely updated to include coverage of President Barack Obama.

2. A new box, "Barack Obama: On the Presidency," features an interview with the President shortly after taking office.

3. New coverage of the Bernie Madoff scandal analyzes the regulatory practices of the Securities and Exchange Commission.

4. An updated chapter on the Congress that includes topics such as Arlen Spector's switch to the Democrats, Nancy Pelosi's House cleaning and the Republicans' upset win of Ted Kennedy's Senate seat.

5. A new case study in Chapter 4 analyzes the 2009 House Climate Bill aimed at controlling global warming.

6. An updated "Presidents and the Court" box looks at the appointment of

Justice Sonia Sotomayor to the Supreme Court.

7. A new feature in the Voters and Political Parties chapter analyzes Barack Obama's use of the Internet during the 2008 presidential campaign.

8. New statistics from the 2008 presidential election examines voter turnout, party spending, and candidate fundraising.

9. Chapter 8, Interest Groups and the Media, has been thoroughly updated to include new statistics on the top donors to Barack Obama's presidential campaign, and the top PAC contributors to candidates in 2008.

10. New features in Chapter 8 look at media mogul Rupert Murdoch, political satirist Jon Stewart's *The Daily Show*, and former congressional members turned healthcare lobbyists.

PEARSON

The Basics of American Politics

FOURTEENTH EDITION

Gary Wasserman
Georgetown University

Longman

Boston Columbus Indianapolis New York San Francisco Upper Saddle River
Amsterdam Cape Town Dubai London Madrid Milan Munich Paris Montreal Toronto
Delhi Mexico City São Paulo Sydney Hong Kong Seoul Singapore Taipei Tokyo

Dedicated To: Ann, Daniel, Adrienne, Laura
To My Students, Arab and American

Editor-in-Chief: Eric Stano
Editorial Assistant: Elizabeth Alimena
Supplements Editor: Donna Garnier
Media Producer: Regina Vertiz
Marketing Manager: Lindsey Prudhomme
Production Manager: Jacqueline A. Martin
Project Coordination, Text Design, and Electronic Page Makeup: Pre-Press PMG
Cover Design Manager: Wendy Ann Fredericks
Cover Designer: Nancy Sacks
Cover Photo: © Stockbyte/Getty Images
Manufacturing Manager: Mary Fischer
Printer and Binder: RR Donnelley & Sons Company/Crawfordsville
Cover Printer: RR Donnelley & Sons Company/Crawfordsville

Library of Congress Cataloging-in-Publication Data
Wasserman, Gary
   The basics of American politics / Gary Wasserman.—14th ed.
      p. cm.
   Includes bibliographical references and index.
   ISBN-13: 978-0-205-78203-1
   ISBN-10: 0-205-78203-5
   1. United States—Politics and government. I. Title.
   JK276.W36 2011
   320.473—dc22   2009050586

1 2 3 4 5 6 7 8 9 10—DOC—13 12 11 10

www.pearsonhighered.com

Longman
is an imprint of

ISBN-13: 978-0-205-78203-1
ISBN-10:   0-205-78203-5

CONTENTS

PREFACE

A couple editions ago a teacher using *The Basics of American Politics* asked one of his students what he thought of the text. The reply: "Well, at least he gets to the point."

If *The Basics* remains true to its origins in helping undergraduates in the introductory class to American government, it is because it is still brief, current, and readable. This is not a book that says everything needed to teach American politics. Hopefully it says enough to start conversations on the subject and encourage students to learn more.

This edition has taken an extra year in order to reflect recent, exciting political changes. Front and center is the Obama presidency. From reviving an economy in meltdown to abandoning unpopular foreign policies, this new administration is covered. In addition there are new approaches by the executive on lobbyists, secrecy, and media outreach, along with policy czars, the creative use of the Internet, and a new First Lady.

The 111th Congress is a big part of these changes. Our discussion includes a description of the new Congress and its leaders, the unprecedented economic stimulus, health reform, bitter partisan divisions, grassroots lobbying, and a case study of the legislation to restrain global warming.

The 2008 election affected all of this. It bolstered the Democratic majorities and raised the argument that there is a party realignment underway. Highlights of the election include the return of young voters, the improvement in turnout, the issues and strategies of the two parties, fundraising, and a case study of Triple O—Obama's Online Operation.

The judiciary hasn't been quiet. It has already seen a new female justice on the Supreme Court, a conservative Roberts Court navigating a liberal government, and changes in affirmative action and in views toward the civil liberties of those caught in the struggle with terrorism.

The upheavals in journalism have merited a completely revised chapter on the media, discussing the decline of newspapers and the ascent of cable news, blogs, twitters, and YouTube. This new media universe includes names like Jon Stewart, Rupert Murdoch, Rush

Limbaugh, 'No Drama 'Obama, and Microsoft vs. Google, as well as a perspective of what all this means for the nation's politics.

These changes are energized by a host of new boxes and stories, such as: Rupert Murdoch's Politics, Is There Life After Congress? The Daily Show Shapes Political Journalism, World Democracies Dissent on U.S. Freedoms, The SEC and the Bernie Madoff Scandal, Obama's Top Donors, How to Tell a Liberal from a Conservative, The Prime Time Prez, Is the Vanishing Young Voter Reappearing? Nancy Pelosi: Madam Speaker, and Barack Obama: On the Presidency.

ACKNOWLEDGEMENTS

Thanks go to a number of people who helped with this edition. My brother, Ed, took time away from teaching journalism ethics at Washington and Lee to help on the media chapter. Excellent research assistance was provided by Elliott Fullmer and Seth Peterson, both of whom reflect the best in Georgetown's graduate school education. Judy Press put together the index; cartoons were drawn by Kjell Nisson-Maki and Mike Philips. Reviewers of this edition included Glynn Ellis of Georgia University, Ervin H. Gilliam of Draughons Junior College, Francis Neely of San Francisco State University, and Rob Wright of the College of Santa Fe.

Production was overseen by Jackie Martin, Steve McDonald, and Aparna Yellai. Eric Stano and Elizabeth Alimena of Longman were supportive and insightful, as usual. I appreciate the support of my colleagues and staff, especially Dean Mehran Kamrava, at Georgetown University's innovative School of Foreign Service in Qatar

My family, especially Ann, helped by keeping me centered, more or less.

Any mistakes are still mine.

What Is Politics?

The First Day of Class

*This class sucks. The first day of American government the pro-
fessor comes in and asks us to sit in alphabetical order. Do you
believe this? Of course all the freshman sheep shuffle off to
their seats. But since I am sitting next to an attractive lady,
I don't want to move. So I ask him whether he might want us
to wear Mickey Mouse t-shirts to his next class. A bit too cute,
perhaps, because he asks me if I think politics goes on in the
classroom.*

*I reply, "No, we study politics, but very few of us actually
participate."*

*"Incorrect," he responds, and would I mind leaving the
class?*

*"Well, yes, I would mind," I say, "considering the costs of
my first seven years at college."*

"Will you please leave?" he says.

*OK, so I start to go. He then stops me and asks why I am
departing. I remind him that while he may have missed it, he has
just asked me to remove myself. But he persists and asks why I'm
doing what he asked. Maybe I have missed something. I respond
that he is the kahuna here. I am just a sometimes- paying student.*

*"In other words," he says, "my position as the teacher
influenced you to do something you didn't want to do. In fact,
it influenced everyone to sit in alphabetical order. So we just
saw a process of influence in this classroom that affected a
group of people. That's politics. . . ."*

"Oh, by the way, do you have a cigarette?"

"Hey, you can't smoke in here."

*"You mean my power as a teacher is limited. In this case by
your right to have a nonsmoking classroom. And of course all
of you have other rights that limit any teacher's power. If this
gentleman here didn't have such a good sense of humor he
might bring me before some university committee for harassment. That too is politics."*

This story reveals a process of influence between the teacher and the students. Their relationship is not only an educational one but a political one as well. It is political in the sense of political scientist Harold Lasswell's famous definition of *politics* as *the process of who gets what, when, and how.* The teacher (who) gets the student to leave the class (what) immediately (when) by using his authority to persuade and threaten him (how). This indeed is politics.

Our definition of politics centers on actions among a number of people involving influence. How do people get others to do what they wish? How does our society or any group (like that classroom) distribute its valued things, such as wealth, prestige, and security? Who gets these *values*, and how? The dialogue hints at answers in the concepts of *power* and *authority*.

Politics and Power

Note that the teacher influenced the student to do something he didn't want to do—leave the class. The teacher demonstrated his power over the student, though limited by the student's rights. *Power* is simply the *ability to influence another's behavior.* Power is getting people to do something they wouldn't otherwise do. Power may involve force (often called *coercion*), persuasion, or rewards. But its essence is the ability to change another's actions. The more power one has over another, the greater the change, or the easier the change is to accomplish. Having more power also could mean influencing more people to change.

Power involves relationships between people and groups. When someone says that a person has a lot of power, one should ask: Power to influence whom to do what? What is the power relationship being discussed? Take the statement "The United States is the most powerful nation in the world today." If this means that because the United States has a military larger than the next 15 countries combined, it can influence any other country however it wishes, the statement is wrong. These resources (including its huge wealth and educated population) can give only a *capacity* for power. Whether this capacity is converted into effective influence will depend on the relationship in which it is applied. Certainly the United States has far greater military capabilities than any adversary in Afghanistan. Yet attempts to stabilize a friendly government seem beyond America's power. The limits of power were shown by the costs—casualties and money—as well as the uncertain outcome of using American resources to influence Afghan behavior.

People generally do not seek power for its own sake. They want it for other values it can bring them—for security or fame or wealth. Power, like money, is a means to other ends. Most people seek money for what it can buy—whether food, clothing, or shelter. Just as some people go after money more intently than others, so too do some people seek power more than others. Of course power, like money, does not come to everyone who seeks it.

Elites

Those who do gain power often are called a political elite. *Elites* are those who get more than others of the values society has available (such as wealth and respect). We could answer the "who" part of the question "who gets what, when, and how?" by saying the elite are those who get the most.

There may be different elites depending on what value is being considered. In a small town, the owner of the largest business may be getting most of the wealth in the community, whereas the poor but honest mayor may have most of the respect. In most cases, however, the values overlap. The wealthy businessman will get plenty of respect, and the mayor will use people's respect for her to make income-producing contacts and investments.

To see the difference between an elite and the rest of us, we can look at one value (wealth) in one society (the United States). Clearly, wealth is not distributed equally among the population; some (the elite) get more than others. The top 5 percent of the American population gets more than 21 percent of the national income while the bottom 20 percent receives only 3.4 percent. More than 37 million Americans live below the official poverty line. Further, inequality seems to be growing. Between 1970 and 2008 the average annual compensation of the top 100 chief executive officers (CEOs) of American corporations went from $1.3 million—31 times the pay of an average worker—to $38 million, more than 4,500 times the pay of the average worker. (See "Guess Who's Coming to Dinner.")

Authority: Legitimate Power

Elites often reinforce their position by gaining authority. *Authority* is legitimate power. By *legitimate* we mean even more than "legal": The word implies something *accepted as right*. This correctness or *legitimacy* is connected in people's minds to both the position and the wishes of the authority. People may think something is legitimate if it was chosen using an agreed-upon procedure, such as an election. People recognize certain others as having the right to influence them in certain ways (say by leaving the class) and not in other ways (by giving them a cigarette to smoke in class). Most people feel that students *should* listen to teachers, children *should* obey their parents, and vice presidents *should* follow the wishes of presidents. People have many reasons for obeying authorities including habit, the authority figure's personal appeal, desire to be accepted by the group, and self-interest. But although they may not always follow it, people widely recognize authority as deserving obedience and that is what gives it legitimacy.

Authority is an efficient form of power. If people feel they *should* follow the wishes of an authority, then there is no need to force or even to persuade them to do so. The cost of influence is lowered for the authority. If, however, people do not respect the authority's legitimacy, its power can disappear quickly. A glance at a newspaper's front page will provide examples of authorities somewhere in the world having their legitimacy challenged. Today there are reports of Uighurs, a non-Chinese people living in western China, protesting the Chinese political and economic dominance of their region. Several days of rioting resulted in widespread damage. Because the police had lost their legitimacy for many in this Muslim ethnic group, the cost to the police of influencing behavior went up. The police could still force people off the street—and an element of force lies behind most authority—but anyone can clear a street with a gun. Only an accepted authority can do it with just a word.

PRIORITIES MENU
IRAQ WAR as of 6/10/09
$830 BILLION

OR 114 MILLION KIDS IN HEADSTART FOR 1YR

OR 128 MILLION COLLEGE SCHOLARSHIPS FOR 1YR

OR 6.5 MILLION UNITS OF PUBLIC HOUSING

SOURCE:
NATIONAL PRIORITIES,
http://www.nationalpriorities
.org

Guess Who's Coming to Dinner

Imagine one hundred people at the banquet seated at six tables. At the far right is a table set with English china and real silver, where five people sit comfortably. Next to them is another table, nicely set but nowhere near as fancy, where 15 people sit. At each of the four remaining tables 20 people sit—the one on the far left has a stained paper tablecloth and plastic knives and forks. This arrangement is analogous to the spread of income groups—from the richest 5 percent at the right to the poorest 20 percent at the left.

Twenty waiters and waitresses come in, carrying 100 delicious looking dinners, just enough, one would suppose, for each of the one hundred guests. But, amazingly, four of the waiters bring 20 dinners to the five people at the fancy table on the right. There's hardly room for all the food. (If you go over and look a little closer, you will notice that two of the waiters are obsequiously fussing and trying to arrange ten dinners in front of just one of those five.) At the next-fanciest table, with the 15 people, five waiters bring another 25 dinners. The 20 people at the third table get 25 dinners, 15 go to the fourth table, and ten to the fifth. To the 20 people at the last table (the one with the paper tablecloth), a rude and clumsy waiter brings only five dinners. At the top table there are four dinners for each person; at the bottom table, four persons for each dinner. That's approximately the way income is distributed in America—fewer than half the people get even one dinner apiece.

Source: From *Equality* by William Ryan. Copyright © 1981 by William Ryan. Reprinted by permission of Pantheon Books, a division of Random House, Inc.

Power and authority, then, are central to politics. They are also central to many other aspects of life; almost all social relations involve people trying to influence others. In a political science course, we could study the politics of a school, a hospital, or a family—who influences, who is influenced, and what is the process and limits of that influence. But most students of politics are interested in a bigger question: How does our society or nation decide who gets what, when, and how? To find out, we need to study the most important organization that decides who gets the values of our society—government.

The Need for Government

Government is one of humanity's oldest and most universal institutions. History records very few societies that have existed without government. *Anarchy* (a society without government) may be an interesting theory, but it seldom has been applied for long. Instead, people have lived under forms of government that vary from the tribal council of a Native American village to the complex party dictatorship of Communist China. Why is government so common?

One answer is that government is as common in society as is *political conflict*—the struggle over distribution of a community's valued things. These values (such as wealth) are limited, but people's demands for them are pretty unlimited. This imbalance means conflict. Whenever people have lived together, they have needed a way to regulate the disagreements. The question is not *whether* there will be conflict, but *how* the conflict will be handled. Who will decide on the rules that determine who wins and who loses? And how does one get the loser to accept the decision? The usual way to channel political conflict and thus preserve society is to have some form of government.

Most governments in the world today claim to be democratic. A *democracy* is a form of government in which most people can effectively participate. Because it is generally impractical for all the people to take part in their government directly, their participation is usually through representatives chosen in free elections. Hence, the people rule themselves indirectly through their representatives, in a form of government often called a *representative democracy*.

An essential part of democracy is a tolerance of different opinions and interests. What many countries call "free elections"—without competing political parties, freedom of speech, and an independent press—would not impress many Americans. Unlike ideologies such as militant Islam or communism, democratic politics doesn't assume that some groups, like Christians or capitalists or socialists, are wrong and shouldn't participate. Politics in a democracy acts like a marketplace, continually reacting to demands by different groups and reaching compromises among them.

Reaching decisions this way is messy. Democratic politics seldom allows clear-cut victories by anyone. Groups must be free to stand up for their own interests and none has a monopoly on the truth. Politicians in a democracy practice an ancient and noble craft—to reconcile conflicting interests in order to promote a common good. As British political scientist Bernard Crick wrote, "democratic politics . . . chooses conciliation rather than violence . . . as a way to maintain order and adapt to change."

Yet establishing governments, even democratic ones, does allow a few great power over many others. This power includes the ability to coerce others more effectively than if government didn't exist. As illustrated by the mass murders of Jews by Nazi Germany and the current genocide of African tribes in Sudan, control of government may even mean the power to kill millions of your own citizens.

As we will see in the next chapter, the skeptical politicians who wrote the Constitution understood the problem of power. The journalist Robert D. Kaplan described our founders as "constructive pessimists" who "worried constantly about what might go wrong in human relations." James Madison's famous quote in *The Federalist Papers* No. 51—"If men were angels, no government would be necessary"— justified the elaborate Constitutional hardwiring of checks and balances, and divisions of power and civil liberties designed to limit the future leaders of the United States. Yet as the Supreme Court decision following the 2000 conflicted presidential vote reminded us, the control of powerful judicial and political offices can allow those in authority to determine the outcome of even the most honored process in a democracy—a free election.

What Is Government?

Government is a political association that does two things:

1. It makes rules determining who will get society's values.
2. It alone regulates the use of legitimate force in society.

The first part of the definition deals with how society distributes the values it has available—wealth, respect, safety, resources, money, and so on. The second part deals with how these decisions are enforced. Government, then, has the final word over who gets what and the ultimate say over how it will be done.

Government does not always *directly* determine who will get the valued things in a society. The United States is a capitalist system, based on the private ownership of the economy. This means that the government doesn't directly decide on what jobs people will do, what products they will make, or who will get the income from the sale of the products. In theory, the U.S. government only protects the private distribution of society's values, with minimal interference. At the same time, the government places higher taxes on those with higher incomes, and gives welfare to people who are getting the least of society's wealth. Both taxes and welfare illustrate the government's authority limiting the private distribution of the value of wealth.

This is not to say that somehow the economy is outside the reach of America's government. During the recent economic meltdown, the Obama administration rescued the nation's largest banks and automobile companies by buying their stock. But even in more normal times the so-called "free" market depends on a framework of public regulations. The American economy is joined at the hip with a complex network of government agencies that make sure that we find comfort in our hotels, meat in our Big Macs and safety in our savings accounts. The trust behind countless economic exchanges in society rests on legal rules and political expectations. When these break down, as many suspected happened during the lax government regulations that led to the recession of 2008–2009, people's confidence in banks and businesses declines as well. Those who proclaim that the strength of the economy lies in maintaining mythical barriers to political "interference" are talking ideology, not analysis. The successful American economy rests not in the detachment of the market from government but in their numerous effective links.

Making and Supporting Decisions

The government may also intervene directly in disputes among its citizens. Folks in a town near a river may not be able to swim there because a paper mill pollutes it. The town residents or the owners of the mill may ask the government to settle the dispute. The appropriate part of the government may respond by passing a law, or by a ruling of an administrative agency such as the Environmental Protection Agency, or by a court decision on whether the town or the paper mill will get the use of the river ("the value").

How the government supports its decision brings us to the second aspect of government—its exclusive regulation of legitimate force. In enforcing its decisions, the government may employ, allow, or prevent the use of force. Either the paper mill or the town's swimmers may be ordered not to use the river and may be fined or arrested if they do so. Only the government is allowed to regulate what kind of force is used, and how.

The government is not the only one in society that can legitimately use force. Parents may discipline their children to keep them from swimming, or the paper mill may employ guards to keep people off their property. But only the government can set limits on this force. Most governments permit parents to spank their kids yet forbid physical abuse of children. The paper mill's guards may be forbidden to use guns to keep swimmers out. Government does not *monopolize* the use of legitimate force, but it alone *regulates* its use.

The Study of Politics

What is the study of politics? One thing to notice about political science is that it's a lot like other *social sciences* such as history, economics, sociology, and psychology. Each studies aspects of the relations among people. In any large group of people, many social interactions are going on. Each of these disciplines may look at the same group and ask different questions about the relationships that are occurring. This division of labor is partly traditional and partly a way of separating complicated human relations into more easily understood parts. Political science fits in by studying one type of interaction between people— that involving power and authority. The following example will make the approaches of the other disciplines clearer and distinguish them from political science.

Political Science and Microsoft

What questions would an economist, a psychologist, and a historian ask about the operations of a "society" like the giant computer software company Microsoft? An *economist* might ask questions about the production and distribution of the various Microsoft operating systems and other programs. In designing its Microsoft Network, how did the company attract subscribers and content providers? How were buyers of the Windows program discouraged from using rival Web browsers? A *psychologist* might concentrate on the motives and goals of Bill Gates, the founder of Microsoft and the richest man in America. What is the psychological makeup of this successful entrepreneur? How does he deal with subordinates and competitors? A *historian* might look at the origins and development of Microsoft. What factors within the industry explain why in a few years its operating systems ran more than four-fifths of the world's computers? Why did it become a multibillion dollar corporation while competitors fell by the wayside?

These different fields of study overlap. Members of one discipline often are interested in the findings of another. Economists may find answers to their questions about how focused and innovative the company is in a psychological study of Bill Gates. The historian might ask the economist about Microsoft's mergers with potential competitors to determine the logic behind its expansion. Certainly the economist and the psychologist would want to know about the history of the corporation before studying their particular parts of it.

A political scientist, although interested in the other disciplines' findings, would most likely focus on the central question: *Who is getting what, when, and how?* How do Bill Gates successors control and manage Microsoft; how do these executives reach decisions and implement them? How did Microsoft gain preeminence in its industry, and how do its leaders keep the company, and themselves, on top? How does the government influence their decisions through regulations, taxes, and occasional legal actions? Political science focuses on the study of power and authority—on the powerful, the ways in which they exercise their authority, and the consequences for the rest of us.

As Lasswell wrote, "The study of politics is the study of influence and the influential." That is the core of what a political scientist would want to find out about Microsoft.

Why Give a Damn About Politics?

After looking at what politics is and what government and political scientists do, you could still be asking one basic question: Who cares? Some students conclude: "Politics is just ego. I don't want to get involved in it." Why *should* any of us give a damn about politics?

The problem is that we are already involved. Apathy is as much a political position as is activism. Either position will influence who gets what in our society. Safe streets, good schools, and clean food are political decisions influenced by who participates in making them, who is prevented from participating, and who chooses not to participate.

Our lives are webs of politics. Think of what you have done today and how politics has influenced you. What you had (or didn't have) for breakfast was probably influenced by the price and availability of the food. The quality of the food you ate was regulated by a government agency that made sure those Grade A eggs were Grade A and that the milk was indeed pasteurized. The cost of those milk and eggs was affected by the decisions of government to aid farmers, as well as the ability of agricultural groups to influence the government by lobbying and campaign contributions. The news you heard on the radio about what the government was doing for the economy was conditioned by what officials felt they should tell the public, what reporters could dig out of unofficial sources, and what media editors felt was newsworthy. The college you attend, the tuition you pay, and the student loans you may or may not receive are all the results of someone's choices in the political game. (See "Who Needs Government?")

Sometimes the influence of politics is subtle. Many of the ways we expect to be treated in our daily lives reflect recent changes in the laws. Identity politics, "Who Is What" as well as "Who Gets What," have risen in public attention as groups have made demands based on their shared identities. These would include the rights of women and homosexuals not to be harassed, or that elderly workers can't be fired because of their age, or the right of nonsmokers to learn in a smoke-free class. These evolving rights can be supported by joining demonstrations, wearing buttons, and going to court. We are rights-bearing citizens often without thinking that these too are the result of political choices.

Of course few of us participate in the government decisions that affect us. Let's take a personal example. Studies of American government have often pointed out that federal regulatory commissions have not effectively regulated the businesses they oversee. These commissions have tended to be closely tied to the powerful economic interests they supervise. This lesson was brought home when I was in graduate school.

Some years ago the cargo door blew off an American Airlines DC-10 flying over Windsor, Canada, causing violent decompression. The pilot managed to land the empty jumbo jet safely. The government's independent National Transportation Safety Board investigated the near disaster. Their recommendations went to the Federal Aviation Administration (FAA), the government regulatory commission in charge of airline safety. The Safety Board recommended that the FAA order that all cargo doors have modified locking devices and that McDonnell Douglas, the plane's builder, be required to strengthen the cabin floor.

The FAA, headed by a political appointee, was operating under a policy of "gentlemen's agreements" with the industries it was regulating. After discussions with the plane's manufacturers (who were large contributors to President Nixon's reelection campaign), they allowed McDonnell Douglas to modify the door on its own instead of under FAA supervision and simply to issue advisory service bulletins for the 130 DC-10s already in operation. McDonnell Douglas was allowed to reject as "impractical" the idea of strengthening the floor.

Somehow the changes were not made on the door of a DC-10 flown by Turkish Airlines. The plane, flying from Paris to London in March 1974, crashed, killing all 346 people aboard. At the time it was the world's worst air disaster. The cargo door had blown off. This loss produced explosive decompression, collapse of the cabin floor, and loss of control. Passengers still strapped in their seats were sucked from the plane. A subcommittee of the House of Representatives, in a report on the crash, attacked the FAA for its "indifference to public safety" and for attempting to "balance dollars against lives."

A teacher and friend of mine, Professor Wayne Wilcox of Columbia University, was on the plane. With him were his wife and two children.

We have no choice over *whether* to be involved in the political game. But we can choose *how* to be involved. We can choose whether to be a *subject* in the political game or an *object* of that game. The question is not whether politics affects us—it does and will. The question is whether we will influence politics. The first step in this decision is choosing how aware we wish to be of the game. This text may, with luck, start that awareness.

Who Needs Government?

Former Senator Ernest Hollings of South Carolina tells this story:

> A veteran returning from Korea went to college on the GI Bill; bought his house with an FHA loan; saw his kids born in a VA hospital; started a business with an SBA loan; got electricity from TVA; and then, water from a project funded by the EPA. His kids participated in the school lunch program and made it through college courtesy of government-guaranteed student loans. His parents retired to a farm on their social security, getting electricity from the REA and the soil tested by the USDA. When the father became ill, his life was saved with a drug developed through NIH; the family was saved from financial ruin by Medicare. Our veteran drove to work on the interstate; moored his boat in a channel dredged by Army engineers; and, when floods hit, took Amtrak to Washington to apply for disaster relief. He also spent some of his time there enjoying the exhibits in the Smithsonian museums.
>
> Then one day he wrote his congressman an angry letter complaining about paying taxes for all those programs created for ungrateful people. In effect, he said, the government should get off his back.

Source: Jonathan Yates, "Reality on Capitol Hill," *Newsweek*, November 28, 1988, p. 12.

What Is This Book About?

In a way this is a scorecard covering the major players in the game of national politics. This first chapter introduces some of the terms and substance of politics—the means (power and authority) and goals (values) of the game. Chapters 2 and 6 cover the formal constitutional rules and the civil liberties and rights under which the competition proceeds. Chapters 3, 4, and 5 deal with the governmental players—the president and bureaucracy, Congress, and the Supreme Court—their history and organization, their strengths and weaknesses. Chapters 7 and 8 are about four important nongovernmental players—voters, political parties, interest groups, and media. Though they are not official parts of the government, they have great influence over the outcome of political conflicts. Finally, the last chapter goes into two different theories of who wins and loses, who plays and doesn't play the game.

Let's be clear about this "game"; it is not "Monday Night Football." It is important, complex, changing, and serious enough to involve questions of life and death. Actually, many games are going on at the same time with overlapping players and objectives. They are games in which the participants often disagree, even on the goals. The goals (unlike the touchdown in football) vary with the objectives of the players. A business may seek higher profits from its involvement in a political issue, a consumer group may want a lower-priced product, and a labor union may demand higher wages for its workers. They may compete over the same issue for different reasons. They all seek to use power to obtain the values they consider important. We can analyze objectively how they play the game, but which side we root for depends on our own interests and ideals.

Another problem is that the players we've grouped together may not see themselves as being on the same team. Each participant, whether the bureaucracy, Congress, or the media, is hardly one player seeking a single goal. They are not only players but also *arenas* in which competition goes on. We may read of Congress opposing the president on an issue, but a closer look will find the president's congressional supporters and opponents fighting it out in the committees of Congress. Some of the media may oppose a certain interest group, while allowing or limiting the use of television news and radio talk shows as arenas for the group's views.

Finally, in a brief introductory text all the political players are not discussed. State and local governments are certainly important in national politics. Ethnic groups and foreign governments may have a role in the outcome of the competition. Someone even more basic may be missing. As one student asked, "Where are the people?" "Whatever happened to the American people in this game?"

Alas, politics today is a spectator sport. The audience is mostly on the sidelines. To be sure, people do influence the players. The president and Congress are selected by election, interest groups depend on their members' support, and media need to please an audience. But the making of foreign policies, the negotiations over legislation, and the discussions of what news the media should cover all get done behind closed doors. Though it is played for the crowd—who certainly pay for the game—the competition itself generally doesn't include them. Whether it will depends on the players, the rules of the game, and the people watching.

THOUGHT QUESTIONS

1. In the opening dialogue of this chapter, we discovered politics in an unlikely place—a classroom. Describe some other unlikely situations where politics takes place.
2. How do authorities gain legitimacy? How do they lose it? Do recent elections provide examples of both?
3. People sometimes justify their apathy by the way politicians behave. Do you think this attitude is justified?

4. When you go shopping, do you notice the role of the government in your choice of what to buy? Do you see it on labels or availability of goods or certain standards that you assume are met?

5. Have any decisions in your life been affected by government action? Did you have anything to say about those actions? If you didn't, do you know who did?

SUGGESTED READINGS

Crick, Bernard. *Democracy: A Very Short Introduction*. New York: Oxford University Press, 2002. Pb.
An intelligent discussion of the definitions, conditions, and development of modern democracy.

Golding, William G. *Lord of the Flies*. New York: Capricorn Books, 1959. Pb.
A pessimistic novel (even before the TV series *Survivor*) on what happens to British children on a deserted island without adults or government.

Kay, John. *Culture and Prosperity: The Truth about Markets*. New York: HarperBusiness, 2004.
An economist's readable account of how markets and governments make some nations rich and some poor.

Orwell, George. *Animal Farm*. New York: Alfred E. Knopf, 1993.
The classic political fable of the communist barnyard where all the animals are equal but some are more equal than others.

Warren, Robert Penn. *All the King's Men*. New York: Harcourt Brace Jovanovich, 1946.
A terrific novel about a terrifically manipulative politician modeled on Louisiana's Governor, Huey Long.

Wasserman, Gary. *Politics in Action: Cases in Modern American Government*. Boston: Houghton Mifflin, 2006. Pb.
Thirteen brief stories of how presidents and lobbyists, editors and judges, students and bureaucrats play the game of modern politics.

CHAPTER 2

The Constitution: Rules of the Game

The Second Day of Class

The second day of class was as bad as the first. This time the prof announces that we're going to be a focus group to test public opinion. We'll be interviewed to see what a small group thinks about American politics. He starts by asking us what words come to mind when we hear "politician"?

Well, this I happen to know the answer to.

"How about 'Slime balls'?"

High fives all around.

Then he says, "What about 'politics'?"

Not too hard—"Corrupt," "Games," "Boring."

So then he says, "What about when I say 'Founding Fathers'?"

"Patriots," "Freedom," "George Washington."

"How about 'The Constitution'?" he asks.

"Liberty," "Equality," "Bill of Rights"...

Some of us are beginning to catch on.

Then he lets us have it. "Didn't the framers of the Constitution run for election and make promises to win people's votes? And not all of them were perfect in their personal lives. Didn't they cut secret deals and wheel and deal to write the Constitution and get it adopted? Many people at the time, perhaps most, were unhappy with the results. And with their leaders.

Sounds to me like our Founding Fathers were a bunch of politicians."

The Constitution did not fall from the sky. It was created by political leaders trying to form a government, solve immediate problems, and compromise conflicting interests, all within the political understandings of their century. The Constitution has lasted because the politicians into whose care it was given proved flexible enough to adapt it to different times, and because it commanded loyalty as a symbol of a nation's traditions and ideals. But the Constitution has never been "above politics." Its words cannot be understood apart from the politics when they were written, and when they are applied.

So far we have discussed the game of politics, what winning means, and why one plays. This chapter deals with the principles and organization of the competition. First, this chapter discusses the politicians who wrote the Constitution, their debates, the regional interests they represented, and the compromises they reached. The Constitution contains the official rules of the American political game; it also establishes three major players and their powers—the president, Congress, and the Supreme Court. Further, it places limits on the game, providing civil liberties protections for both players and people. By creating a central government that shares power with state governments, the Constitution establishes the playing field of federalism.

What led to the adoption of the Constitution, its meaning, how it has changed, and its political influence today are the topics of this chapter.

Background to the Constitution

On July 4, 1776, the Declaration of Independence proclaimed the American colonies "Free and Independent States." This symbolized the beginning not only of a bitter fight for independence from Great Britain but also of a struggle to unite the separate, often conflicting interests, regions, and states of America. Only after a decade of trial and error was the Constitution written and accepted as the legal foundation for the new United States of America.

The politicians who gathered in Philadelphia in May 1787 to write the Constitution were not starting from scratch. They were able to draw on (1) an English political heritage, (2) American models of colonial and state governments, and (3) their experience with the Articles of Confederation.

The framers were inheritors of an English legal heritage that included the *Magna Carta,* which, in 1215, declared that the power of the king was not absolute. It also included the idea of natural rights, expressed by English philosophers, most notably John Locke, who wrote that people were "born free" and formed society to protect their rights. Many colonists felt that they were fighting a revolution to secure their traditional rights as Englishmen, which they had been denied by an abusive colonial government.

Their 150 years as colonies had taught the states much about self-government, which they used in the Constitution. From their earliest days, the settlers had been determined to live under written rules of law resting on the consent of the community: The *Mayflower Compact* was signed by the Pilgrims shortly before they landed at Plymouth in

1620. Similar documents had been written in other colonies, most of which had their own constitutions. Other aspects of colonial (and English) governments, such as two-house legislatures, were later to appear in the Constitution. After the American Revolution, in reaction to the resented authority of the royal governor, the colonists established the legislature as the most important branch in their state governments.

Most of the colonies had a governor, a legislature, and a judiciary—a pattern that would evolve into the Constitution's separation of powers. Most had regular elections, though generally only property-owning white males could vote. There was even an uneasy basis for the federal system of local and national governments in the sharing of powers between the American colonies and the government in England. Perhaps most important was the idea of limited government and individual rights written into the state constitutions after the Revolution.

However, unity among the colonies was slow in coming. Attempts to tighten their ties during the Revolution were a limited success. Most political theorists of the time thought democracy could only exist in small states. This idea added to the reluctance of many leaders to give up their states' powers to a presumably undemocratic central government. The First Continental Congress in September 1774 had established regular lines of communication among the colonies and gave a focus to anti-British sentiment. The Second Continental Congress, beginning in Philadelphia in May 1775, created the Declaration of Independence. At the same time a plan for confederation—a loose union among the states—was proposed. The Articles of Confederation were ratified by the states by March 1781 and went into effect even before the formal end of the American Revolution in February 1783.

The Articles of Confederation (1781–1789)

Looking back, the shortcomings of the Articles of Confederation are pretty apparent. No real national government was set up in the articles. Rather, they established a "league of friendship" among the states, which didn't have much more authority than the United Nations does today. The center of the federation was a *unicameral* (one-house) legislature, called the *Confederation Congress*. Each state had one vote, regardless of its size. Most serious actions required approval by 9 states. Amendments to the articles needed unanimous approval by all 13.

The confederation had no executive branch and no national system of courts. Perhaps most important, the Congress had no ability to impose taxes; it could only *request* funds from the states. Each state retained its "sovereignty, freedom, and independence." Nor did the Congress have any direct authority over citizens who were subject only to the government of their states. In short, the Congress had no ability to enforce its will on either states or citizens.

The confederation did have some muscle. Unlike the United Nations, it had the power to declare war, conduct foreign policy, coin money, manage a postal system, and oversee an army made up of the state militias. The Articles of Confederation were also anti-elite in requiring compulsory rotation in office, what we would today call *term limits*—no member of the Congress could serve more than three years in any six. Finally, real achievements were made under the Articles, such as the start of a national bureaucracy and the passing of the *Northwest Ordinance*, which established the procedure for admitting new states into the Union.

But by 1787, the weakness of the articles was more apparent than its strength. Too little power had been granted to the central authority. Many people worried that Britain, France, or Spain would attack America because of its feeble central government. The confederation was in deep financial difficulty: Not enough funds were coming from the states, the currency was being devalued, and the states were locked in trade wars, putting up tariff barriers against each other. In late 1786 Shays's Rebellion, an angry protest by Massachusetts farmers unable to pay their mortgages and taxes, reinforced the fears among the property-owning elite that a strong central government was needed to avoid economic decline and "mob rule".

The Constitutional Convention

Against this background, the convention met in Philadelphia from May 25 to September 17, 1787. The weather was hot and muggy, making tempers short. All the meetings were held in secrecy, with the windows shut and the press excluded. This was because Congress had reluctantly called the convention together "for the sole purpose of revising the Articles of Confederation." Yet within five days of organizing, the convention had adopted a Virginia delegate's resolution "that a national government ought to be established consisting of a *supreme* legislative, executive, and judiciary." In other words, the convention violated the authority under which it had been established and proceeded to write a completely new U.S. Constitution in a single summer.

The Constitution was the product of a series of compromises. The most important compromise, because it was the most divisive issue, was the question of how the states would be represented in the national legislature. The large states proposed a legislature with representation based either on the taxes paid or on the number of people in each state—both of which gave them more power. The small states wanted one vote for each state no matter what its size—giving them more influence. After a long deadlock, an agreement called the *Great Compromise* established the present structure of Congress—representation based on population in the lower house (House of Representatives) and equal representation for all states in the upper house (Senate).

Other compromises came more easily. Southern delegates feared the national government would impose an export tax on their agricultural goods and interfere with slavery. An agreement was reached that gave Congress the power to regulate commerce but not to tax exports. In addition, the slave trade could not be banned before 1808. The slave issue also was central in the weirdest compromise—the Three-Fifths Formula. Here the debate was over whether slaves should be counted as people for purposes of representation and taxation. The South, which did not want to treat slaves as people, did however want to count them that way. It was agreed to continue the Confederation rule that a slave should be counted as three-fifths of a person for both. (This provision was later removed by the Thirteenth and Fourteenth Amendments.) Another issue, the right of a state to withdraw or *secede* from the Union, was simply avoided. The questions of secession and slavery had to wait for a later generation to answer in a bloody civil war.

The Framers

It is a bit surprising how quickly and relatively painlessly the Constitution was drafted. No doubt the writing went so smoothly partly because of the qualities of the leaders in Philadelphia. The universally respected General Washington chaired the meetings, bringing with him the pragmatism of a successful businessman and the commitment of a nationalist. Alexander Hamilton, the self-assured financial genius, frequently dominated the debates, whereas the shy but equally brilliant James Madison often secured a consensus at discussion's end. Benjamin Franklin, at 82 years old, added the moderation and insights of age.

The delegates possessed a blend of experience and learning. (See "Colonial Drinking and Voting.") Of the 55 delegates, 42 had served in the Continental Congress. More than half were college educated and had studied political philosophy. As a relatively young group, the average age being 40, they may have reflected a generation gap of their own time. Having politically matured during the revolutionary period, they were less tied to state loyalties than were older men whose outlook was formed before the war. They were nationalists building a nation, not merely defending the interests of their states.

But there was more to the consensus than this. The framers were not exactly representative of the American people at the time. They were wealthy planters, merchants, and lawyers. Fifteen of them were slaveholders; 14 were land speculators. The small farmers and workers of the country, many of whom were suffering from an economic downturn, were not represented in Philadelphia. Nor did leaders who spoke for this poorer, more radical majority, such as Thomas Jefferson (who was in Paris as ambassador and disliked the face-to-face disputes in political meetings) or Patrick Henry (who stayed away because he "smelt a rat"), attend the convention. Only 6 of the 56 men who signed the revolutionary Declaration of Independence were at the convention. The delegates were a conservative, propertied elite, worried that continuing the weak confederation would only encourage more and larger Shays's Rebellions. Thus the debates at the convention were not between the "haves" and the "have-nots," but between the "haves" and the "haves" over their regional interests.

Motives Behind the Constitution

Much scholarly debate has gone on about the motives of the framers since Charles Beard published his book *An Economic Interpretation of the Constitution of the United States* in 1913. Beard argued that the convention was a counterrevolution engineered by the delegates to

 ## Colonial Drinking and Voting

[James] Madison . . . believed deeply in a government based on the consent of the people, *as long as the direct involvement of the people was strictly limited.* Early in his political career he had seen the ways of popular politics, and the experience made him uncomfortable. In Madison's Virginia, men got elected to office by plying the freeholders with bumbo—in the vernacular of the day. Rum punch was preferred, accompanied by cookies and ginger cake and occasionally a barbecued bullock or a hog. For one election, in 1758, George Washington supplied 160 gallons of liquor to 391 voters—a stiff one and a half quarts per voter.

That was the way it was done. Though good enough for the likes of Washington, Jefferson, Henry, Mason, and the rest, to young Madison it was a "corrupting influence," inconsistent with the "purity of moral and republic principles." During his second run for the Virginia House of Delegates, in 1777, he decided to set an example. He refused to supply the bumbo.

Madison lost that election—to a tavernkeeper.

Source: Fred Barbash, *The Founding.* New York: Simon & Schuster, 1987, p. 131.

protect their own property holdings by transferring power from the states to an unrepresentative central government. Certainly the 40 delegates who held nearly worthless confederation bonds stood to profit from a new government committed to honoring these debts. Certainly their interests as creditors and property holders would be better protected by a strong central government. Nor did the delegates particularly favor democracy. Most thought that liberty had to be protected *from* democracy (which they thought of as "mob rule") and agreed with Madison's statement in *The Federalist Papers* No. 10 that "those who hold and those who are without property have ever formed distinct interests in society."

Critics of Beard's theory argue that the framers' motives were more varied. They conclude that the delegates wanted to build a new nation, to reduce the country's numerous political disputes, and to promote economic development that would benefit all. They point out that having a central government able to raise an army to protect the states from foreign attack appeared to be the most important reason that General George Washington, among others, backed the Constitution.

But the arguments of the two sides don't necessarily cancel out each other. The framers' *public* interest of building a strong nation and their *private* interest of protecting their property could work together. Like

 ## Is the Constitution Antidemocratic?

There is an argument that the Constitution was an antidemocratic attempt to limit popular participation in government. Many of the framers saw liberty and democracy as very separate, with people's liberties needing constitutional protections from democratic pressures. Certainly how presidents, senators, and Supreme Court justices were selected were restraints on democracy. Critics often quote an antidemocratic framer like Roger Sherman of Connecticut who wrote that the people "should have as little to do as may be about the government. They . . . are constantly liable to be misled."

The late Thurgood Marshall, the Supreme Court's first black justice, pointed out that the Constitution's preamble that begins "we the people," did not include the majority of citizens—women and minorities. He called the Constitution "defective from the start" because it required tremendous social upheaval "to attain the system of constitutional government, and its respect for the individual freedoms and human rights, we hold as fundamental today." He warned against a complacent belief in the original vision of the founders. Instead, Marshall praised those who, through the Civil War, created virtually a new constitution using the Fourteenth Amendment to ensure the rights of all Americans.

most people, they believed that what was good for them was good for society. It was not surprising by the standards of the day that most of the population (workers, the poor, blacks, women) was not represented at Philadelphia. Nor should it be surprising that the delegates' ideas for a government did not work against their own economic interests and, in many cases, aided them. (See "Is the Constitution Antidemocratic?")

Federalists vs. Anti-Federalists

The framers were divided. Many of the debates during the writing and ratification of the Constitution separated the elite into two camps: the Federalists and the Anti-Federalists.

The *Federalists* generally favored a strong federal (national) government, with protection of private property rights and limits on popular participation in government. (Alexander Hamilton, a leader of the Federalists, once described the people as "a great beast.") In the debates over the Constitution, the Federalists pushed for high property qualifications for voting, an indirectly elected Senate modeled after the English aristocratic House of Lords, a lofty indirectly elected president, and a strong nonelected judiciary. The Federalists, being more pessimistic about human nature (including the nature of the rulers), wanted these "cooling-off" devices in the government to filter down the popular will and create guardians of the people's real interests.

The *Anti-Federalists* were more optimistic about human nature though just as suspicious about the nature of those in power. Led by men like Patrick Henry and George Mason, they favored strong state governments because they felt the states would be closer to public opinion than a central government. They wanted fewer limits on popular participation and pushed for the legislative branch to have more power than the executive and judicial branches. Believing that the majority was responsible, though agreeing that it needed cooling off, Anti-Federalists wanted government to be accountable to officials elected by the people.

The Constitution is a compromise between these two positions. It was designed to prevent tyranny from the bottom—the people (whom the Federalists feared)—and from the top—the rulers (whom the Anti-Federalists feared). Neither side could foresee a federal government of the size and complexity that exists today. Both generally agreed that the government that governed best governed least.

Ratification and the Bill of Rights

The struggle for ratification of the Constitution focused the debate between the Federalists and Anti-Federalists. Conventions in nine states had to approve the Constitution before it could go into effect. Because a majority of the people were likely against the Constitution, the fight for ratification wasn't easy. The Anti-Federalists wanted a more rigid system of separation of powers and more effective checks and balances. Fearing that the president and Senate would act together as an aristocratic clique, they proposed compulsory rotation in office (as under the Articles of Confederation).

The Federalists' had a problem. They were making the very arguments that they had *opposed* during the Revolution against the British—taking powers away from the states and supporting a strong central government that could tax and endanger people's liberties. They criticized the Anti-Federalists for ignoring the advantages of a national union. Their propaganda campaign in the newspapers pointed out the failures of the confederation, reassured people that the proposed president would be more like a governor than a king, and dismissed charges that the judiciary would be a threat to individual liberties. A series of their essays in a New York newspaper written by Madison, Hamilton, and John Jay was later republished as *The Federalist Papers*. The book stands today as the most famous commentary on the framers' thinking about their Constitution.

The debate over whether to include the *Bill of Rights,* the first 10 amendments in the Constitution, became a key issue in the struggle over ratification. The Philadelphia convention, dominated by Federalists, had failed to include a bill of rights in the original document, not so much because of opposition to the goals of the bill, but from a feeling that such a statement was irrelevant. (A proposed bill of rights was voted down unanimously near the end of the convention partly because everyone was worn out and wanted to go home.) The Federalists, from their conservative viewpoint, believed that liberty was best protected by the *procedures,* such as federalism, and checks and balances, established by their constitutional government. No matter what ideals were written down, such as freedoms of speech, press, and religion, the Federalists argued that support for them would depend on the "tolerance of the age" and the balance of forces established by the Constitution.

For the Anti-Federalists, the Bill of Rights was a proclamation of fundamental truths—natural rights due to all people. No matter whether future generations might ignore them, these rights were sacred. Any government resting on the consent of its people must honor them in its constitution. Although the Anti-Federalists had lost the battle over the Bill of Rights in Philadelphia, they eventually won the war. Massachusetts and Virginia agreed to accept the Constitution with the recommendation that such a proclamation be the first order of business of the new Congress. It was, and the Bill of Rights became the first 10 amendments to the Constitution on December 15, 1791.

Four Major Constitutional Principles

The U.S. Constitution did three things in creating a government. First, it *established the structure* of government. In setting up three branches of government within a federal system, it gave the country a political framework that has existed to the present time. Second, the Constitution *distributed certain powers* to this government. Article I gave legislative powers, such as the power to raise and spend money, to Congress. Article II gave executive powers to the president, including command over the armed forces and wide authority over foreign policy. Article III gave judicial power, the right to judge disputes arising under the Constitution, to the U.S. Supreme Court. Third, the Constitution *restrained the government* in exercising these powers. Government was limited, by the Bill of Rights for example, so that certain individual rights would be preserved.

The Constitution, then, both *grants* and *limits* governmental power. This can be shown by looking closely at four major constitutional principles: separation of powers and checks and balances, federalism, limited government, and judicial review.

Separation of Powers and Checks and Balances

The first major constitutional principle is actually two: separation of powers and checks and balances. However, the two principles cannot be understood apart from each other, and they work together.

Separation of powers is the principle that the powers of government should be divided and put in the care of different parts of the government. Although never exactly stated in the Constitution, this principle was in practice in the governments of the colonies. The idea that power was needed to balance other power was a key concept of the French political theorist Baron de Montesquieu who was often quoted in Philadelphia. (See "Madison on Separation of Powers and Government.") The writers of the Constitution separated the federal government into three branches to carry out what they saw as the three major functions of government. The *legislative function*—passing the laws—was given to Congress; the *executive function*—carrying out or executing the laws—was given to the president; and the *judicial function*—interpreting the laws—was given to the Supreme Court.

Though nice and neat, the principle is probably unworkable in practice. The purpose of separation of powers was to allow ambition to counter ambition, to prevent any one authority from monopolizing power. Yet simply dividing the powers of government into these three branches would probably make the legislature supreme—as it had been in the colonies. As the starter of the governmental process, the legislature could determine how, or even if, the other branches played their roles. Although Congress was accepted as the most important branch, something was needed to curb legislative power. That something was checks and balances.

Checks and balances create a mixture of powers that permits the three branches of government to limit one another. (A *check* is a control one branch has over another's functions, creating a *balance* of power.) The principle gives the branches constitutional means for guarding their functions from interference by another branch. Checks and balances mix together the legislative, executive, and judicial powers, giving some legislative powers to the executive, some executive powers to the legislative branch, and so on, to keep any branch from dominating another.

There are a number of examples of checks and balances in the Constitution. The president is given legislative power to recommend measures to Congress and to call Congress into special session, and some judicial power like the right to pardon (which presidents have sometimes used to excuse political allies from the judgment of the courts). The presidential veto gives the chief executive a primarily legislative power to prevent bills he dislikes from becoming law. Congress can check this power by overriding the veto by a two-thirds vote. The Senate is given an executive power in its role of confirming presidential nominations for major executive and judicial posts, which is also the power *not* to confirm. Further, Congress can refuse to appropriate funds for any executive agency, thereby preventing the president from acting. President Obama learned this early in his administration when the Senate in May 2009 voted to strip $80 million from a military spending bill that was designed to close the military prison at Guantanamo Bay, Cuba. Senators, worried that prisoners would be moved to their states, demanded a detailed plan outlining what would be done with the suspected terrorists after the base was closed.

The system of separation of powers and checks and balances is even more elaborate than this mixture of functions. The way each branch of government is set up and chosen also checks and balances its power. Congress is divided into two houses, and both must approve legislation before it becomes law. Limited terms of office and varied methods of selection keep any one person or branch from becoming too strong. The House of Representatives was to be popularly elected for two-year terms; senators were elected for six years, originally by their state legislatures (changed by the Seventeenth Amendment to popular election); the president was elected for four years by an electoral college not a popular vote; and federal judges were to be

Madison on Separation of Powers and Government

The great security against a gradual concentration of the several powers in the same department consists in giving to those who administer each department the necessary constitutional means and personal motives to resist encroachments of the others. . . . Ambition must be made to counteract ambition. The interest of the man must be connected with the constitutional rights of the place. . . . If men were angels, no government would be necessary. If angels were to govern men, neither external or internal controls on government would be necessary. In framing a government, which is to be administered by men over men, the great difficulty lies in this: You must first enable the government to control the governed; and in the next place, oblige it to control itself.

Source: James Madison, *The Federalist Papers* No. 51.

appointed by the president, confirmed by the Senate, and to serve for life during good behavior. All these procedures were designed to give government officials different interests to defend, varied bases of support, and protection from too much interference by other branches.

The institutions that result from this dividing and mixing of powers are separate bodies that in practice *share* the overall power of government. Each needs the others to make government work, yet each has the means to check the powers of the others. This elaborate mechanism of separation of powers and checks and balances was certainly not designed to be the most efficient form of government—as we can see today with the frequent complaints about political "gridlock." Rather, it was established "to control the abuses of government"—to oblige the government to discipline itself. It set up a structure that historian Richard Hofstadter has called "a harmonious system of mutual frustration."

Federalism

Federalism calls for political authority to be divided between a central government and the governments of the states. Both the federal and state governments may act directly on the people and each has some *exclusive powers.* Federalism, like separation of powers, distributes political authority to prevent power from being concentrated. It is a constitutional principle around which major political debates continue to the present day.

Actually, the men who wrote the Constitution had little choice. The loose confederation of states had not operated well in their opinion and centralizing all government powers would have been unacceptable to the major governments of the day—those of the states. Federalism, then, was more than just a reasonable principle for governing a large country separated by regional differences and slow communications. It also was the only realistic way to get the states to approve the Constitution.

American federalism involves two somewhat contradictory ideas. The first, expressed in Article VI, is that the Constitution and the laws of the central government are supreme. This condition was necessary to establish an effective government that would be able to pass laws and rule directly over all the people. The second principle of states' rights ensures the independence of the state governments: The Tenth Amendment *reserved powers* not delegated to the central government to the states or the people. These substantial reserved powers include control of local and city governments, regulation of business within a state, supervision of education, and exercise of the general "police power" over the safety of the people.

The conflict between the two principles—national supremacy and states' rights—came to a head in the Civil War, which established the predominance of the national government. That is not to say that the question was settled once and for all. Even today on issues such as gun control and immigration, state governments often clash with the federal government. Such conflicts can be expected from a constitution that not only divided the powers of government into a federal system but also set up the basis for national union.

As political issues—whether regulating the economy or protecting the environment—became national, so too did solutions gravitate toward Washington. In practice there are few domestic programs today that are solely run by the federal government. Almost all require cooperation by the states and often the cities. In the best cases, this arrangement helps adjust the programs to local conditions; in the worst, it may delay or hinder needed changes, even in a natural catastrophe. (See "Federalism Caught in a Storm: The Katrina Disaster.")

Whether harming or helping, federalism now exists far less as separate boxes of powers than as a mix of overlapping relations between the states and the federal government, sometimes called a *marble cake,* because of its swirl of different colored batter. This blending of relations can be seen in public education. Public schools in this country are governed by local school boards. The boards set teachers' salaries and make the basic decisions concerning day-to-day operations of a public school system. Local taxes on property in the school district are usually the major source of public school funds.

Public education in the United States is not, however, solely a local government responsibility. State governments provide a large part of the funds for local education. These funds from state taxes are partly supplied to school districts according to financial need. This equalizes local revenues from property taxes, which vary widely from poorer to wealthier school districts. In addition, state governments usually control teacher qualifications, set educational standards in public schools, and approve the textbooks used.

The federal government gets involved in public education through aid programs that help equalize state funding, just as state funds are used to reduce the differences among local school districts. Some "strings" are attached to these federal funds. In the education reform, "No Child Left Behind," the federal government set standards for student achievement, backed by tests, and left it to the states to implement them. Federal monies would both help states achieve these goals and penalize them if they didn't. This same kind of funding and regulation of public education is found in government programs ranging from pollution control to traffic safety. (See "No Child Left Behind and Federalism.")

No Child Left Behind and Federalism

The first bill sent to Congress by President Bush was the education reform called "No Child Left Behind." It passed both houses of Congress and was signed by the president in January 2002. The law increased the federal government's role in education, even if it undermined the conservative position of strengthening federalism by giving more powers to the states.

The approach in "No Child Left Behind" was to hold states, districts, and schools accountable for student performance. The federal government would reward improved student achievement, as measured by annual reading and math tests. There were also penalties to states for failure. If after a few years these schools did not meet performance goals, federal funds would be provided to parents to help them relocate their children in other schools.

The reform's impact on education has been debatable; student scores rose in some states, while antagonism from state and local officials was apparent almost everywhere. Many, including conservative Republicans, felt that Washington was stepping over traditional lines of federalism. A number of states had difficulty providing qualified teachers in classrooms or having their students pass the required tests. President Obama supported the goals of the reform but criticized its lack of funding and flexibility for the states. He called No Child Left Behind "one of the emptiest slogans in the history of American politics."

The Debate Over Modern Federalism

At first glance *modern federalism* appears far different from the original creation. While the Constitution remains a limit on centralized power, the federal government has grown stronger than the framers could ever imagine. Yet most nonmilitary government services are supplied by state and local governments in a complex tapestry of relationships with Washington. In some ways federalism makes it easier for citizens to participate in decisions because they occur closer to home. In other ways it's more difficult because people need to keep track of separate decisions being made in a variety of places. (See Table 2.1.)

Are local and state governments closer to the people and therefore produce better policies than the national government? Historically, the answer to this question has depended on how satisfied people have been with what the government does. The growth of the federal government has been fueled by big problems and popular demands for their solution. As the economy became national, issues like regulating business, protecting workers, providing housing, and guarding the environment seemed beyond the states' capacities to solve. By responding to these challenges the national government appeared both

TABLE 2.1   90,000 GOVERNMENTS IN THE UNITED STATES, 2009

Types and Numbers of Governments

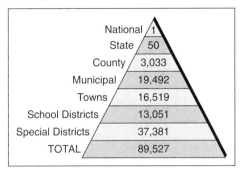

National	1
State	50
County	3,033
Municipal	19,492
Towns	16,519
School Districts	13,051
Special Districts	37,381
TOTAL	89,527

Source: U.S. Census Bureau, *Statistical Abstract of the United States: 2009*: Washington, DC: Government Printing Office, 2009), Table No. 410.

efficient and representative, certainly an improvement over state and local governments.

These liberal programs produced opponents. Business opposed encouragement for labor unions, environmental restrictions, and consumer protections that curtailed the marketplace. Wealthy and middle-class families disliked paying taxes for programs that benefited poor people. Elected officials worried about expanding government spending that led to more bureaucracies. Public opinion began to shift; more people trusted state and local governments than trusted Washington and wanted them to take the lead in solving national problems.

In the 1980s, Republican President Ronald Reagan pioneered a "New Federalism" that gave large block grants to states and localities to use with few controls from Washington. Democratic President Bill Clinton continued this conservative trend. Clinton's welfare reform legislation reduced federal programs and shifted more responsibility to the local level. It ended the federal government guarantee of support for needy children and transferred control over welfare to the states by giving them block grants to use at their discretion.

Before being elected, George W. Bush declared himself in favor of local and state policymaking. But as president he went in the other direction—resisting state and local initiatives, and centralizing policymaking in the federal government. Besides expanding the federal role in his education reforms, the Republican administration blocked state efforts to buy prescription drugs in Canada, challenged Oregon's assisted-suicide law, and resisted states' attempts to issue tougher air pollution standards. Opponents of the proposed constitutional amendment to ban gay marriages pointed out that it would limit a traditional state responsibility to regulate marriage. In short, where federalism clashed with Bush administration objectives, federalism lost.

Facing the greatest economic crisis since the Depression, President Obama was initially quiet on federalism. He did generally endorse the idea of "cooperative federalism," where Washington would look to states for new ideas and guidance. In practice this meant policies like supporting California's pollution standards for cars and trucks that were tougher than the federal guidelines. Under this liberal approach federal regulations would be treated as a floor not a ceiling, thereby encouraging more activism by the states.

Still, federalism seemed alive and well. State and local governments employed some 16 million people, while the federal payroll fell to under 2 million employees. Despite the economic crisis, the public supported local government involvement in spending their taxes. The Supreme Court joined in with decisions favorable to shifting power away from the central government. Ambitious state and local officials grabbed headlines by suing tobacco companies, helping senior citizens pay for prescription drugs, and encouraging same-sex marriages. Even the rise of deficits in the national government and the cutbacks in state and local programs because of budget shortfalls did not immediately reverse this trend.

Almost 100 years before, Woodrow Wilson, the only political scientist to become president, wrote that the relations of the states and federal government cannot be settled "by one generation, because it is a question of growth, and every new successive stage of our political and economic development, gives it a new aspect, makes it a new question." To see federalism as a flexible system for representing the varied interests of a large, diverse country is not far from what we have today. Actually it is not far from what the framers of the Constitution had in mind. (See "Federalism at 55 MPH.")

Limited Government

The principle of *limited government* means that the powers of government are limited by the rights and liberties of the governed. This principle is basic to the very idea of constitutional government: The people give the government listed powers and duties through a constitution, while reserving the rest to themselves. This *political compact* means that government actions must rest on the *rule of law,* approved, however indirectly, by the consent of the governed. Furthermore, the Constitution sets up procedures, such as separation of powers and federalism, to ensure that the government remains limited to its proper duties and powers. As an example, the president may not exercise powers given by the Constitution exclusively to Congress.

Federalism at 55 mph

A 55 mph speed limit has been praised as policy and seldom followed in practice. It was first passed by Congress in the 1970s, during the Arab oil embargo, to conserve fuel and protect public safety. (While under federalism, Congress could not directly legislate state speed limits, it could threaten to withhold federal money from states that didn't comply.) By 1995, times had changed, and a bill raising the limit to 65 mph was before Congress. Residents of Western states, with long distances to travel, especially hated the 55 mph limit, and the newly elected Republican majority saw a popular way of getting a "paternalistic" federal government off the backs of the states.

In a vote that was seen by the press as a strong endorsement of federalism, Congress quickly repealed the 55 mph speed limit. Less noticed was the Senate vote on the same day that approved the federal government's 55 mph limits on big trucks, which were seen as more dangerous than cars. The next day, the Senate voted *not* to repeal popular federal requirements that people use seat belts. Later in that session, the Senate overwhelmingly passed a bill requiring tough new state laws against drinking and driving by minors. Any state not adopting such "zero tolerance" laws would lose up to 10 percent of its federal highway funds.

Confusing? Perhaps, because federalism must compete with other policy choices, in this case concerns for safety and the environment. This makes the modern application of federalism, as the 55 mph limit illustrates, only as consistent as the politics swirling around it.

Limited government guarantees citizens their *rights against* the government as well as *access to* the government. Civil liberties and rights guarantee the openness and competitiveness of the political process, which is not only the right to vote but also the freedom to dissent, demonstrate, and organize to produce alternatives. These rights make voting meaningful. Civil liberties protect citizens from arbitrary governmental power. Under civil liberties would fall a citizen's right to a fair and speedy trial, to have legal defense, and be judged by an impartial jury of his or her peers. Further, government cannot take life, liberty, or property without due process of law, nor interfere with a citizen's right to practice religion, nor invade one's privacy. In short, the people who make the laws are subject to them. (See Chapter 6 on civil rights and liberties.)

Judicial Review

An important means of keeping government limited and of maintaining civil rights and liberties is the power of judicial review vested in the Supreme Court. *Judicial review*, the last constitutional principle, is the judicial branch's authority to decide on the constitutionality of the acts of the various parts of the government (local, state, and federal). The political importance of judicial review can be seen in the Court's rulings that ended racial segregation in schools, that prevented laws banning abortion in the first trimester, and that stopped the recounting of votes in Florida in the 2000 presidential election.

Although judicial review has become an accepted constitutional practice, it is not actually mentioned in the document. There was some debate in the first years of the Constitution over whether the Court had the power merely to give nonbinding opinions or whether it had supremacy over acts of the government. Most people at that time agreed that the Supreme Court did have the power to nullify unconstitutional acts of the state governments, but opinion was divided over whether this power extended to the acts of the federal government. In 1803, the case of *Marbury v. Madison* clarified this power. The Supreme Court for the first time struck down an act of Congress. This power has since become a firmly entrenched principle of the Constitution, though limited by the Supreme Court's own practices and by the other branches of government.

Judicial review not only makes the Court a watchdog limiting the central government but also the guardian of federalism. The latter function, reviewing the acts of state and local governments, has historically been the Supreme Court's most important use of judicial review. Though relatively few federal laws have been struck down by the Court, hundreds of state and local laws have been held to violate the Constitution. As Justice Oliver Wendell Holmes said over 80 years ago, "The United States would not come to an end if we lost our power to declare an act of Congress void. I do think the Union would be imperiled if we could not make that declaration as to the laws of the several states." (See Chapter 5 on the judicial branch.)

How Is the Constitution Changed?

To say that the Constitution has lasted over 200 years is not to say it is the same document that was adopted in 1789. The Constitution has changed vastly. Most of the framers would scarcely recognize the political process that operates today under their constitution. Changes in the Constitution have been made by four major methods: formal amendment, judicial interpretation, legislation, and custom.

Amendments

Although the amendment process is the first way we usually think of for changing the Constitution, it is actually the least common method. Only 27 amendments (including the first 10 amendments, which can practically be considered part of the original document) have been adopted. (The Equal Rights Amendment and the Washington, D.C., Voting Rights Amendment were proposed by Congress but not ratified by the needed three-fourths of the state legislatures.) As those recently proposing an amendment banning gay marriages have discovered, adopting amendments is meant to be difficult. Though the Constitution's framers recognized the need for change in their basic document, they wanted to protect it from temporary popular pressure. Hence, they required unusually large majorities for adopting amendments.

Article V of the Constitution provides a number of methods for adopting amendments. (See Figure 2.1.) Amendments may be *proposed* by a two-thirds vote of each house of Congress or (if requested by two-thirds of the state legislatures) by a national convention called by Congress. They must be *ratified* by conventions in three-fourths of the states, or by three-fourths of the state legislatures (the choice is up to Congress).

The national convention has never been used; all amendments have been proposed by Congress. The most recent attempt occurred

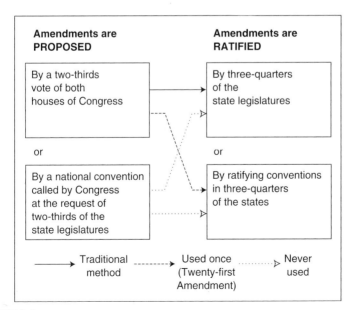

FIGURE 2.1
Amending the Constitution.

in the late 1980s, when 32 states of the needed 34 passed resolutions calling for a constitutional convention to draft a new amendment requiring a balanced budget. Only the Twenty-first Amendment, repealing Prohibition in 1933, was ratified by state conventions. The idea behind this one use of state conventions was that the state legislatures were still full of the same representatives who had passed Prohibition in the first place and conventions seemed likely to be the fastest way to change it. A major reason that the national convention method has never been used to propose amendments is Congress's jealousy toward another body trespassing on its powers. Another is worry over how many other amendments might be proposed by such a convention. After all, the Constitution was written by an earlier runaway convention set up only to amend the Articles of Confederation.

Judicial Interpretation

If the amendment process is the least-used method of changing the Constitution, interpretations by the Supreme Court are the most common. Practically every part of the Constitution has been before the Court at some time or another. The justices have shaped and reshaped the document. Modern Supreme Court decisions have allowed Congress great scope in regulating the economy, prohibited legal segregation of races, allowed local communities to determine the limits of obscenity, and established "one man, one vote" as a constitutional principle governing election to the House of Representatives. The Supreme Court has also given practical meaning to general constitutional phrases such as "necessary and proper" (Article I, Section 8), "due process of law" (Amendments 5 and 14), and "unreasonable searches and seizures" (Amendment 4). No wonder the Supreme Court is sometimes called "a permanent constitutional convention."

Legislation

Although legislation is passed under the Constitution and does not change the basic document, Congress has been responsible for filling in the framework of government outlined by the Constitution. Congress has established all the federal courts below the Supreme Court. It has determined the size of both the House of Representatives and the Supreme Court. The cabinet and most of the boards and commissions in the executive branch have been created by congressional legislation. Most of the regulations and services we now take for granted, such as social security, have come from measures passed by Congress.

Custom

Custom is the most imprecise way in which the Constitution has changed, yet one of the most widespread. Many practices accepted as constitutional are not actually mentioned in the document. The growth of political parties and their role in Congress, the presidential nominating conventions, the breakdown of an independent electoral college, and the committee system in Congress are just a few customary practices not foreseen by the Constitution.

Custom also has changed some practices that, at least on the surface, seem to have been clearly intended by the framers. The Eighth Amendment, forbidding "excessive bail," has not prevented courts from setting bail for serious offenses that is too high for the accused to raise. Although Congress has the right to declare war (Article II, Section 8), presidents have entered conflicts that looked very much like wars (Korea, Vietnam, Iraq) without such a declaration. Customs also have been broken and reestablished by law. The custom that a president serves only two terms was started by Washington and cemented by Jefferson. Franklin D. Roosevelt broke the tradition—with much debate and with war looming—by running for a third term in 1940, and then a fourth term four years later. The custom was made law in the Twenty-second Amendment, adopted in 1951, to keep FDR's example from being followed in the future.

Why Has the Constitution Survived?

How the Constitution has been changed does not entirely explain why it has survived. Indeed, many of the framers saw the Constitution as an experiment not likely to outlive their generation. Various explanations have been offered for why the Constitution has endured to become the oldest written constitution of any country.

The major reason it has lasted probably lies not in the Constitution itself, but in the stability of American society. Upheavals like the Civil War, the Indian campaigns and massacres, and foreign wars all have been handled within the same constitutional structure. The Constitution has been made more democratic to include "out" groups, such as immigrants, former slaves, women, and the poor, that were originally excluded from political participation. The Constitution's emphasis on

A British View on the Constitution's Survival

The nineteenth-century British scholar and diplomat, James Bryce, believed the Constitution deserved "the veneration" bestowed on it. He thought much of its value came from the "political genius" of the Anglo-American race.

> The American Constitution is no exception to the rule that everything which has the power to win the obedience and respect of men must have its roots deep in the past and that the more slowly every institution has grown, so much the more enduring it is likely to prove. There is little in the Constitution that is absolutely new. There is much that is as old as Magna Carta.

Source: James Bryce, *The American Commonwealth.* New York: Macmillan, 1910, vol. 1, p. 28.

procedures has served it well through the wars and depressions as well as the peace and prosperity of various ages.

Other explanations for the Constitution's durability focus on the document. One maintains that it is a work of genius. William Gladstone, the nineteenth-century British prime minister, described it as "the most wonderful work ever struck off at a given time by the brain and purpose of man." Incorporating centuries of English political traditions as well as the framers' own experience, the Constitution set out the principles and framework of government in concise, well-written phrases. (See "A British View on the Constitution's Survival.")

The shortness of the document (some 7,000 words with all its amendments) is another major reason for its durability. Although it sets out the basic principles and structures of a government, the Constitution leaves much only generally stated or not mentioned at all. In a word, the Constitution is *vague.* Many of the most enduring constitutional phrases ("freedom of speech," "due process of law," "all laws which shall be necessary and proper," "privileges or immunities of citizens") have been applied differently at different times in our history. Other principles, such as majority rule and individual liberties, sometimes seem contradictory. It is left to the political players of each age to resolve the conflicts between groups claiming constitutional support. Ambiguity and flexibility have been the Constitution's major strengths in adapting to new political pressures and allowing people to reach compromises under competing principles.

CASE STUDY

Federalism Caught in a Storm:
The Katrina Disaster

On Monday morning, August 29th, 2005, Hurricane Katrina hit the coast of Louisiana about 63 miles southeast of New Orleans. Although missing the brunt of the storm, the city suffered one of the nation's worst natural disasters. Its levees collapsed, flooding much of the area. The failure of these flood walls reflected both shoddy engineering and a historic lack of political will to maintain them. The threat of a hurricane to a city built largely below sea level was well known, with the federal government in 2001 listing it as one of the three most catastrophic events the country could face. But preparations remained, to say the least, inadequate.

In the days that followed the deluge, the response and conflicts of the different levels of government—federal, state, and local—would compound New Orleans' pain. Katrina would illustrate the inconsistencies, the politics, and the hazards surrounding modern federalism. Among the many failures was the failure of communications between leaders of the city, state, and nation.

ON THE GROUND

Katrina overwhelmed New Orleans. It left 80 percent of the city underwater, with no ground transportation, little shelter for those who lost their homes, 75,000 stranded—many on their roofs waiting for rescue—and masses of citizens, mostly poor, heading for the Superdome where promised food, water, and medicine were dwindling. While TV was showing the chaos, and exaggerating reports of crazed looters on the loose, local political leaders running on no sleep were trying to cope with a unique disaster. Mayor Ray Nagin, who had waited until less than 24 hours before the storm struck to call for a mandatory evacuation, seemed shell-shocked.

On Monday evening, President Bush telephoned Kathleen Blanco, Democratic governor of Louisiana. The desperate governor told the president that the worst had happened. "We need your help," she pleaded. "We need everything you've got." The vagueness in the request led the president to not respond with immediate actions. He privately regarded her as incompetent and worried that the partisan divisions between them would lead to the White House being blamed for the difficulties. In the days that followed, administration spokesmen were notably upbeat in describing the situation in New Orleans as "going relatively well." Unfortunately the president was relying on a federal agency that was not up to the huge challenge.

The Federal Emergency Management Agency (FEMA) had been absorbed in the Homeland Security Agency created in a 2003 reorganization designed to elevate antiterrorist programs. This reduced the importance of disaster relief within the administration. Further weakening FEMA was the appointment of Republican allies of the president to run the agency. Bush appointed his campaign manager as the head of FEMA, and when the campaign manager resigned he passed on the position to a college friend with little experience. Trained disaster relief experts tainted by service in the previous administration lost their jobs. FEMA was a bureaucracy crippled by cronyism.

Not surprisingly, both advanced planning and immediate relief efforts were poor. Frightened by reports of lawlessness, the head of FEMA on Monday actually advised emergency responders to *stay home* until requested by local authorities. FEMA also turned down offers of support from other federal agencies because of its concern for security. Examples of incompetence were abundant. In early September, as thousands still awaited help, 600 firefighters from across the nation who had volunteered for rescue duties in New Orleans were taken to Atlanta to sit in a hotel listening to FEMA lectures on customer service and sexual harassment. "This is ridiculous," one yelled at a speaker.

At the same time, local leaders in New Orleans faced a situation where civilization seemed to have dissolved in the rising waters. Police officers deserted their posts, looting was widespread, buses were not available to transport evacuees out of the city—hundreds of school buses had been unthinkingly left in parking lots submerged by the flood. Command and control by local government was sporadic at best. Mayor Nagin avoided the governor in a state where the politics were described as "dysfunctional." Instead the mayor spoke directly to White House officials about his city's needs. He used frequent news conferences to communicate to a national audience. The mayor, who was notably emotional during the days after the storm, soon left the city for Dallas for five days. Before that he had called into a radio talk show to declare to the levels of government above him, "Now, get off your asses and do something, and let's fix the biggest goddamn crisis in the history of this country."

SEND IN THE TROOPS

The need for troops to restore order and allow relief efforts was clear to everyone. But this too got bogged down in the politics of federalism.

On Wednesday, Governor Blanco had called the president requesting 40,000 troops. She expected that these would be mainly National Guard units officially under her control. The president requested that they be federalized, which would put them under the president's authority. Blanco did not think that this would help the rescue and relief efforts, which she felt that FEMA was already botching. The possibility that this would provide a public opportunity to scapegoat her for the post-Katrina mess undoubtedly figured into the calculation. Handing over responsibility for the troops to the president meant minimizing her own role. Why should she let George Bush play hero, leading the cavalry to the rescue?

The president may have had a similar view, seeing no reason why he should help a Democratic governor enhance her profile. (The issue of federalizing National Guard troops in neighboring Mississippi, with a friendly Republican governor, never came up.) Though he had the authority, the president was reluctant to federalize Louisiana's troops without the governor's permission. Such an action would bring back memories of the 1950s and 1960s, when southern governors had been forced to do that in school desegregation fights with Democratic presidents. He was also reluctant to send in regular army units because they were not allowed to perform domestic law enforcement, clearly needed to reestablish order in the streets. While Mayor Nagin supported the president's increased role, it was not a decision that the mayor could make.

Eventually, in a meeting held in Air Force One parked at New Orleans international airport, the governor and president reached a private understanding. She refused to sign a document that would have handed over state control of the National Guard troops to the president. The president dispatched the troops anyway, and Blanco maintained her authority over them. Only with the arrival of federal troops supplementing the state forces some five days after the storm could the immediate crisis be considered to have ended. It may have been that the widespread media reports of federal mismanagement of the rescue efforts motivated the president to reach an agreement.

AFTER THE DELUGE

". . . the infuriating, unmistakable and unnerving lesson of the continuing tragedy is the fundamental failure of government at all levels to protect its citizens, the most vulnerable chief among them."

Editorial, The Washington Post, September 5, 2005.

Blame for the inadequacy of the government's response to the Katrina disaster belongs on all three levels of the federal system. Neither the mayor nor the governor had adequately prepared for the disaster, nor had they plans or people in place to respond in the days following the flood. But the government in Washington cannot avoid a singular fact: It had the resources to meet the challenge. Whether it was troops or emergency responders or relief supplies, the federal government had its hands on what was needed. State and local authorities were overwhelmed. They looked for support to the national government, which, because of mismanagement, as well as politics, was not in a position to respond competently. Federalism complicated the efforts, but political leaders were ultimately responsible for the ineffectiveness of the response.

WRAP-UP

In looking at the writing of the Constitution, we saw how the colonists drew from English political thought, the models of colonial government, and their own experiences with the Articles of Confederation in shaping the Constitution. The framers also were influenced by who they were. As a wealthy elite, they sought to establish a government that would further their own economic concerns as well as the interests of the nation. They divided into Federalists and Anti-Federalists over how strong the government should be and how best to protect individual rights. Ratification and the addition of the Bill of Rights forged an uneasy agreement between the two groups.

The Constitution that has developed centers on four major principles: separation of powers and checks and balances, federalism, limited government, and judicial review. Although these principles remain fundamental, the Constitution has been greatly changed by four main methods: formal amendment, judicial interpretation, legislation, and custom. The changes it has undergone have enabled the Constitution to endure. Perhaps more important to its survival, however, is the stability of American society and the ambiguity of the document itself. The flexibility of the document can be seen in the modern application of the principle of federalism. Still, the question of "who's in charge" is at times not answered quickly or competently enough to prevent the disaster seen in New Orleans in the confusion following Hurricane Katrina.

Does the ambiguity of the document mean that the Constitution, as a body of rules governing the American political game, is meaningless? That essentially it serves the interests of those in power, and its interpretations change only as those interests change? Perhaps. Certainly any document that has legitimized a political system that imported and enslaved its black residents, placed its citizens of Japanese descent in detention camps, allowed sweatshops and child labor, and ignored great wealth alongside extreme poverty has much to answer for. Is the Constitution a grab bag of obsolete principles used to rationalize domination by the few?

As Chapter 1 made clear, politics is not primarily about words—it is about power and ideals. We can't blame a body of principles and procedures for the power or lack of power, for the ideals or lack of ideals of the players in the game. All great historical documents, from the Bible to the Constitution, have been applied differently by different leaders at different times.

More than the rules of the game, then, the Constitution stands as a symbol of the ideals of a people. But it is a symbol with power. That a president is accused of violating the law does mean that he has to answer to impeachment charges in Congress. That people have a constitutional right to elect representatives can change what laws are passed and whether the government continues an unpopular war. That the press has the right to report and publish officials' mistakes—from a Watergate break-in of opposition party headquarters to pictures of Iraqi prisoners being tortured—does affect whether voters keep an administration in power. Even the hypocrisy of officials in bowing to principles they may wish to ignore shows the strength of the symbol.

Yet the substance of the principles in the Constitution must ultimately rest on the political relationships of the players. The *right* to vote is meaningless without the *will* to vote. Freedom of speech means nothing if no one utters any informed criticism of authorities. Judicial safeguards, such as the right to a lawyer, could be lost (and indeed was ignored in the government's treatment of some accused terrorists) without anyone necessarily changing a word of the Constitution. Power without principle may be blind, but principle without power is lame.

The rules of this game, then, are not fixed or unchanging. Though written in the traditions of the past, they live in the politics of the present. They are not only historical guides but future goals as well. Therefore, they remain unfinished as must any constitution setting out to "secure the Blessings of Liberty to ourselves and our Posterity."

THOUGHT QUESTIONS

1. How did the Constitution, as written by the framers, reflect the politics of the time and their need to resolve sectional differences? Give examples of the impact of these politics in how each branch of government is set up.
2. Could the Constitution be adopted today? How would the drafting process be different? What might be changed in the document?
3. How effective are the political structures set up by the Constitution in dealing with contemporary problems? Do the goals of efficiency and democracy in the Constitution work against each other?
4. "Americans can afford optimism partly because their institutions, including the Constitution, were conceived by men who thought tragically." Discuss.
5. How important in the bungled response to the flooding of New Orleans was the federal division of government? Could competent leaders have overcome the obstacles?

SUGGESTED READINGS

Beard, Charles A. *An Economic Interpretation of the Constitution of the United States.* New York: Macmillan, 1935. Pb.
The famous criticism of the framers' economic motivations in writing the Constitution.

Berkin, Carol. *A Brilliant Solution: Inventing the American Constitution.* New York: Harcourt, Inc., 2002.
A historian gives a lively account of the human stories behind the writing of the Constitution.

Brinkley, Douglas. *The Great Deluge.* New York: William Morrow, 2006.
An American historian's record of the incompetence, heroics, and tragedies occurring in the first days after Hurricane Katrina hit New Orleans.

Dahl, Robert. *How Democratic is the American Constitution?* New Haven: Yale University Press, 2001.
An insightful, short read by a noted political scientist that discusses the problems of the Constitution and why the framers wrote it the way they did.

Ellis, Joseph J. *Founding Brothers: The Revolutionary Generation.* New York: Vintage Books, 2000. Pb.
Well-written Pulitzer Prize–winning stories of the flawed but fascinating fraternity of men who unexpectedly made the new American republic work.

Hamilton, Alexander, James Madison, and John Jay. *The Federalist Papers.* New York: New American Library, 1961.
The classic work on what the framers thought about their Constitution.

Sunstein, Cass R. *Designing Democracy: What Constitutions Do.* New York: Oxford, 2001. Pb.
A challenging comparative study by a leading scholar of how constitutions help democracies.

CHAPTER 3

The Executive Branch: The Presidency and Bureaucracy

Presidents are the superstars of the American political game. The president is the only official—along with the vice president—elected by the entire country. Although the head of just one of the three branches of the federal government, in times of crisis he stands as a symbol of the nation. Yet the presidency is an intensely political office, the target of partisan attacks and filled by the leader of a political party.

Historically Americans have idolized their president. He often represents the country's belief in its religious mission as "the last best hope of mankind," and is expected to act on his own for the good of the nation. However, he is selected by voters who like to think that he is still "one of the folks," both king and kin. And of course he is expected to solve many of the nation's problems. These roles create conflicts, especially when they clash with the reality of the limited executive power granted by the Constitution. The result is presidents who disappoint.

Not surprisingly Americans swing back and forth in how powerful they want their presidents. In times of crisis, people demand strong leadership, yet this often leads to popular concerns about the consequences of that strength. In more peaceful periods the call is heard for a less vigorous executive, an inactivity that is soon dismissed as weakness. Today President Obama has attempted to use the policy and publicity tools of his office to pull the country out of a severe recession and implement his program of change. With his considerable power over the nation's economy has come responsibility for the results, both good and bad. (See "Obama: On the Presidency.")

Modern presidents have faced this tension between too much and too little power with varying success. Often they enter office by contrasting themselves with their predecessors. Underlying Richard Nixon's resignation in 1974 was the public's fear of the president's growing—and illegal—use of his authority, revealed by the Watergate scandal. Distancing himself from Nixon, a more open Jimmy Carter fell victim to the popular view that the president was too weak to solve the country's problems of hostages in Iran, gas shortages, and inflation. Ronald Reagan brought a smiling conservatism to the office. His efforts to extend the powers of the office in order to limit the growth of the federal government seemed to achieve more, at least in raising the popularity of his Republican party. Inheriting the optimism of the Reagan years, George Bush Sr.'s low-key concentration on governing proved popular at first, and less so later on.

President Bill Clinton, with his populist charm, shaped an administration that emphasized youth and change. While bogged down in scandals and investigations, Clinton was propelled by a buoyant economy, the excesses of his opponents, and his own political skills.

Obama: On the Presidency

Comfort

"I feel surprisingly comfortable in the job. The challenges are big. But one thing that I'm absolutely convinced about is that you want to be president when you've got big problems. If things are going too smoothly, then this is just another nice home office."

Compromise

"My natural instinct is not to beat the other person down, but rather to understand their point of view and make sure they understand my point of view, and then see if we can find common ground."

"If you've got a working majority, if the American people are behind you, then you can fear no man. You can walk into a room with a sunny disposition. You can smile and say yes sir, no sir, yes ma'am and no ma'am. And if they don't agree with you, you've got the votes and you will beat them and you can do it with a smile on your face."

Captain

"I'm the captain of a ship, I am not the builder of a ship. So there's certain constraints, in terms of the ship's capacities. I can't transform an old steamer into a nuclear submarine. I can't steer the thing faster than its capacities. And most importantly, I don't control the weather or the oceans. On the other hand, given what the oceans are and what the weather is and what the constraints of the ship are, I can be a better captain or a worse captain."

Communications

"And I think that if you think of the presidency just as a bureaucratic job, then you will not be effective. If you think of it only as a rhetorical, political job, you will not be effective. . . . But let's not lose sight of the fact that we also have to persuade the American people as to where the country needs to go."

Confidence

Asked whether he wore boxers or briefs—a question that Bill Clinton had been asked and made the mistake of answering, he replied: "I don't answer those humiliating questions. But whichever one it is, I look good in 'em!"

Sources: Liz Sidoti, Associated Press, April 24, 2009; Richard Wolffe, *Renegade,* New York, NY: Crown Publishers, 2009, pp. 190, 302, 304, 321.

George W. Bush's projected a more businesslike leadership style that didn't quite remove the doubts about the disputed 2000 election and his intellect. The 9/11 attacks silenced dissent in a flurry of patriotism. But after winning a close reelection in 2004, Bush's popularity suffered from the unresolved war in Iraq, a flurry of scandals within his party, his own strident tone, and a financial panic that dragged down the economy. The 2008 election was seen as a striking rebuke both for the Republican who ran, Senator John McCain, and the Republican president who left office.

President Barack Obama inherited a nation deeply pessimistic about the future and suffering the worst recession since the Great Depression of the 1930s. Not surprisingly the new president made his break with the past as sharp as possible. At his inauguration he stated, "On this day, we gather because we have chosen hope over fear, unity of purpose over conflict and discord." He emphasized change not just in politics but in the debate over politics, calling for a bipartisan approach in policies at home and abroad. Whatever the doubts and dissent, a new president was making history.

This chapter is about the president and the executive branch he heads. The growth of the presidency starts from the limited powers granted to the office by the Constitution. Next, we will discuss the different approaches to being president and the various roles of the office. Then there are the departments of the federal bureaucracy under the president, and the problems of controlling the bureaucracy. Finally, a case study looks at the president under the worst of circumstances, the days following September 11, 2001.

The President and the Constitution

The Constitution in Article II grants a president far less power and far fewer duties than it gives Congress in Article I. Nevertheless the opening sentence of the article ("The executive Power shall be vested in a President of the United States of America") and other broad phrases ("he shall take Care that the Laws be faithfully executed") have been used by presidents to justify enlarging their powers. As we will see, presidential practice has vastly expanded the Constitution's ideas of executive powers.

The Constitution requires that the president must be at least 35 years old, a resident of the United States for 14 years, and a native-born citizen. The president can be removed by impeachment or, because of the Twenty-fifth Amendment, if he is disabled. The term of office is fixed at four years. Under the Twenty-second Amendment, passed in 1951, presidents are limited to two terms.

During the last months of his final term the president often is called a *lame duck:* Because he cannot be reelected, his influence— and his accountability—are lessened. For political reasons, the term often is expanded to label presidents in their last term as being power-less, as many Democrats tried to do to President Bush. Strictly speak-ing, only between the election in November 2008 and his successor's inauguration in January 2009 was President Bush a lame duck.

The Electoral College

Presidents are not chosen by direct popular elections. All the votes across the United States are not added up on election day, with the can-didate receiving the most declared the winner. Rather, presidents gain office through the *electoral college.* Each state is granted as many *electors*—members of the electoral college—as it has senators and rep-resentatives combined (the District of Columbia gets three votes). After a presidential election the votes *within each state* are added up, and the candidate with the most votes receives *all* that state's votes in the elec-toral college, except for Maine and Nebraska, which do not use this "winner-take-all" system. If any candidate has a national majority of elec-toral college votes—270, which is 50 percent plus 1—he or she becomes president. If no candidate wins a majority—because several candidates have split the votes—the Constitution provides that the election will be decided by a majority vote in the House of Representatives, with each state delegation casting one vote.

Sometimes the presidential electoral system does not work. In 1800 and 1824 the House of Representatives had to decide on a pres-ident because no candidate received a majority of the vote. In 1876 Democrat Samuel Tilden lost to Rutherford Hayes when a Republican-dominated Electoral Commission awarded the Republican the elec-tion even though Tilden had won the popular vote. Then in 2000 Al Gore won the popular vote by over 500,000 votes yet lost the electoral college, and the presidency, to George W. Bush by 271 to 267. It was an election that came down to a difference of a few hundred votes in Florida and a contested recount halted by the U.S. Supreme Court.

In a uniquely close race like 2000 the messiness of an election is exposed to public view. This mess includes the states determining their own election laws as well as designing and supervising the ballots. It also includes the electoral college. A product of compromises at the Constitutional Convention, the electoral college reinforces federalism by strengthening the smaller states. It was designed to keep partisans— whether state officials, legislators, or Supreme Court justices—from deciding who will be president. As Alexander Hamilton wrote in

The Federalist Papers No. 68, "They have not made the appointment of the President to depend on any preexisting bodies of men who might be tampered with beforehand to prostitute their votes."

The electoral college was created by the authors of the Constitution as another way of filtering the prejudices of the mass of voters. The development of political parties (see Chapter 7) has undercut the purpose of the college, for electors are now pledged to one party's candidate at the time of the elections. After the 2000 election there were calls for a constitutional amendment to replace the "outmoded" electoral college with a direct popular vote. Since many states and interests benefit from the present system these voices for change quickly faded.

Vice President

The major constitutional duties of the vice president are to preside over the Senate and to succeed the president if the office should become vacant. (The Speaker of the House of Representatives and the president *pro tem* of the Senate are next in line.) Traditionally the vice presidency has been seen as a limited, frustrating office. John Nance Garner, Franklin Roosevelt's vice president, commented that his position was "not worth a pitcher of warm spit." But this view is out of date. Just the fact that seven vice presidents became president in the twentieth century has increased the political importance of the office.

Today scholars speak of a "new vice presidency." Vice presidents such as Al Gore, Dick Cheney, and Joe Biden have played key roles in their administrations. They have represented the chief executive in visits overseas, lobbied for him in Congress, and served as the chief presidential adviser. Al Gore was treated as a partner of President Clinton and became the president's chosen successor.

George W. Bush elevated his vice president to become the most powerful in the nation's history. Dick Cheney brought his long experience as a Washington insider—former White House chief of staff, secretary of defense during the 1991 Persian Gulf War, and a congressman from Wyoming. He made the vice president's office the center for a web of like-minded conservative officials throughout the executive branch, many of whom he put in their jobs. Cheney's staff was known for its muscle and its secrecy in moving the Bush administration toward hardline positions on national security issues. His misleading arguments for the war in Iraq and the disasters that followed caused popular disillusionment with the policies and the vice president.

Joe Biden promised to shrink the office closer to its traditional role. Biden explained that the vice president would be an "Adviser in Chief" to the president rather than running what Democrats referred to as Cheney's separate "shadow operation." President Obama has used Biden's decades of Senate experience and his years as chair of the Foreign Relations Committee to help him with congressional relations and national security issues. Less useful was the vice president's tendency to speak candidly off the cuff to the press, which led to problems at times with his more disciplined boss.

History of the Presidency

Forty-four men have been president of the United States, from George Washington, who took office in 1789, to Barack Obama, who became the nation's first African-American president on January 20, 2009. (See Tables 3.1 and 3.2 on pp. 55–56.) Between the two, the influence and duties of the presidency have expanded considerably, if not always in a pattern of constant growth.

Most members of the Constitutional Convention in 1787 did not see a *political* role for the president. They pictured the president as a gentleman-aristocrat—probably because they had George Washington in mind—who would stand above politics as a symbol of national unity. He would be selected by an electoral college to ensure that he was not dependent on popular support. Congress, not the president, was to be the leading branch. Yet strong presidents confronting national problems soon increased these powers, although at times less assertive presidents and popular sentiment have reduced executive power. In the twentieth century, presidential power has irregularly expanded as a result of wars and domestic crises, such as economic depression.

George Washington sent troops to put down a rebellion among farmers in western Pennsylvania who were angered by a tax placed on whiskey. Washington's action in the Whiskey Rebellion was later claimed as the precedent for a president's *residual power* (also called *inherent power*)—powers not spelled out in the Constitution but that are necessary for the president to be able to carry out other responsibilities. The third president, Thomas Jefferson, had fought against establishing a strong executive in the Constitution. Yet as president, he expanded the powers of the office. By negotiating and signing the Louisiana Purchase, gaining the approval of Congress only after the fact (perhaps inevitable in an age of slow communication), Jefferson weakened the principle of checks and balances. Congress played a minor role in doubling the size of the country and then couldn't easily reverse the president's action once it had been taken.

Abraham Lincoln, the sixteenth president, disregarded parts of the Constitution when he led the North in the Civil War. Lincoln raised armies, spent money that Congress had not appropriated, freed slaves

TABLE 3.1 PRESIDENTS OF THE UNITED STATES

Year	President	Party
1789	George Washington	
1792	George Washington	
1796	John Adams	Federalist
1800	Thomas Jefferson	Democratic-Republican
1804	Thomas Jefferson	Democratic-Republican
1808	James Madison	Democratic-Republican
1812	James Madison	Democratic-Republican
1816	James Monroe	Democratic-Republican
1820	James Monroe	Democratic-Republican
1824	John Quincy Adams	Democratic-Republican
1828	Andrew Jackson	Democratic
1832	Martin Van Buren	Democratic
1836	Andrew Jackson	Democratic
1840	William H. Harrison	Whig
1841	John Tyler[a]	Whig
1844	James K. Polk	Democratic
1848	Zachary Taylor	Whig
1850	Millard Fillmore[a]	Whig
1852	Franklin Pierce	Democratic
1856	James Buchanan	Democratic
1860	Abraham Lincoln	Republican
1864	Abraham Lincoln	Republican
1865	Andrew Johnson[a]	Democratic (Union)
1868	Ulysses S. Grant	Republican
1872	Ulysses S. Grant	Republican
1876	Rutherford B. Hayes	Republican
1880	James A. Garfield	Republican
1881	Chester A. Arthur[a]	Republican
1884	Grover Cleveland	Democratic
1888	Benjamin Harrison	Republican
1892	Grover Cleveland	Democratic
1896	William McKinley	Republican
1900	William McKinley	Republican
1901	Theodore Roosevelt[a]	Republican
1904	Theodore Roosevelt	Republican
1908	William H. Taft	Republican
1912	Woodrow Wilson	Democratic
1916	Woodrow Wilson	Democratic
1920	Warren G. Harding	Republican
1923	Calvin Coolidge[a]	Republican
1924	Calvin Coolidge	Republican
1928	Herbert C. Hoover	Republican
1932	Franklin D. Roosevelt	Democratic
1936	Franklin D. Roosevelt	Democratic
1940	Franklin D. Roosevelt	Democratic
1944	Franklin D. Roosevelt	Democratic
1945	Harry S. Truman[a]	Democratic
1948	Harry S. Truman	Democratic
1952	Dwight D. Eisenhower	Republican
1956	Dwight D. Eisenhower	Republican
1960	John F. Kennedy	Democratic
1963	Lyndon B. Johnson[a]	Democratic
1964	Lyndon B. Johnson	Democratic
1968	Richard M. Nixon	Republican
1972	Richard M. Nixon	Republican
1974	Gerald R. Ford[a]	Republican
1976	James E. Carter	Democratic
1980	Ronald W. Reagan	Republican
1984	Ronald W. Reagan	Republican
1988	George H. Bush	Republican
1992	William J. Clinton	Democratic
1996	William J. Clinton	Democratic
2000	George W. Bush	Republican
2004	George W. Bush	Republican
2008	Barack H. Obama	Democratic

TABLE 3.2 VICE PRESIDENTS OF THE UNITED STATES

Year	Vice President	Party	Year	Vice President	Party
1789	John Adams	Federalist	1904	Charles W. Fairbanks	Republican
1792	John Adams	Federalist	1908	James S. Sherman	Republican
1796	Thomas Jefferson	Democratic-Republican	1912	Thomas R. Marshall	Democratic
1800	Aaron Burr	Democratic-Republican	1916	Thomas R. Marshall	Democratic
1804	George Clinton	Democratic-Republican	1920	Calvin Coolidge	Republican
1808	George Clinton	Democratic-Republican	1924	Charles G. Dawes	Republican
1812	Elbridge Gerry	Democratic-Republican	1928	Charles Curtis	Republican
1816	Daniel D. Tompkins	Democratic-Republican	1932	John N. Garner	Democratic
1820	Daniel D. Tomkins	Democratic-Republican	1936	John N. Garner	Democratic
1824	John C. Calhoun	Democratic-Republican	1940	Henry A. Wallace	Democratic
1828	John C. Calhoun	Democratic	1944	Harry S Truman	Democratic
1832	Martin Van Buren	Democratic	1948	Alben W. Barkley	Democratic
1836	Richard M. Johnson	Democratic	1952	Richard M. Nixon	Republican
1840	John Tyler	Whig	1956	Richard M. Nixon	Republican
1844	George M. Dallas	Democratic	1960	Lyndon B. Johnson	Democratic
1848	Millard Fillmore	Whig	1964	Hubert H. Humphrey	Democratic
1852	William R. King	Democratic	1968	Spiro T. Agnew	Republican
1856	John C. Breckinridge	Democratic	1972	Spiro T. Agnew	Republican
1860	Hannibal Hamlin	Republican	1973	Gerald R. Ford[b]	Republican
1864	Andrew Johnson	Democratic (Union)	1974	Nelson A. Rockefeller[b]	Republican
1868	Schuyler Colfax	Republican	1976	Walter F. Mondale	Democratic
1872	Henry Wilson	Republican	1980	George H. Bush	Republican
1876	William A. Wheeler	Republican	1984	George H. Bush	Republican
1880	Chester A. Arthur	Republican	1988	Dan Quayle	Republican
1884	Thomas A. Hendricks	Democratic	1992	Albert Gore Jr.	Democratic
1888	Levi P. Morton	Republican	1996	Albert Gore Jr.	Democratic
1892	Adlai E. Stevenson	Democratic	2000	Richard Cheney	Republican
1896	Garret A. Hobart	Republican	2004	Richard Cheney	Republican
1900	Theodore Roosevelt	Republican	2008	Joseph R. Biden Jr.	Democratic

[a]Vice presidents who became president on the death or the resignation (in the case of Richard Nixon) of their predecessor.

in the South, suspended certain civil rights, and generally did what he felt was necessary to preserve the Union. He even sent money and troops to promote a rebellion in Virginia that created West Virginia, all without participation by Congress. Congress later approved these actions, but the initiative was clearly with the president.

This pattern of *crisis leadership* continued into the twentieth century. Most visible were aggressive presidents like Theodore Roosevelt, who pushed his pro-environment and anti-monopoly policies, and Woodrow Wilson, who led the country into World War I. They were followed, however, by a series of passive presidents in the 1920s (Harding, Coolidge, and Hoover), reflecting a national mood in the country that favored less government activity presided over by less assertive chief executives.

Franklin D. Roosevelt's coming into office in 1933 confronted the Great Depression of the 1930s. FDR's tenure saw a president taking virtually full responsibility for the continual shaping of both domestic and foreign policy. His administration's programs in response to the Depression (called the *New Deal*), and his command of the United States in the international role it would play during and after World War II, firmly established the strong leadership we find today in the presidency. FDR influenced the shape of the office more than anyone else in the twentieth century. Thus Roosevelt is called the first modern president.

Types of Presidents

This growth of the presidency has not been a straight-line expansion of presidential powers. There have been cycles in which the power of the office has waxed and waned, reflecting presidents' personalities and national politics. To simplify matters we will discuss three general approaches that presidents have adopted toward the office and see which chief executives fit into each category.

Buchanan Presidents

The first category is called *Buchanan presidents*, after James Buchanan, known mainly for his refusal to end southern secession by force in 1860. Presidents in this group view their office as purely administrative: The president is aloof from politics and depends on leadership from Congress. Buchanan presidents adopt a *custodial* view of presidential powers: The president is limited to those powers expressly granted to him in the Constitution. Otherwise, they argue, there would be no limits on presidential power. Presidents who have followed this approach generally have been less active chief executives. They include William Howard

Taft, Warren Harding, Calvin Coolidge, and Herbert Hoover—all Republican presidents in the early twentieth century.

Lincoln Presidents

Second, there are the *Lincoln presidents*. In this approach, the president is an active politician, often rallying the country in a crisis. Abraham Lincoln did so in the Civil War; Theodore Roosevelt did it later when he moved to restrain the large business monopolies called trusts. In this century, the Lincoln president also originates much of the legislation Congress considers, he leads public opinion, and he is the major source of the country's political goals.

Lincoln presidents do not interpret the Constitution as narrowly as do Buchanan presidents. In their view the presidency is a *stewardship;* its only limits are those explicitly mentioned in the Constitution. The president's powers, then, are as large as his political skills. Following this approach have been activist presidents such as Andrew Jackson, Theodore Roosevelt, Franklin Roosevelt, Lyndon Johnson, and Ronald Reagan.

Eisenhower Presidents

These two approaches to the presidency were outlined by Theodore Roosevelt who, as the energetic twenty-fifth president, expanded the influence of the office. Another style of presidential leadership is a combination of the first two called the *Eisenhower president.* While General Eisenhower was a skilled leader, he concealed his own involvement in political business. He delegated responsibility widely, which allowed others to take the blame for policy failures while he preserved his own reputation of being "above" politics. This *hidden-hand leadership* hurt Eisenhower's ability to transfer his personal popularity to his party or his chosen successor in 1960—his vice president, Richard Nixon. Many recent presidents since Eisenhower have tried to copy his pose of remaining aloof from partisan politics, with less success.

Modern Presidents

While presidents never fall into exact boxes, modern presidents have leaned toward activism. Lyndon Johnson sought not only to represent a national consensus but also to create and guide this coalition as well. A master politician, President Johnson was known for his midnight phone calls and political arm-twisting to gain support for his proposals. Richard Nixon tried to create an image of the presidency being above politics while using his powers as president for partisan and sometimes illegal activities, climaxing in the Watergate scandal. After Nixon's resignation in

1974, Gerald Ford served a calm, brief presidency. Ford was the nation's first nonelected vice president—he had been selected by Nixon and confirmed by Congress under the Twenty-fifth Amendment.

Jimmy Carter, though respected as a hardworking honest manager, was criticized for his lack of political leadership. Trained as an engineer, Carter spent time privately submerged in policy details. By the end of his term a widespread feeling that national problems—gas lines and inflation at home, Soviet aggression in Afghanistan, and hostages in Iran—were not being solved led to the Democrat's defeat for reelection in 1980.

Ronald Reagan came to the presidency with a career as an actor and two terms as a conservative Republican governor of California behind him. He excelled in the ability to communicate through the media, while delegating broad powers to subordinates. His relaxed, sunny attitude toward the office and his advanced age (76 when he left office) led critics to accuse him of being a "nine-to-five" president. Reagan's public relations and political skills led to decreases in social programs, increases in defense spending, and large tax cuts. His hard line toward the Soviet Union arguably contributed to the fall of communism in Eastern Europe and Russia. His state funeral in June 2004 revealed Reagan's popularity almost two decades after he had been in office. (See "Presidential Mama's Boys")

Reagan's public support helped elect his vice president, George Bush Sr., to the presidency in 1988. This Bush I administration had two faces. The one looking out to foreign affairs beamed with success; the domestic side paled in comparison. Foreign policy gave Bush notable victories, some of his own doing (pushing Iraq out of Kuwait), and some through a mixture of his and others' efforts (the end of the cold war). His domestic claims of being the "education president" and the "environmental president" just added to critics' complaints that he neglected these national concerns. A stalled economy lowered his popular support, and he lost his 1992 bid for reelection.

Bill Clinton brought a youthful zeal for campaigning to the White House plus 12 years experience as governor of Arkansas. With Democrats in control of both houses of Congress in his first two years in office, he passed drastic deficit reductions, but the defeat of his health care reform in 1994 followed by the Republican takeover of Congress limited Clinton's objectives. A moderate "New Democrat," Clinton compromised with Republicans in areas like welfare reform while denouncing their cuts in social programs.

In his second term, Clinton used the president's "bully pulpit" to speak out on issues like race and the Middle East conflict. While

Presidential Mama's Boys

One overlooked part of many presidents' emotional makeup has been their extraordinarily close relationship with their mothers. Harry Truman had a portrait of his mom hung in the White House, and Calvin Coolidge died carrying a picture of his mother. In Richard Nixon's Watergate farewell address, he called his mother a "saint." Lyndon Johnson declared his mother "the strongest person I ever knew." Sara Roosevelt rented an apartment in Cambridge to be near Franklin at college. Years later when some New York political bosses asked him to run for office, he responded, "I'd like to talk with my mother about it first." George W. Bush is described as inheriting his mother's decisive good versus bad instincts. A recent biography of Barack Obama concludes that he "adored and idealized his mother" and quotes him as saying, "what is best in me I owe to her."

It is no accident that most of our presidents were their mother's first son. These strong, often religious women dominated the raising of their favorite, pushing them to overcome the failures of their husbands. Alas, our presidents' fathers were not great role models: Truman's lost his farm in speculation; both Eisenhower's and Nixon's dads were unsuccessful storekeepers; and Reagan's dad had a drinking problem, as did Bill Clinton's stepfather. Obama's Kenyan father left when he was an infant, and the president's memoir revolves around his search for a father and a missing identity.

The sons of these laid-back fathers and dynamic mothers were hardly sissies. Rather, they became self-confident men who took their mothers' belief in them and turned it into real success.

handicapped by scandals—and character lapses—President Clinton's public approval remained high enough to defeat the Republican effort to impeach him. But neither his popularity nor the nation's prosperity was enough to elect his vice president, Al Gore, in 2000.

The man who was elected, George W. Bush, took office as the first president since 1888 to lose the popular vote. Bush's controversial election, his lack of experience in Washington, the appearance of undeserved advancement from being the son of former president, George H. W. Bush, and his bouts of garbled speeches cast early doubt on his performance as president.

These low expectations elevated Bush's achievements. In domestic affairs he won broad income tax reductions, education reform, and Medicare expansion. He put a twist on conservatism by decreasing taxes while increasing the cost and scope of government, which, not surprisingly, caused a large rise in the federal deficit.

Following the 9/11 attacks Bush rallied the nation for the war against terrorism. After an impressive victory in Afghanistan, the intensifying violence and misleading justifications for invading Iraq raised questions about his "gut" judgments. President Bush overcame this opposition in his 2004 reelection campaign by mobilizing his conservative base, attacking Senator John Kerry's wavering leadership, and raising fears of another terrorist attack. Whatever moderation his second term showed, it was not enough to save his party from defeat in the 2006 midterm elections, throttled by doubts about the costly war in Iraq. By the time of the 2008 elections, the economic meltdown, lobbyists' scandals, and near-universal overseas loathing for Bush's aggressive foreign policies combined to heap popular dismay on the departing president. (See "The White House Spins")

The White House Spins

"Spin" is political slang for putting a favorable interpretation on information. In late winter of 2007 the Bush White House used this skill to handle the news that the British were withdrawing 1,600 of their 7,000 troops from southern Iraq.

The withdrawal of troops by America's staunchest ally in Iraq was in sharp contrast to President Bush's controversial "surge" that sent 21,000 more American troops to Baghdad in early 2007. Prime Minister Tony Blair, facing popular opposition in England to the war, announced the withdrawal. He admitted that conditions in southern Iraq were not what he had hoped they would be. At the least, having our principal ally subtracting troops the same month the United States was adding troops was bad timing.

The White House spin was to contend that this was "basically a good-news story." A Pentagon spokesperson declared that the British withdrawal reflected their "success" in stabilizing southern Iraq. The White House Press Secretary said that ultimately this was what the United States wanted to see throughout Iraq—turning control over to the Iraqis. Vice President Cheney added that this shows "things are going pretty well" in some parts of Iraq.

The administration spin wasn't the last word. The *New York Times* responded to the vice president that "nothing in Iraq is 'going pretty well'" and that Cheney was "disconnected from reality." A Republican senator accused the White House of acting like Alice in Wonderland. One editorial concluded, "Spin it any way you like" this withdrawal is not good news for Bush.

Source: The *Washington Post*, February 22, 2007; *New York Times*, February 22, 2007.

The Obama Presidency

It would be difficult to invent a less likely president than Barack Hussein Obama. He is literally an African American, the child of a Kansas mother and a Kenyan father who returned to his country when his son was two. Obama was raised in modest circumstances largely by his grandparents. Obama would later write about his heritage and his search for identity in his remarkably candid memoir, *Dreams from My Father.* His journey of self-discovery took him to Harvard Law School, community organizing in Chicago, the Illinois state legislature, and election to the U.S. Senate in 2004, at which point he was talked about as a candidate for the White House.

How did this long-shot freshman senator in his mid-40s become president? The political setting in 2008 included a battered Republican party, a deeply unpopular president, and a collapsing economy, making any Democratic candidate a likely winner. In seizing the Democratic nomination Obama mounted a disciplined insurgent campaign, raising record amounts of money, organizing energized volunteers nationwide, and creatively using the Internet. His message of change was in sync with the political climate and his own personal history as an outsider. Obama himself possessed that overused term "charisma"; an articulate intellectual who could both inspire and reassure an audience. (See Chapter 7, Case Study: Obama's Online Operation.)

As president he has lived up (or down) to his nickname, "No-Drama Obama." His approach has been that of a pragmatic opportunist, seeking bipartisan solutions or at least justifying liberal programs with moderate rhetoric. He has set broad goals for his administration without micromanaging the details. His early popularity at home and abroad helped him build support for his ambitious program of economic recovery. But it remains to be seen whether a middle way can be found to resolve America's domestic conflicts and foreign dilemmas in the early twenty-first century.

The war with radical Islam has continued in Iraq and Afghanistan, while allies' support has remained uncertain. Ambitious domestic efforts to rescue a faltering economy, conserve energy, protect the environment, and reform health care have faced stern if sometimes kneejerk opposition. The culture war that plagues American politics has continued and intensified, jeopardizing Obama's hopes for bipartisan compromises. The danger facing the president has been that he will not gather enough political consensus to solve problems, but rather just enough to raise these issues and then get stuck. To many Americans President Obama seems like the greatest change their political system could produce. Whether American politics will allow him to achieve enough to meet the country's very real challenges is less clear.

Presidential Hats

The reasons the presidency has expanded lie not only in the history of the office and the personality of the officeholder but also in the increasing expectations focused on the president. When a national problem arises—declining student test scores, rising unemployment, or terrorist threats—the president is expected to respond. He also is legally required to handle a number of important duties, such as presenting the federal government's annual budget to Congress. In meeting these responsibilities, the president wears six hats, often more than one at a time.

Chief of State

The president is the symbolic chief of *state* as well as the head of *government*. (In England, the two positions are separate: The queen is chief of state, a visible symbol of the nation, and the prime minister is head of government, exercising the real power.) As *chief of state*, the president has many ceremonial functions, ranging from throwing out the ball to start the All-Star game to shaking hands with the pope when visiting the Vatican. Because of this role, many people see the president as representing the nation, blessed with extraordinary abilities. This perception raises public expectations, often unrealistically, but also gives him a political advantage. The difficulty in separating ceremonial from political actions was evident after September 11. President Bush rallied the nation at nationalist and religious ceremonies, where he spoke as a nonpolitical chief of state, and yet it was a role with clear partisan consequences. A somewhat sillier example occurred when President Obama addressed the nation's schoolchildren to urge them to work hard and stay in school, but was accused of pursuing a political agenda.

Chief Executive

On his first day in office President Obama signed rules making it easier for the public to get information from government agencies. Reversing Bush administration policies, Obama replaced a presumption of secrecy for a presumption of disclosure in releasing government documents. In keeping his campaign promise to bring transparency to government, Obama was wearing a president's second hat of managing the huge federal bureaucracy in the executive branch. His authority as *chief executive* comes from Article II of the Constitution, which states: "The executive Power shall be vested in a President of the United States of America." Executive power in this instance means the ability to carry out or execute the laws. By the end of 2009 this meant the president headed a bureaucracy spending $2.5 trillion a year and employing just under 2 million civilians (down from 2.2 million in 1990). The federal government, with revenues larger than those of the top 40 U.S. corporations combined, ranks as the largest administrative organization in the world.

Criticism of the bureaucracy is widespread. Presidential candidates in every election inevitably pledge to restrain and reform "Washington." They follow a long bipartisan tradition of promising to get government "off the backs of the American people." Most presidents, Republicans and Democrats, have found that accomplishing their political goals required an increase in the federal budget and bureaucracy, not a reduction.

Chief Diplomat

In his 2002 State of the Union address President Bush condemned Iraq, Iran, and North Korea as an "axis of evil." President Obama delivered a speech in Cairo, Egypt, in June 2009 that stressed American respect for Islam and Arab culture. Both speeches illustrated the importance of the president's role as chief diplomat. As leader of the world's only superpower, a president's words matter.

Under the Constitution, the president has the power to establish relations with foreign governments, appoint U.S. ambassadors, and sign treaties that take effect with the consent of two-thirds of the Senate.

The Senate has traditionally been the legislative branch most involved in foreign affairs. Its power to approve or reject treaties has been limited because most international agreements never reach the Senate. These *executive agreements* do not require the approval of the Senate, and their use has increased to where a president may sign hundreds of them a year. Presidents argue that these agreements usually concern only minor matters and that important issues are still submitted to the Senate.

Modern presidents and the national security agencies in the executive branch remain dominant over American foreign policy. Despite the Senate's power to approve treaties and Congress's power to appropriate money for weapons and foreign aid and to declare wars, the president reigns supreme in foreign relations. The political restraints on the president's power in foreign affairs are far fewer than the checks and balances on domestic matters.

At times this authority over foreign policy has elevated the president's power in the domestic arena. The war on terror, as overseen by the Bush administration, led to infringements of civil liberties, including the tapping of phones without a court order, the jailing of citizens suspected of ties to terrorism without constitutional protections, and the use of torture. This led to resistance by other legislative, judicial, and media players concerned about this striking expansion of presidential powers. Shortly after taking office President Obama created a new detainee policy, prohibited torture, and ordered the detention camp at Guantanamo to be closed within a year.

Commander-in-Chief

Whether it is President Obama sending 17,000 additional American troops to Afghanistan shortly after taking office or George W. Bush mobilizing U.S. military forces to invade Iraq in the spring of 2003, the role is the same: The president is the commander-in-chief of the armed forces. The principle behind this presidential hat lies in *civilian supremacy* over the military: An elected civilian official is in charge of the armed forces. In practice, this authority is given to the secretary of defense, who normally delegates command to military officers. This is not limited to actions abroad, as shown by President Bush's tardy use of federal troops in New Orleans to help victims of Hurricane Katrina. Its political importance has been increased by a war on terror that frequently involves the executive in issues of privacy rights, local policing powers, and freedom of the press. The economic importance of the military is reflected in the FY2010 budget, which spends $556 billion or about 15.6 percent on defense programs.

Although the Constitution gives Congress the power to declare war, Congress has not done so since December 1941 when the United States entered World War II. Presidents, in their role as commander-in-chief, initiated the country's involvement in the Korean and Vietnam wars. Congress supported both actions by appropriating money for the armed forces. Criticism of the president's role in Vietnam led to the *War Powers Act* of

1973 to restrict the president's war-making powers. The law, passed over President Nixon's veto, limited the president's committing of troops abroad to a period of 60 days, or 90, if needed for a successful withdrawal. If Congress does not authorize a longer period, the troops must be removed.

The effectiveness of the War Powers Act is questionable, though presidents generally feel the need to gain congressional approval for any major use of the military. In the first Gulf War (1991), Congress frequently referred to the act while former President Bush cited it as unconstitutional. But Bush Sr. implicitly respected it by seeking a congressional resolution of approval for sending troops to recapture Kuwait.

In gaining approval for using force against Iraq, Congress passed a resolution in October 2002 authorizing the president to use the military "as he determines to be necessary and appropriate" to defend the nation against "the continuing threat posed by Iraq." George W. Bush was encouraged to work with the United Nations and to report to Congress within 48 hours of any military action. The resolution described itself as "specific statutory authorization" under the War Powers Act. Mr. Bush argued that he already was permitted to act as commander-in-chief without a formal declaration of war, but that he wanted a congressional vote to reflect national unity. Many Democrats later argued that this resolution was not the equivalent of a declaration of war, and that they had been duped by the administration's use of faulty intelligence. In short, Congress and presidents have agreed to disagree on the War Powers Act.

Chief Legislator

The Constitution gives the president the right to recommend measures to Congress, but it was not until the twentieth century that presidents regularly participated in the legislative process. The president delivers a *State of the Union address* to a joint session of Congress at the beginning of every year to present the administration's annual legislative program. He also gives an annual budget message, an economic message and report, and  frequently sends special messages to Congress supporting specific legislation. On occasion he will address Congress on bills of particular importance as President Obama did on health care reform. Historically, most bills passed by Congress start life in the executive branch.

The president's main constitutional power as chief legislator is the *veto*. If a president disapproves of a bill passed by Congress, he may refuse to sign it and return it to Congress with his objections. The president can also *pocket veto* a bill by refusing to sign it within 10 days of

Congress adjourning. Congress may override the veto by a two-thirds vote of those present and voting in each house. Only about 1 out of every 5 vetoes is overridden by Congress. In practice the veto is used as a threat to influence a bill while it is still being considered by Congress. President Obama threatened to veto the entire military spending bill in the summer of 2009 to pressure Congress not to fund a jet fighter, the F-22, that the Air Force didn't want but that senators from states that manufactured the plane favored. He won that fight.

Note that President Obama had to threaten to veto an entire spending bill to get one item removed. This is because presidents have no line-item veto. In 1996, the Republican Congress passed a law allowing the president to veto sections of some money bills. Supporters hoped that this line-item veto would reduce federal spending. During its 1997 term the Supreme Court ruled that the line-item veto unconstitutionally expanded presidential powers (*Clinton* v. *City of New York*). Because the Supreme Court had the last word, presidents must still accept or reject the entire bill before them.

Presidents often try to lead Congress by controlling the *national agenda*, which consists of the important political issues that the public concentrates on at any one time. With large Democratic congressional majorities President Obama established a pattern of setting broad goals for legislation without micromanaging the details of the process. In areas like economic stimulus, energy and health reform the White House worked through Democratic leaders on the Hill, especially committee chairs, to act on the president's priorities.

Presidents are frequently unsuccessful in gaining support for their national agenda. An indifferent public, a skeptical press, and entrenched interest groups can combine to derail this legislative strategy. Despite the new president's popularity and his party's dominance of Congress, agreement between independent branches of government isn't always easy. As Senate Majority Leader Democrat Harry Reid said, "I do not work for Barack Obama. I work with him."

The president lobbies the Hill in support of his legislation. He pressures individual members, offers to fund pet projects for states, and tolerates changes in his bills to allow for congressional views. Obama's White House also campaigned to elect Democrats, which included recruiting new candidates to run for Congress, taking polls for them, raising money, and giving them the publicity that comes from a president's visit to their states. Presidents are noted for "killing Congress with kindness"—inviting members to dine at the Camp David retreat, watching basketball games with them, and phoning their sick relatives. Such courtesies build loyalties. More forceful leverage may also prove useful. (See "Presidential Arm-Twisting.")

Presidential Arm-Twisting

West Virginia Senator Robert Byrd, who has had his arm twisted by presidents of both parties, offers a dialogue of what a White House phone call is like:

"Hello, Mr. President."

"Bob, I have been wanting to talk to you about something. . . . I know you have some moneys in the appropriations bill for the Gallipolis Locks and Dam."

"Yes, sir."

"The people of West Virginia, in my opinion, are to be complimented in having you as their Senator. I know you have worked hard for that funding. . . . By the way, Bob, we have this piece of legislation that is going to be coming up in the Senate in a few days to authorize moneys for the Contras in Central America. Gee, I wish you would support that, Bob. . . . It will be used only for food and medicines. . . . I respect you for your opposition to that funding, but I wish you would see your way to vote with us next time on that. Can you do it?"

"Well, I will certainly be glad to think about it, Mr. President. . . ."

"Well, Bob, I hope you will. And by the way, that money for the heart research center in Morgantown that you have worked for, I will bet your people love you for that."

"Yes, Mr. President. There is a lot of support for that in West Virginia."

"Bob, I have given a lot of thought to that. Be sure and take another look at that item we have, funds for the Contras."

Source: New York Times, July 26, 1985, p. A10. Copyright © 1985 by The New York Times Company. Reprinted by permission.

Party Leader

A president leads his party. Wearing his party hat, the president faces a number of major duties: to choose a vice president after his own nomination; to distribute a few thousand offices and numerous favors to the party faithful; and to demonstrate that he is trying to fulfill the *party platform,* the policy program adopted at the nominating convention. The president also is the chief campaigner and fundraiser for his party. He names the national chair and controls the national party machinery.

The president's grip on his party has traditionally been limited by the decentralized nature of American parties. Members of Congress are selected by voters in their districts and states, and serve as long as they're reelected. A president has no direct power to refuse members of Congress their party's nomination. However, the Republicans under

President Bush pioneered a strengthened national organization and exercised a great deal of influence over a party that, until 2006, dominated the national government. While President Obama has frequently promoted bipartisanship, he has not let this weaken his ties to Democrats, in part because of his dependence on congressional party members for passing his administration's programs.

The Public Presidency

A major result of the president's many powers and roles is his influence over mass opinion. The president's visibility, standing as a symbol of the nation, and position as a single human being compared with a frequently impersonal government give the chief executive a great deal of public support in the political game. The White House offers what Theodore Roosevelt called "a bully pulpit."

"Going public" has become an essential part of presidential power. A president with visible public support can increase his overall prestige within Washington as well as his influence on a specific issue. By rallying public opinion, pressure can be brought on official Washington—usually Congress—to support the chief executive.

Mobilizing public opinion behind the president results from careful planning. The White House staff sells the president's message through techniques used in election campaigns. Polling of public opinion will first be used to determine which issues and arguments have the greatest positive impact. Then the topic may be presented in a nationally televised speech, or the president may hit the road to push his plan through local media. Cabinet secretaries and allies in Congress may meet with groups to reinforce the message. All of this can be directed from the White House staff as a coordinated national campaign. These tactics were used by President Bush following 9/11 to maintain public support for his response to the attacks. The strategy of "going public" is a key weapon in keeping popular backing for the public presidency. (See "9/11: A President's Trial by Fire.")

This visibility may work against him. After all, a president is chosen by election and has to keep the voters' support to keep himself and his party in office. This means accomplishing his administration's goals as well as maintaining his own personal popularity. But these two aims are not always compatible. Two presidents, Lyndon Johnson—despite domestic legislative successes—and Richard Nixon—despite foreign policy achievements—left office widely unpopular. Johnson was unpopular because of the Vietnam War; Nixon, because of Watergate. In both cases the public attention focused on them by the mass media hastened their decline. George W. Bush completed his second term confronting a public unhappy with a costly war in Iraq, an economy in rapid decline, and administration policies that seemed ineffective at home and abroad. (See "Presidential Privacy and the Press: FDR.")

Some presidents have been luckier. President Reagan, with his career as a Hollywood actor behind him, was one of the most skillful chief executives at using the media to gain public support. President Clinton's folksy manner and detailed command of issues did not quite overcome press suspicion of his honesty. He preferred going around national reporters by favoring out-of-Washington speaking and their local reporters—a practice continued by Bush and Obama.

President Obama has used his position of national leadership to mobilize public support and travel "to the people." He has made frequent TV appearances, including giving informal interviews like *The Tonight Show*, and has held at least one public event daily to guarantee news coverage. Despite journalists' concern that he has been overexposed most people haven't minded, at least not initially. Not surprisingly he has been attacked for everything from a "socialist" healthcare reform to winning the Nobel Peace Prize. Like chief executives before him Obama has positioned himself to the public as representing the national interest against the "special interests" found inside the Beltway around Washington. As he stated in one weekly radio address, "The system we have now might work for the powerful and well-connected interests that have run Washington for far too long. But I don't. I work for the American people."

While keeping up his standing with other branches of the government and the public at large, the president must carry out the tasks of his office and the goals of his administration. In doing so, his most critical

Presidential Privacy and the Press: FDR

Franklin Roosevelt, a polio victim, could not walk. He was protected by the press in ways that seem amazing to modern presidents. Of 35,000 press photographs of FDR in the archives only two showed him confined to a wheelchair. When he occasionally fell in public, photographers would take no pictures and live radio broadcasts would not mention it.

The press's rule of thumb was that a president's private life should stay private unless it seriously interfered with his job performance. But this rule extended into 1944 (the year before his death) when FDR's failing health was a legitimate concern. His hearing had deteriorated to where he had to have questions at his press conference repeated for him. Publishers like Henry Luce of *Time Magazine*—a strong Republican—refused to print photos showing the president's poor health. World War II was going on and this was seen as giving comfort to the enemy.

relationship is with the bureaucracy, the huge organization that manages programs ranging from launching shuttles into orbit to testing drugs. What makes up this bureaucracy and how the president tries to control it is the focus of the rest of this chapter.

The Federal Bureaucracy

The federal bureaucracy carries out much of the work of governing. Despite the negative sound of the word, a *bureaucrat* is simply an administrator, a member of the large administrative organization—the bureaucracy—that carries out government policies. The U.S. bureaucracy is generally competent and uncorrupt, distinguishing it from many other bureaucracies around the world. It is what makes the country well governed—with notable exceptions like the Hurricane Katrina relief efforts. The great historical growth of the national government has produced an administrative system unequaled in size and complexity. Whether this bureaucratic organization is the servant or master of government varies from case to case.

Most of the bureaucracy is within, or close to, the executive branch. Its structure can be broken down into the executive office of the president, the cabinet departments, the executive agencies, and the regulatory commissions. (See Figure 3.1.)

Executive Office of the President

In 1939 the *executive office* was established to advise the president and to assist him in managing the bureaucracy. It has grown steadily in size and influence and today it includes over a dozen agencies and some 1,400 people. (See Figure 3.2.) Three of the most important agencies of the executive office are the White House office, the National Security Council, and the Office of Management and Budget. The *White House office* is a direct extension of the president. Its staff is not subject to Senate approval. In recent years, centralization of executive power has increased the authority of the White House staff at the expense of the cabinet officers. White House Chief of Staff Rahm Emanuel, who came into office with President Obama, has a reputation of being a hard charging, demanding boss. He manages the staff, keeps the paperwork flowing, and serves as the gatekeeper to the president. Rahm (called Rahmbo behind his back) is more likely than his boss to apply the pressure in negotiations over policy, which of course allows Obama to appear more reasonable. The staff, often veterans of the campaign team, perform a variety of tasks from speech writing and press briefings, to relations with Congress and drawing up the president's schedule.

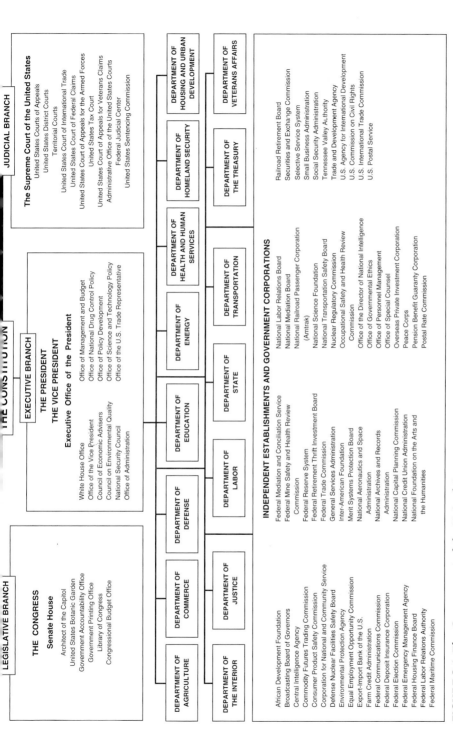

FIGURE 3.1 The Government of the United States. Source: U.S. Government Manual.

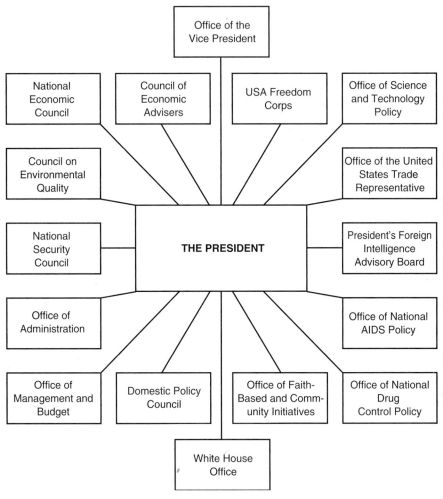

FIGURE 3.2
Some of the Offices in the Executive Office of the President.
Source: http://www.whitehouse.gov

The White House staff is frequently part of the problem of a president losing touch with reality. In the past strong chiefs of staff have alienated Congress and the media with their arrogance. The president's
residence has taken on the trappings of a royal castle with the staff acting like a palace guard isolating the president from the outside world. A
special assistant to Lyndon Johnson described the staff's relationship to
the president as that of a doting mother to a spoiled child—"Whatever
he wants is brought to him immediately." Many people have spoken
of the intimidation that comes from speaking to a president, and the

First Ladies in History

There is no position of first lady mentioned in the Constitution. Yet presidents' wives have often been their husbands' key advisor.

Dolly Madison, wife of the fourth president, was the only first lady threatened by war. Responding heroically during the War of 1812, she refused to leave the White House—which the British later burned. She retreated only after she took with her documents including the Declaration of Independence and the Constitution.

Eleanor Roosevelt, during World War II, maintained that America could not fight for democracy abroad without strengthening it at home. As history's most active first lady she flew with Tuskegee Airmen to show her confidence in black pilots and toured an internment camp for Japanese Americans to press for their release.

Hillary Rodham Clinton was deeply involved in presidential policymaking, from leading a major, if unsuccessful, health care reform to human rights overseas. Her experience propelled her to the senate from New York, to become a serious candidate for the White House, and to her current job as secretary of state.

Laura Bush kept her private life private. A pro-choice secret smoker, she quietly exercised real power in the Bush White House. She got increased funding for AIDS in Africa, nixed at least one cabinet appointment, and regularly advised her husband on his public performances.

Michelle Obama has said she wants to focus on being "mom-in-chief" to her two young daughters. She initially avoided policy matters and opted for a more traditional role as the nation's first black First Lady, while urging a young generation toward public service.

difficulty of dissenting in front of him. That may be one reason that presidents have come to rely on their wives for frank opinions. (See "First Ladies in History.")

The current White House reflects its president's calm personality. President Obama has repeatedly said that he doesn't want a team full of people who agree with him. He admires historian Doris Kearns Goodwin's book *Team of Rivals*, which describes how Lincoln assembled a war cabinet of political opponents. To some extent Obama has followed this model. He named Hillary Clinton secretary of state and kept Republican Robert Gates as secretary of defense, and then allowed them to manage their own departments. Unlike the previous administration where the president valued internal harmony, Obama enjoys the rigor of a back-and-forth debate on issues. As he said to a reporter, "The lesson is to not let your ego or grudges get in the way of hiring absolutely the best people." Obama takes pride in his pragmatic approach to finding the best candidate for the job, not necessarily the candidate who shares his ideology.

Obama's reassuring manner permeates the atmosphere at the current White House. He has been described as radiating an "Aloha Zen" of a man not too full of himself. The environment is a bit less formal than under Bush, with casual dress on the weekends the standard. The president likes to have breakfast with his daughters in the morning and exercise before his 30-second commute to the Oval Office downstairs. But no one would call the place "relaxed." The norm is 14-hour workdays, a constant flood of demanding issues, inevitable stress, and the threat of staff burnout.

The *National Security Council (NSC)* was established early in the cold war (1947) to coordinate American military and foreign policies for the president. These policies mainly involve the State and Defense departments, which are represented on the council. Presidents have varied in how much they wished to use the NSC. In President Bush's first term, National Security Adviser Condoleezza Rice became a key player, coordinating agency input to the White House and planning for the war on terrorism and the invasion of Iraq. President Obama's national security advisor, former Marine General Jim Jones, has played a less visible role in policymaking.

The *National Economic Council (NEC)* was established in 1993 because President Clinton decided that the United States needed an organization similar to the NSC to manage orderly economic policymaking. In its formal structure the NEC includes cabinet members plus various top aides, and coordinates the executive branch's economic activities. Under its director, Larry Summers, it has been a key actor in shaping Obama's economic recovery policies.

The *Office of Management and Budget (OMB)* was created by President Nixon in 1970 to replace the Bureau of the Budget. Departments of the executive branch submit competing claims for shares in the federal budget to OMB. Besides preparing the budget, OMB is an important general-management arm of the president. It helps control the executive branch by overseeing the agencies and their success in accomplishing their programs. Preparing and administering the annual budget, which is then submitted to Congress for approval, gives OMB tremendous power within the government. OMB has a well-deserved reputation for brutally reducing spending requests by government agencies. Obama's OMB is led by Director Peter Orszag.

The *Council of Economic Advisers* is another important unit of the executive office. Its three-member council of economic experts, appointed with Senate approval, helps the president form a national economic policy and predicts future economic developments. Christina Romer currently serves as chair.

Obama's Czars have been the president's most notable organizational change. Sometimes referred to as ad hoc government (from the Latin term "for this purpose"), Obama by mid-2009 had appointed 33 "czars." Under this innovation in presidential management, a top-level official, or czar, is assigned responsibility for a current foreign or domestic issue requiring swift action. Examples include an energy czar, who promotes smooth cooperation among energy groups and agencies; a stimulus accountability czar, who monitors wasteful spending; and a compensation czar, who oversees the salaries of executives of companies that receive bailout money. Because they are outside formal channels, not confirmed by the Senate and only reporting to the White House, some have seen this as a presidential power grab. One Democratic senator declared that Obama's system of czars threaten the Constitution's checks and balances.

The Cabinet Departments

The *cabinet departments*, created by Congress, are the major agencies of the federal government. At first there were only 3 (the departments of State, War, and the Treasury); today there are 15. The expansion of the cabinet has been due largely to the growth of problems that political interests and public opinion wanted the federal government to deal with.

The newest cabinet department, Homeland Security, came out of the widespread frustration with the bureaucratic "turf wars" that hindered the nation's security both before and after 9/11. While originally pushed by congressional Democrats over the administration's objections, it was soon embraced by the Bush White House. The Homeland Agency combined 22 agencies and some 170,000 employees in a cabinet department that aimed to centralize domestic security. It was the biggest government reorganization since the creation of the Defense Department in the late 1940s. The complexity of blending various agencies with different workplace cultures and physical locations behind a common mission was reflected in the criticism of the department's bungled efforts that followed Hurricane Katrina. FEMA, which was placed under Homeland Security, complained that its budget, people, and mission of emergency assistance were buried by the superagency's focus on combating terrorism. Efforts to reorganize bureaucracy usually promise more than they deliver. (See Chapter 2, Case Study: "Federalism Caught in a Storm.")

Each cabinet department is headed by a secretary, who is appointed by the president with the consent of the Senate, which is usually given. Cabinet secretaries hold office as long as the president wishes. Pressures from their staff and constant involvement with the problems of their agencies may cause secretaries to act more like lobbyists for their departments than delegates of the president. Because of this detachment they often play a secondary role to the White House office. Cabinet secretaries in more than one administration have been heard complaining that they were excluded from important administration decisions, that young White House staffers with large egos were blocking their access to the president.

The cabinet has no power as a body. How much the president uses the cabinet as a whole is strictly up to him. Although many presidents entered office promising to give the cabinet more power, things have not worked out that way. Neither Clinton nor Bush used the cabinet as a whole, except for ceremonial photo opportunities. President Obama continued this tradition by inviting the press in to his first official Cabinet meeting to call for a $100 million cut in government spending, and then not doing much else with the group. As one White House scholar, Bradley Patterson, wrote, "The Cabinet is for pictures and stories and publicity." This traditional lack of a policymaking role underlines a story about President Lincoln being opposed by his entire cabinet on an issue. He remarked, "Seven nays, one aye; the ayes have it."

A cabinet department may only be a loose structure containing strong, independent groups. For example, the attorney general has authority over the FBI, which is part of the Justice Department. Yet the reports on FBI missteps in tracking the Arab terrorists who hijacked American planes in 2001 and the difficulty in steering the bureau from crime detection to terrorist prevention illustrated the independence of the FBI from any administration's control. The FBI's ability to keep itself separate from the Homeland Security Department showed that this autonomy was likely to continue.

Much of the work of cabinet departments involves serving the interests of clients for whom they were established in the first place. Departments like Labor (unions), Commerce (business), and Agriculture (farmers), are designed to promote and develop the goals of their industry. Their regional offices are set up to better serve these clients, with Agriculture's "extension agents," who encourage better farming practices, being the best known. Back in Washington these departments, and others like Education and Transportation, operate like a *client agency,* lobbying for the bills and regulations that their industries need.

The Executive Agencies

Executive agencies are simply important agencies of the executive branch that are not in the cabinet. Their heads are appointed by the president with approval of the Senate, but they are not considered major enough to be part of the cabinet. Examples of these are the Office of Personnel Management (OPM), the National Aeronautics and Space Administration (NASA), and the Central Intelligence Agency (CIA).

Under executive agencies we might include *government corporations,* which began as semi-independent but have come increasingly under presidential control. Government corporations, like private corporations, perform business activities such as operating a transportation system or developing and selling electricity. They are usually governed by a board of directors, have limited legislative control over them, and allow for flexible administration. The Tennessee Valley Authority (TVA) is a government corporation, set up in the 1930s to develop electricity for the Tennessee Valley. The U.S. Postal Service was established in 1970 when Congress abolished the post office as a cabinet department and set it up as a semi-independent, government-owned corporation. Amtrak is also a government corporation overseeing what passes for train service.

The Regulatory Commissions

Regulatory commissions are charged with regulating and making rules for certain parts of the economy. Examples are the Federal Trade Commission (FTC), which oversees unfair business practices and consumer protection, and the Federal Communications Commission (FCC), which regulates telephones, radio, Internet, and TV. Although the president appoints the members of the commissions and chooses who chairs them, the commissions are relatively independent of all branches of the government. They are bipartisan (members come from both parties)—the president has only a limited right to remove commissioners, who generally serve longer terms than the president—and there is no presidential veto over their actions. These commissions have all three capacities of government: They make rules that have the force of law (legislative), administer and enforce these regulations (executive), and conduct hearings and issue orders (judicial). Their decisions can be reviewed by federal courts, while their authority and budget can be reduced by Congress.

The important Federal Reserve Board (Fed), under Chairman Ben Bernanke, is a special type of regulatory agency that determines general monetary policies, like short-term interest rates, for Federal Reserve Banks. During the financial meltdown of fall 2008 the Fed was unusually active in arranging, in cooperation with the Treasury Department, rescue packages for large banks and insurance companies threatened with extinction. Fed Chairman Bernanke also ensured that enough money was in circulation to keep the stalled economy from slipping into a depression. The Fed played a crucial role in calming panicked stock, bond, and currency markets by playing this role of lender of last resort, which may have been its most important task. Some banks, such as Bank of America, were saved; others, such as Lehman, were allowed to fail. After the crisis was over, observers generally gave the Fed good marks for its efforts to preserve the banking system, or at least the biggest Wall Street banks.

The logic behind these commissions was the idea that the economy required oversight on complicated matters on which Congress didn't have the technical expertise. They were made independent because their decisions were not supposed to be made on a partisan basis. Their independence from the rest of the government has left the public with little control over their activities. The commissions are pressured by the groups they are regulating, and the lack of governmental controls has led them to negotiate with, rather than regulate, important economic interests. They have been charged with serving powerful economic clients rather than exercising oversight. Following the Bernie Madoff scandal, the Securities and Exchange Commission (SEC) was accused of not closely regulating the financial industry and mutual funds. While it was a valid criticism, the SEC during President Clinton's administration had been accused of overregulation by the same business groups that now blamed lax government supervision. (See "The SEC and the Bernie Madoff Scandal.")

Problems of Bureaucracy

When most Americans hear the word *bureaucracy,* they think of incompetence and red tape, of faceless administrators blindly following rules regardless of their impact on people's lives. Yet bureaucracies are set up to apply standardized rules, to treat people the same or at least according to some standard operating procedure (SOP). The problems with bureaucracies seem to be related to their size rather than the nature of the public or private organizations they serve. The complexity of any large bureaucracy makes it hard to tell who is responsible for a particular action, which inhibits public oversight.

Franklin Delano Roosevelt created the modern American bureaucracy. The only president to be elected to four terms, FDR brought the United States through the Great Depression of the 1930s and World War II. To fight the depression, Roosevelt started 30 new federal agencies, including well-known ones like the Social Security

The SEC and the Bernie Madoff Scandal

In the last decade deregulation dominated Washington. Efforts were made to deemphasize government rules over business and the marketplace. The Securities and Exchange Commission, which was established in the 1930s to regulate the stock market, changed under Republican Chairman Christopher Cox. The SEC limited its staff to collecting penalties from corporations violating regulations. Staff morale was considered poor.

In June 2009 one of the world's largest financial frauds ended with Bernie Madoff convicted of fleecing investors of $50 billion. In Madoff's "ponzi scheme" earlier investors were paid with money from new clients, with no money actually invested. It had gone on for years. Despite repeated complaints that Madoff's profits were impossibly high, the SEC had failed to uncover wrongdoing and had not pursued many credible complaints. Blame was placed on an agency that was short of staff and underfunded—all in keeping with an emphasis on deregulation. It was not the SEC but Madoff's own sons who alerted the FBI. Madoff was sentenced to 150 years in prison. The Obama administration replaced Chairman Cox.

Administration and the Securities and Exchange Commission (SEC). Later, to pay for the war, payroll deductions allowed the government to automatically collect income taxes. As a result, taxes poured into Washington at six times the rate as before the war and, of course, the bureaucracy expanded.

This growth in government has continued since FDR. Federal taxes now take 20 percent of the nation's gross domestic product, four times more than in Roosevelt's first years. The federal budget is three times what it was when Jimmy Carter was president. Under conservative George W. Bush, the cost and scope of government increased even more than under his more liberal predecessor. And in Barack Obama's effort not only to reverse the severe recession he inherited but also to invest in infrastructure, health care reform, and energy alternatives, he has increased the budget, the deficit, and, of course, the bureaucracy.

In the 1980s and 1990s public distaste for the bureaucracy helped antigovernment politicians gain positions of power. They then faced the dilemma of both denouncing bureaucrats and depending on these experts to carry out public policies. Bureaucrats also proved a useful scapegoat for failed policies. Whether in 2003 the CIA bureaucracy misjudged the presence of weapons of mass destruction in Iraq, or whether it was pressured by the Bush White House to shape its findings to support administration policies has became an issue in assessing blame for the war.

At times dissenting bureaucrats have risked their careers by leaking information to the press that their superiors preferred to keep from the public. In recent years, torture in military prisons, experts' widespread doubts about Iraq's alleged nuclear weapons, and wiretapping Americans' phone calls only became known because government employees leaked to the media, which had the freedom to publish the classified information. Policy battles among bureaucratic agencies frequently result in leaks to the press and a more open public debate than many high government officials would prefer.

Rise of the Civil Service

In the federal government's first century, the usual method of choosing bureaucrats was known as the *spoils system*. Taken from the phrase "to the victor belong the spoils," the spoils system meant that victorious politicians filled government jobs with their supporters. This system of patronage became widespread during the administration of Andrew Jackson (1828–1836) and peaked under Abraham Lincoln (1860–1865). These appointees did not need to be educated in their fields, but as the skills expected of bureaucrats became more complex and corruption grew, pressure for reform increased.

In 1881 President James Garfield was assassinated by a disappointed (and crazy) office seeker. The new president, Chester Arthur, backed by public outrage over the murder, supported the Civil Service Reform Act (also known as the *Pendleton Act*), which was passed by Congress in 1883. The law set up a bipartisan Civil Service Commission under which government employees were chosen by merit through examinations. At first only about 10 percent of federal employees were covered by civil service, but the system has grown and now covers practically the entire bureaucracy. This has considerably diminished the spoils system and has added stability to government. The president today fills only about 5,000 patronage jobs, of which fewer than one-third are policymaking. While weakening the spoils system, it also has weakened presidential control of the bureaucracy; the bureaucrats know they will have their jobs long after the current administration passes into history.

Bureaucrats as Policymakers

The traditional idea of *public administration* was that *policy* and *administration* were two different functions of government. Elected officials, the president and Congress, should make policy. The unelected bureaucracy should carry it out. The goal of bureaucracy was "efficiency." According to this ideal model, bureaucrats only administer policy and provide their expert knowledge to elected policymakers. Today political scientists consider this traditional view inadequate, if not a bit naïve.

Politics does not end when a law is passed. Conflicts continue in the administration of the law. In order to pass a bill, Congress may reach a battle-scarred compromise, resulting in vaguely worded requirements. That leaves it to the administrators to referee the debate—on, say, how clean is clean water or what towns can do with their stimulus funds—in applying the law. Before the bill is passed, bureaucrats may have had an influence by their advice and information, even shaping the bill with congressional staff. Afterward they may apply the law in changed political and economic situations not foreseen by those who drafted it. And, of course, bureaucracies have interests of their own, such as increasing their budget or protecting their "turf." The result is that the model of a bureaucrat as a politically neutral administrator looks like a single musical note in a symphony of sounds. Bureaucrats carry other tunes as well.

Bureaucracies are involved in policymaking by exercising legislative, judicial, and executive powers. For example, the Internal Revenue Service (IRS) holds hearings on tax cases, makes judicial findings, and issues regulations. These legislative and judicial powers have been delegated by Congress. In exercising executive power, federal bureaucracies draw up long-range plans and then make decisions about day-to-day operations: Which schools should get education aid in Pakistan? Will roads harm this Oregon national forest? Should accused terrorists born in America get constitutional protections? Decisions made by administrators in the executive branch include the government's most important policy choices.

The President and the Bureaucracy

Curiously, the bureaucracy is both an important support for the president and a major limit on his actions. The agencies of the federal government give the president access to more information than anyone else is likely to have, and allows him to initiate actions to which others must react. But in carrying out his administration's policies, the president must rely on the information, advice, and activities of many others. Keeping control over the 2 million employees of the executive branch is a full-time job in itself. As political scientist Richard Neustadt commented, the president spends much of his time finding out what his subordinates are doing in his name.

Members of the bureaucracy may work to protect their own agencies or may respond to pressures from economic interests threatened by presidential policies. They may ignore the president's orders and delay or even sabotage him, even on trivial matters. (See "The President and the Mouse.") Often executive departments have long-standing rivalries with each other: Labor versus Agriculture on food prices or State Department versus Defense Department over national security policies. The president must judge these conflicts yet maintain close ties with both sides.

Cabinet officials appointed by the president may represent their own departments' interests against those of the president. Does the secretary of defense represent the president to the Defense Department, or the department to the president? Clearly both, but conflict often results.

 ## The President and the Mouse

The problems presidents have with their bureaucracies are not always earth-shaking policies. An example from the Carter presidency:

> When a couple of mice scampered across the president's study one evening last spring, an alarm went out to the General Services Administration, housekeeper of federal buildings. Some weeks later, another mouse climbed up inside a wall of the Oval Office and died. The president's office was bathed in the odor of dead mouse as Carter prepared to greet visiting Latin American dignitaries. An emergency call went out to GSA. But it refused to touch the matter. Officials insisted that they had exterminated all the "inside" mice in the White House and this errant mouse must have come from outside, and therefore was the responsibility of the Interior Department. Interior demurred, saying that the dead mouse was now inside the White House. President Carter summoned officials from both agencies to his desk and exploded: "I can't even get a damn mouse out of my office." Ultimately, it took an interagency task force to get rid of the mouse.

Source: Hedrick Smith, "Problems of a Problem Solver," *New York Times Magazine,* January 8, 1978. Copyright © 1978 by The New York Times Company. Reprinted by permission.

Those benefiting from specific programs don't want them touched, whatever a president may want. And whether they are retired people or doctors or oil companies, these groups are usually intent on preserving their benefits. Government programs create and reward beneficiaries, who in turn support continuing the program seemingly forever. President Ronald Reagan entered office promising to abolish two cabinet departments—Education and Energy. He left office having created one, Veterans in 1988, with Education and Energy still there. As one member of congress remarked, bureaucrats may have discovered the secret of eternal life—government programs.

However attractive the public finds the general idea of limiting their government and restraining the bureaucracy, when challenges arise—whether from hurricanes or recessions or terrorists—Americans, and their president, understand the need to act. If growth in the economy is to be restored, if unemployment is to be reduced, if the financial giants of Wall Street are to be rescued and restrained, then government will be involved. The problems facing America at home and abroad may well require a president to respond. That response may be financial or political, educational or military, but if it is to be more than words it will call on the skills and resources that only a large organization, the bureaucracy, can bring.

Especially in a crisis.

9/11 Viewed as History

Historian Joseph J. Ellis assessed 9/11's place in American history. His first question was where the attacks ranked as a threat to the survival of the republic. At the top of the list he put the War for Independence, the War of 1812, the Civil War, World War II, and the cold war, specifically the Cuban missile crisis of 1962 with its risk of nuclear conflict. Ellis concluded that 9/11 did not rise to the highest level of danger because it did not threaten the survival of the republic.

He then asked what history told us about earlier responses to these traumatic events. Here he mentioned, as precedents for the Patriot Act and government wiretapping of citizens, the 1798 Alien and Sedition Acts, the denial of habeas corpus during the Civil War, the Red Scare of 1919, the internment of Japanese Americans in World War II, and the Senator McCarthy "witch hunts" of the 1950s. He thought that none of these reactions to perceived national security threats seemed justified. To modern historians, they appeared "excessive, even embarrassing."

"History suggests that we have faced greater challenges and triumphed, and that overreaction is a greater danger than complacency."

Source: Joseph J. Ellis, "Finding a Place for 9/11 in American History," OpEd, *The New York Times,* January 28, 2006.

CASE STUDY

9/11: A President's Trial by Fire

It was a horrible day, for the nation and the president. On Tuesday morning, September 11, 2001, four teams of 19 Arab terrorists took control of four California-bound jets at three East Coast airports. Using the planes as "smart bombs" they crashed into both towers of the World Trade Center and the Pentagon. (The fourth plane, United 93, apparently thwarted by passengers, dove into a field in Pennsylvania.) The huge 110-story towers had imploded to the ground, thousands were killed, and a stunned nation watched the doomsday images repeated endlessly on television. The nation's airports were closed, Congress evacuated the capital, rumors of further attacks spread, and Americans struggled to regain a lost sense of security.

A Challenged Leader

At first President Bush had problems appearing in command. His day had begun in an elementary school in Sarasota, Florida, where he had been reading to the kids and plugging No Child Left Behind. He had waited seven minutes after the second attack before leaving the class, and then took 12 hours to get back to the White House. Relying on his staff's security fears, his jet had taken a zigzag course first to an Air Force Base near Shreveport, Louisiana, and then to a command post in Omaha, Nebraska, where he had conducted a meeting of the National Security Council by video phone to Washington. While the secret service worried that the attacks had not ended, the president's political aides had to face another issue: How could Mr. Bush appear in control and reassure the nation from a bunker in Nebraska? Or as a USA *Today* reporter sarcastically noted, "Not since the British burned the White House in 1814 has a President been persuaded by security concerns to avoid the Capital."

Arriving back at the White House that night, President Bush addressed the nation from the Oval Office. In his brief talk a "somber" chief executive sitting alone at his desk assured his audience that "Our country is strong. . . . Terrorist acts can

shake the foundation of our biggest buildings, but they cannot touch the foundation of America." He declared that the government would continue "without interruption," that the search was underway to find those behind these evil acts, and that "America has stood down enemies before, and we will do so this time." (See "9/11 Viewed as History.")

In the coming days the president expanded on these themes. He would be shown offering sympathy, demonstrating national unity, defining an unseen enemy, and executing a strong response. Underlying his activities was a nagging doubt: Was this commander-in-chief, barely eight months in office, elected by a minority of voters, with no foreign policy experience, up to the enormous task? With the nation traditionally rallying around the president in a time of crisis, many of his actions in this first week were designed to answer that unspoken question.

Congress, for its part, was reminded of its physical dependency on the executive on the very day of the attacks. Vice President Cheney ordered that the leaders of Congress be taken to a secure location— rumored to be West Virginia. Later one Republican senator demanded that the leadership be returned to Washington, but the vice president refused. The senator pointed out that Congress was not under executive control. Cheney replied, "We control the helicopters."

THE PRESIDENT RESPONDS

On September 12, his first full day back in the White House, President Bush focused on defining the issue, rallying an international coalition, and asserting his presence in the midst of the tragedy. He escalated his language, calling the attacks "more than acts of terror; they were acts of war," thus laying the foundation for military action. He was shown calling world leaders, meeting security advisors, and discussing with congressional leaders new defense spending. The House passed a resolution of support, and administration officials, led by Secretary of State Colin Powell, sent stern public messages to other countries— "You're either with us or against us."

As the week went on the president overcame his tentative first day. He did this in a way that only an individual chief of state could do: by personally connecting to the range of emotions most Americans felt, from sadness to anger. He comforted victims, thanked rescue workers at the still-smoking sites and reflected stunned feelings of outrage. On Thursday when he got off the phone after talking with New York Mayor Rudolph Giuliani, a *Boston Globe* reporter described him this way: "The president's eyes glistened and welled with emotion as he blinked to hold back tears. 'I'm a loving guy,' he said. 'And I'm also someone, however, who's got a job to do and I intend to do it. And this is a terrible moment.'"

A president's religious role as a "democratic priest-king" was also visible. The president declared Thursday a national "day of prayers and remembrance." His proclamation read, "In the face of all this evil, we remain strong and united, one nation under God." During a televised service at Washington Cathedral on September 14, Bush said, "We ask almighty God to watch over our nation and grant us patience and resolve in all that is to come."

He was also the commander-in-chief, rallying the country for what lay ahead. In that same cathedral service Bush talked tough, "This conflict was begun on the timing and terms of others; it will end in a way and at an hour of our choosing." Two days after the attack the president declared that "The nation must understand this is now the focus of my administration." He asked Congress to authorize the use of force against those responsible for September 11, while adding that he did not need prior approval to launch a military attack. Congress for its part quickly passed $40 billion in emergency spending. By September 15 the president had approved an antiterrorist global strategy involving intelligence, finance, diplomacy, and the military. The CIA became the lead agency in the overthrow of the Taliban government in Afghanistan for harboring the Al Qaeda terrorists.

In the coming days the president pointedly did not do certain things. He did not blame anyone in the government for allowing the attack. Although the hijackings represented an enormous intelligence failure the president made clear his confidence in the CIA by meeting with its director. Bush also tried to separate the terrorists from the religion of Islam they claimed to represent. He publicly met with American Islamic leaders, declaring that the hijackers had nothing to do with peaceful Muslims. When professional baseball resumed, he went to throw out the first pitch. The president made clear that he didn't want the national agenda disrupted by terrorism. He emphasized that his education reform, "No Child Left Behind," remained a top domestic priority.

A CALL TO ARMS

The climax of the country's initial response to the terrorist attack came in President Bush's speech to a joint session of Congress on September 20. Using the Capitol as the stage and Congress as his cheering chorus, a president not known for eloquence gave an inspiring speech. He issued an ultimatum to the Afghan leaders to turn over the Al Qaeda terrorists responsible for the attack, and called on the nation and world to unite to destroy terrorism. "Tonight we are a country awakened to danger and called to defend freedom. Our grief has turned to anger, and anger to resolution. Whether we bring our enemies to justice, or bring justice to our enemies, justice will be done."

He framed the challenge not as a mere policy difference but as a challenge to America's core values. "They hate our freedoms—our freedom of religion, our freedom of speech, our freedom to vote and assemble and disagree with each other. . . . We have seen their kind before. They are the heirs of all the murderous ideologies of the 20th century . . . they follow in the path of fascism, and Nazism and totalitarianism. And they will follow that path all the way, to where it ends: in history's unmarked grave of discarded lies."

And when Bush concluded "In our grief and anger, we have found our mission and our moment," he was speaking for more than a generation of Americans. He was speaking of his presidency.

WRAP-UP

This chapter has introduced the executive players in the political game—the president and the bureaucracy. We have seen how the presidency has irregularly but vastly grown in influence from a limited grant of constitutional powers, and we have looked at three different presidential styles as well as how some modern presidents have carried out the duties of their office. The six major hats a president wears—chief of state, chief executive, chief diplomat, commander-in-chief, chief legislator, and party leader—show how broad and public presidential power has become. In the last century, government power has been centralized, in the federal government relative to the states, and in the presidency relative to the Congress.

The bureaucracy within the executive branch generally reinforces the president's power. Yet its size, its influence over policymaking, the economic clients it serves, its complexity and the rivalries between agencies—from the executive office to the cabinet departments, executive agencies, and regulatory commissions—limit the president's control. In the aftermath of the 9/11 terrorist attacks we saw a president use the powers of his office to unify, defend, and rally a country stunned by a sudden and terrible blow.

The president as both an individual and an institution will continue to play a central role in the American political game. Often presidents have seemed ineffective in managing the bureaucracy and getting their programs passed by Congress. Dissatisfaction with government has often focused on the personalities of individual presidents. (Too arrogant? Too conciliatory?) Most of us still look for a presidential Moses to lead us out of a wilderness of domestic and foreign troubles, which is part of the problem.

Presidents are political leaders. They hold a powerful office limited by history, politics, and law. They may mislead us by overpromising, they may disappoint us by stubbornly holding to failed policies, and they may do great damage through their own character flaws. But we also play a part. If we child-ishly expect heroes or symbols, priests or kings, we are bound to be frustrated. We may have to chill our expectations of what presidents can do to change our country and improve our lives. In that way we can, as citizens in a democracy, more realistically judge the head of the executive branch of government.

THOUGHT QUESTIONS

1. What are the major reasons for the growth in the power of the president? Why do you think that presidential candidates claim to want to limit this growth but then change when they take office?
2. Do you think the president is too powerful or not powerful enough? Should a president's power expand in a crisis like that of 9/11? Should it be limited afterward? How?
3. Many people expect more out of a government where the executive and leg-islative branches are controlled by the same party. Given that situation today, do checks and balances still operate to limit President Obama? Give examples.
4. How can the president gain more control over the executive branch bureaucracy? Is that a good idea?
5. Should bureaucracies, like Agriculture and Labor, serve the interests of the clients in the economic areas they govern? What is the danger in this relationship? How can it be counterbalanced?

SUGGESTED READINGS

Bacevich, Andrew J. *The Limits of Power*. New York: Holt, 2008. Pb.
  A powerful critique that American democracy and its foreign policy have been hijacked.
Cabbage, Michael, and William Harwood. *Comm Check. . . . The Final Flight of Shuttle Columbia*. New York: The Free Press, 2004.
  An interesting case study of the Columbia space shuttle disaster and the bureaucratic problems that led to it.
Greenstein, Fred I. *The Presidential Difference: Leadership Styles from FDR to George W. Bush,* 2nd ed. New York: Free Press, 2000.
  Shrewd insights describing why 12 modern presidents succeed or fail based on skills ranging from public communication to emotional intelligence.
Harris, John F. *The Survivor: Bill Clinton in the White House*. New York: Random House, 2005. Pb
  This *Washington Post* reporter gives a critical evaluation of the forty-second president.
Pious, Richard M. *Why Presidents Fail*. New York: Rowman & Littlefield, 2008. Pb
  Nine case studies from the U-2 to Iraqi weapons of mass distraction incisively trace why presidents fail over and over again.
Risen, James. *State of War: The Secret History of the CIA and the Bush Administration*. New York: Free Press, 2006. Pb
  Disturbing reporting by a Pulitzer Prize–winning journalist on the abuse of power by the Bush administration and its struggle with the spy bureaucracy.

Weisberg, Jacob. *The Bush Tragedy*, New York: Random House, 2008. Pb.
   A journalist studies the president's personality and failures only to find another president, his Dad, at the core.
Wolffe, Richard. *Renegade: The Making of a President.* New York: Crown Publishers, 2009. Pb
   A reporter gets inside the Obama campaign and is impressed with what he sees.

The Legislative Branch: Congress

ongress, according to the Constitution, is at the center of the American political game. The framers' experience with the King of England and his autocratic governors had left the framers suspicious of a strong executive. As a result, the Constitution gives many detailed powers and duties to Congress but far fewer to the president.

The powers of Congress limit those of the president. The president is the commander-in-chief of the military, but cannot declare war or raise armies—only Congress can. The president is the chief administrative officer of the government, but there will be no government to administer if the Congress does not create it. He can appoint executive officials and negotiate foreign treaties only if the Senate consents. Both the raising of money through taxes and the spending of it by the government requires congressional approval. Finally, as President Clinton was reminded, Congress has the power to impeach and then remove the president.

Through its major function, making laws, Congress creates the rules that govern all the political players. Article I of the Constitution gives Congress the power to tax, borrow money, raise armies, declare war, create the federal courts, regulate commerce, coin money, and "make all Laws which shall be necessary and proper for carrying into Execution the foregoing powers . . . "

Through most of the nineteenth century, Congress was the major player in shaping government policies. By the end of the nineteenth century, Woodrow Wilson proclaimed, "Congress is the dominant, nay, the irresistible power of the federal system." Wilson was later to change his mind. And, since the Great Depression and World War II, the presidency generally increased in influence compared with Congress with periods of weak executives and strong legislatures.

Two of the most important power centers in Congress are not mentioned at all in the Constitution—political parties and congressional committees. Both are vital for initiating legislation and providing a specialized means of getting Congress's business done. Recent congresses have seen the political parties becoming more powerful and the committees getting weaker. Party leaders, especially in the House, are key in shaping legislation and in choosing who will become chairs of committees.

Democratic majorities in the House and Senate have been bolstered by their party's leadership of the executive branch in the person of President Obama. In major legislation of his first year—the stimulus bill, global warming, and health care reform—the president has publically outlined major principles and then let Congress work out the details of the laws. However a closer look at health care reform, for example, showed the president's people in constant negotiations with key members of Congress during the legislative process. This reflects a political fact of life: Representative assemblies depend on executive leadership to tackle major issues. The legislature remains necessary to govern, but not sufficient to shape the nation's policies on its own—exactly what the Constitution intended.

In this chapter we will examine the structure and activities of Congress, both how it was designed and how it actually operates today.

Makeup of the Senate and House

The Congress of the United States is *bicameral,* made up of two houses: the Senate and the House of Representatives. The Senate consists of two senators from each state, regardless of size. House members are distributed according to population so that the larger the state's population, the more representatives it gets. The Constitution requires that each state, no matter how small it may be, have at least one representative. These provisions are the result of a political compromise between the small states and the large states during the writing of the Constitution.

As the country has grown, so too has the size of Congress. The first Congress consisted of 26 senators and 65 representatives. With each new state added to the Union, the Senate has grown by two, so that it now has 100 members from 50 states. As the nation's population grew, the size of the House of Representatives also grew. In 1922 the Congress passed a law setting the maximum size of the House at 435 members, where it remains today. In the first House each member represented 50,000 citizens. The average representative now serves districts of around 650,000 people.

Role of the Legislator

There are many questions about the role of a legislator, questions as old as the idea of representative assemblies. Should representatives follow their own judgments about what is best, or do only what their constituents wish ("represent" them)? What should representatives do if the interests of their district conflict with the needs of the nation as a whole? Should legislators recognize a "greater good" beyond their own voters?

Members of Congress are in fact both *national* and *local* representatives. They are national representatives who make up one branch of the national government, are paid by the federal government, and are required to support and defend the interests of the nation. However, they are chosen in local districts or states. In running for election, legislators must satisfy *their* constituents that they are looking out not only for the national interest but for local interests as well. In controversial areas, such as cutting the defense budget by closing military bases, national views may be very different from local popular opinion. In 2008, many Republican representatives running for reelection tried to distance themselves from an unpopular war in Iraq that they once actively supported. They were mindful of a warning heard often in Congress: "You have to save your seat before you can save the world"—a reminder that usually gives local voters' opinions the upper hand.

Casework, or helping constituents solve individual problems with the government, is a vital part of what senators and representatives do. Most of a member's staff work not on legislation but on constituency service for local voters. Given the growing role of government in people's lives and the ease of contacting congressional offices via e-mail, casework has increased. Casework gives people access to an often impersonal bureaucracy. It also helps incumbents get reelected.

Casework includes assisting veterans in getting information about government programs for the disabled, or intervening with an agency so a surviving child can get an overdue Social Security check. These are not always the most earth-shaking issues. One Georgia congressman tells a story about receiving a call from a constituent that her garbage hadn't been picked up. The congressman asked her why she hadn't called the director of the Department of Sanitation. "Well, Congressman," she replied, "quite frankly, I didn't want to go up that high." (See "The Image of Congress.")

Who Are the Legislators?

To be a member of the House of Representatives you must be at least 25 years old, a citizen of the United States for seven years, and a resident of the state electing you. As a Senator you must be 30 years old, a citizen for nine years, and a resident of the state. State residency is a loose requirement. Hillary Clinton first won her Senate seat from New York in 2000 despite never living in the state before. Other states, like Arizona, have a five-year residency requirement to run for office.

Members of the House of Representatives (called *representatives* or *congressmen/women*) serve two years, and all of them need to run every two years. They are elected from congressional districts that are drawn within the states. No congressional district ever crosses state borders.

Senators serve six-year terms and are elected by the entire state's population. Every two years, during national elections, one-third of the

The Image of Congress

Congress's lousy image is not new. In the nineteenth century Mark Twain remarked that "there is no distinctly native American criminal class except Congress." At best the public today sees Congress as chaotic and unresponsive to national needs. At its worst Congress is a place of partisan plotting and scandal. The media darkens this view by finding the misdeeds of a few members easier to report than complicated legislation. As the respected reporter, David Broder said, "Scandals in Congress even of a petty nature are easier to sell to most editors than the stories of larger consequences." Part of the problem is that Congress *is* doing what the framers intended—slowing down the policy process to debate the issues of the day.

Ironically many members of Congress intentionally worsen the image of their own institution. There's a long tradition of members running *for* Congress by running *against* Congress. By pandering to negative views of Congress, members can present themselves as lonely fighters against a corrupt legislature. The result: voters dislike Congress but reelect their own members of Congress, over and over.

Senate seeks reelection. The other senators do not run because they are only one-third or two-thirds of the way through their terms.

The Constitution originally provided that members of the Senate would be elected by their state legislatures. This was done to remove the choice from the public and ensure that more conservative elements would pick the senators. The Seventeenth Amendment changed this in 1913, and senators now are elected by the voters of their state.

Congress is composed overwhelmingly of white males, and it tends to reflect the values of upper-middle-class America. Almost half of the members of Congress are lawyers. Other common professions are business, banking, education, farming, and journalism. Women and minorities have historically been underrepresented in Congress for many reasons, including the selection of candidates by party organizations and voter apathy. Recent elections have increased the number of women, African Americans, and Hispanics in Congress. (See "The 111th Congress.")

Careerism—the tendency for legislators to serve in Congress as a lifetime career—still exists. Tradition holds that the leadership of committees in both houses consists of the most senior members. Recent speakers of the House have only occasionally broken with the seniority tradition in the appointment of committee chairs. The new Democratic speaker angered her committee chairs by continuing a Republican rule that limited them to six years as head of their committees. The

The 111th Congress

The Democrats strengthened their majorities in both houses of Congress in the 2008 congressional elections. In the House they picked up 22 seats going from 236 to 258. That gave them a margin of 81 votes over 177 Republicans. In the Senate the Democratic numbers kept changing. At one point 58 Democrats were joined by two independents to give them a 60-40 margin over Republicans. This filibuster-proof super majority was a decided improvement over their razor-thin advantage of 51-49 after the 2006 elections, and helped them pass their key health care reform measure in the Senate in late 2009. The margin didn't last long. Massachusetts Senator Ted Kennedy's death in August 2009 led to a January 2010 special election where his seat was filled in an upset by Republican Scott Brown, leading to a reduced 59-41 Democratic majority in the Senate.

Women continued to be represented by their first House Speaker, Nancy Pelosi. The percentage of women in both houses was exactly the same—17%, or 75 in the House and 17 in the Senate. The only African American in the Senate was Roland Burris, who filled Barack Obama's Illinois seat. Protestants formed a slight majority in Congress, as they do in the country; Catholics formed Congress's single largest religious group. Seven out of 10 Republicans were Protestant compared with less than half of Democrats. Jews, who make up less than 2 percent of the U.S. population, were almost 10 percent of Congress. Two Muslims in the House were joined by two Buddhists. There were no Hindus, nor has there ever been. The least represented religious belief may have been the one-sixth of the population who claimed no religious affiliation. Only five members of Congress were willing to say the same.

current unpopularity of *incumbents* has led many new members of Congress—calling themselves "citizen legislators"—to vow to stay in office for only a few terms. Some have broken that promise.

It does seem ironic that although executive branch administrators and members of the judiciary may be appointed from outside fields, it is a lifetime career to become a leader in a representative assembly. The problem with careerism is that although it may guarantee loyalty to their institution, it also may separate members from a changing society.

Popular disgust for entrenched government grew into proposals for *term limits* on members of Congress. Twenty-three states limited the number of times their representatives and senators could run for re-election. Congress tried to pass several different constitutional amendments to restrict members to 6 or 12 years in office. They all failed. Even more damaging for supporters was a 1995 Supreme Court decision (*U.S. Term Limits* v. *Thornton*) rejecting term limits by the states because they added to the qualifications for office and thus needed an amendment to the Constitution. Since then support has cooled. As one senator said, "I don't think there's any way to get two-thirds of the people in this place who are willing to say good-bye to their jobs."

Malapportionment and Reapportionment

The drawing of House districts is up to the state governors and state legislatures, who use these powers to boost their own party and penalize the party that is out of power. In the past, *malapportionment* (large differences in the populations of congressional districts) was common in many areas of the country. Districts would be drawn up so that minority-party districts included more voters than majority-party districts. In this way, each minority-party voter would count for less. In 1960, Michigan's sixteenth district had 802,994 people, whereas the twelfth district had only 177,431. Both elected just one representative.

In addition, the art of *gerrymandering*—drawing district boundaries for partisan advantage—was practiced. The name comes from Massachusetts Governor Elbridge Gerry, who in 1812 helped to draw a long, misshapen district composed of a string of towns north of Boston. When painter Gilbert Stuart saw a drawing of the oddly shaped district, he penciled in claws, wings, and a head and said, "That will do for a salamander!" His editor replied, "Better say a gerrymander." The two most common forms of gerrymandering are "packing" and "cracking." *Packing* involves drawing up a district so that it has a large majority of supporters, to ensure a "safe" seat. *Cracking* means splitting up opponents' supporters into minorities in a number of districts to weaken their influence.

Such practices have long been attacked by reformers. In 1962 a Supreme Court decision (*Baker v. Carr*) held that legislative districts must be as close to equal in population as possible. Many of the worst abuses of malapportionment were ended by this and later Court decisions. But politics remains vital to the drawing of districts, as seen in the conflicts following each census.

At the beginning of each decade the Census Bureau counts the nation's population and the House of Representatives is reapportioned to reflect the change in each state. In recent counts, including the 2000 census, the population grew and shifted toward the South and the West of the country. Because the number of seats in the House is limited by law to 435, states in the northeast lost seats while the so-called Sunbelt gained congressional members. Florida, Georgia, Arizona, and Texas gained two congressional seats, while New York and Pennsylvania lost two apiece. Several midwestern and northern states lost one each, while a number of southern and southwestern states gained one. (See Figure 4.1.)

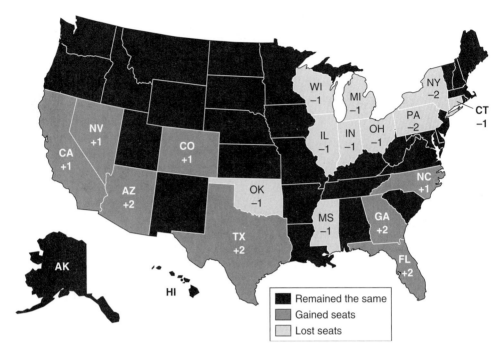

FIGURE 4.1
State Gaining and Losing Congressional Seats Following the 2000 Census.
Source: U.S. Bureau of the Census, "News Release," December 28, 2000.

The redistricting following the 2000 census was as partisan as ever with each party seeking an advantage in the states they controlled. Overall the Republicans were considered the winners with a seven-seat gain in the House resulting from redistricting. Recent court decisions have allowed these partisan gerrymanders. In mid-2006 the Supreme Court rejected a challenge to Texas's redistricting by which the Republican majority in the state legislature had helped the state's congressional delegation go from 17 Democrats and 15 Republicans in 2002 to 11 Democrats and 21 Republicans after the 2004 election. Despite the turnovers in the 2006 and 2008 elections, incumbents in the House of Representatives—which the Constitution designed to be the part of the national government closest to the people—remain shielded by the ability to gerrymander districts. (See "The Incumbent Protection Game.")

Organization of the House of Representatives

Parties are the key to how Congress is organized. The *majority party* in each house is the one with the greatest number of members. The majority party of each house of Congress chooses the officers, controls debate on the floor, selects all committee chairs, and has a majority on

The Incumbent Protection Game

The advantages of holding office—an incumbent—are considerable. Incumbents have wide name recognition. Just by speaking or issuing "official" statements, they can get free publicity that their lesser-known opponents can't get. House members have office and staff budgets of $350,000 a year; senators are given at least that and often considerably more if their states are large. Both receive 32 government-paid round trips to their districts each year. Facilities for making television or radio tapes are available in Washington at a low cost. And there is the *frank,* the privilege of official mailing enjoyed by Congress, under which 200,000,000 pieces of mail, much of it quite partisan, are sent free every year. The local press joins the parade by generally treating incumbents like hometown heroes. And there's always lots of "pork" to pass around.

Adding to the advantages of House incumbents is reapportionment. Changing the shape of the playing field often maximizes the number of districts favorable to incumbents. Coupled with the usually low voter turnout in congressional races and the one-party dominance of most congressional districts, House incumbents usually, but not always, win. Only 21 were defeated in 2008.

all committees. Until 1994 the Democrats had controlled both houses of Congress for 40 years, except for the years 1980–1986 when the Republicans ran the Senate. From 1994 to 2006 the Republicans were the majority in both houses, with a brief 18-month interim from June 2001 to January 2003 when the Democrats took back the Senate after a Republican senator left his party. Then in the 2006 midterm elections the Democrats raised their numbers in the House by over 30 seats and became the majority party, a position they increased in the 2008 elections.

In the House of Representatives, the majority party—the Democrats—chooses the *Speaker of the House* from among its members. He—and now for the first time in history, she—does not have to be the oldest or longest-serving member but will certainly be well respected and is likely to have served in other party posts. During some periods, such as 1890 to 1910, the Speaker exercised almost dictatorial powers. The Speaker still retains power through control over the majority party. She influences how the committee system operates, including who becomes committee chairs.

The selection of the Speaker takes place every two years, at the beginning of Congress. The majority party votes for its leader in its party caucus, and then he or she becomes their candidate for the Speaker, voted on by the entire House. Since this is one time when party discipline must hold, the leader of the majority becomes the Speaker.

In 1994 Newt Gingrich of Georgia became the first Republican Speaker of the House since 1954. He ushered in many rule changes, cutting staffs, eliminating committees, strengthening party control, and increasing the power of the Speaker. Within a few years, the limits of the Speaker's powers became apparent. When Republicans lost five seats in the House in the 1998 elections, after Gingrich had predicted a gain, he was pushed into resigning. Dennis Hastert, from Illinois, emerged as the Speaker in 1999, pledging more power to committee chairs and a low-profile tenure in office. When the GOP lost their majority in 2006, in part due to scandals among House Republicans, Hastert was replaced as Speaker by Nancy Pelosi, who had been minority leader of the Democrats when they were in fact the minority. (See "Nancy Pelosi: Madam Speaker.")

The *caucus* of each political party in the House or Senate is simply a gathering of all the members of that party serving there. (A caucus may also refer to organized groups in Congress such as the farm bloc, blacks, women, and Hispanics.) The Democratic majority caucus in the House chooses a *majority leader*, who is second in command to the Speaker. The majority leader, now Steny Hoyer of Maryland, works closely with the Speaker, organizes party members, and schedules legislation.

Nancy Pelosi: Madam Speaker

The first female Speaker of the House started life in a political household. The daughter of the mayor of Baltimore, she was the youngest of six, and the only girl. She entered Democratic politics as a fundraiser and was first elected to Congress from a San Francisco district at age 47. By then she was the mother of five; when she made it to Speaker she was a grandmother of six.

Her background may not be totally irrelevant to her position, second in line to the presidency after the vice president. Early in the Obama administration Pelosi, who is a fierce partisan Democrat, became an easier target than a popular president for opponents of her liberal programs. In response Pelosi stressed the importance of discipline to party members, a lesson she may have learned at home. When she is asked how she puts up with the arguments and multitasking she confronts in Congress, she offers a reply unique to this Speaker of the House, "I had five children in six years."

The Speaker and majority leader are assisted by *majority whips.* (The word *whip* comes from English fox hunting, where the "whipper-in" keeps the dogs from running away.) The whips help coordinate party positions on legislation, channel information between the leadership and party members, persuade wavering representatives to vote with the leadership, and conduct informal surveys on the likely outcome of votes. Being at the center of the congressional process, these leaders possess more information than other legislators, adding to their power. Recent congresses have increased the influence of the majority party leadership in the House.

The minority party caucus in the House, currently the Republicans, selects a *minority leader* and *minority whips.* Like the majority party's leader and whips, their duties are to coordinate party positions. Minority leaders are usually their party's candidate for Speaker should it become the majority. John A. Boehner of Ohio is now the Republican's leader in the House and is assisted by Roy Blunt of Missouri, the minority whip.

The Democratic and Republican caucuses in the House run their affairs slightly differently. The Democrats have a two-headed executive committee. One, the *Steering Panel,* nominates committee chairs, as well as committee members, all of whom must be approved by the caucus. The other, the *Policy Committee,* studies issues, writes bills, and publicizes them. (Of course with a Democratic president the White House staff is likely to be coordinating closely with them.) The Republican party chooses a *Steering Committee* to function as an executive committee of the caucus. The Steering Committee helps chart party policy in the House, and assigns Republican members to committees.

Organization of the Senate

The Senate has no speaker. The *president of the Senate* is the vice president of the United States, in the present case, Democrat Joe Biden. He has the right to preside over the Senate chamber, which he does only on significant votes. He is allowed to vote in case of a tie. In the period from January to June 2001 when there was a 50–50 party split in the Senate, the vice president's vote was of unusual importance—it determined the majority party. Now the Democrats are an overwhelming majority, so the vice president resumes his mainly figurehead position.

The honorary post of president *pro tem* (from *pro tempore*, meaning "for the time being") of the Senate is given to the senator from the majority party who has served longest in the Senate—currently Democrat Robert Byrd of West Virginia. His only power is to preside in the absence of the vice president, but he hardly ever does so. Because most Senate work takes place in committees, the boring job of presiding over a Senate chamber that may be nearly vacant falls to a junior senator, who is asked to do so by the Senate majority leader.

The *Senate majority leader* is the closest equivalent to the Speaker of the House. However, because the Senate is smaller and not tightly organized, the majority leader has less control over the Senate than the Speaker has over the House. The majority leader schedules debate on the Senate floor, assigns bills to committees, coordinates party policy, and appoints members of *special committees*. But senators value their independence, including a bit of detachment from their leaders' directions. Harry Reid, Democrat of Nevada, became Senate majority leader in 2007 when the Democrats became the majority party. Number two in the Senate is Richard Durbin, Democrat of Illinois, who is the majority whip.

Because they are the majority party the chairs of all senate committees are now Democrats. Both the majority and minority leaders are assisted by a whip, as well as assistant whips who coordinate party positions and floor strategy. In the Senate the Democrats' caucus is organized into a Steering Committee that appoints chairmen and members to committees, and a Policy Committee that coordinates party strategy. Unlike the Republican organizations, the Senate Democratic leader chairs the Democratic caucus (called the *Democratic Conference*), the Steering Committee, and the Policy Committee.

Republicans are led by their senate minority leader, now Mitch McConnell of Kentucky. The GOP has a *Committee on Committees*, which assigns members to committees, and a Policy Committee, which charts legislative tactics. The party caucus, called the *Republican Conference*, consists of all Republicans in the Senate. Unlike the Democrats where the majority leader chairs their party groups, each of these groups is chaired by a leading Republican senator.

How Congress Works

Power in the legislature has changed in recent years. Congress has gone from a strong committee system and weak political parties, to one with stronger parties and weaker committees. Members' loyalty to their party has replaced loyalty to their committee as the chief route to advancement. The majority party leaders—and that now means the president—drive the legislative agenda; they decide which bills are given priority and voted on, not always passed of course. Committees bend with the prevailing wind. This is less true in the Senate where committees, committee chairs, and individual senators have more autonomy.

Either the House or the Senate, or both houses at the same time, may introduce legislation. The only exceptions to this rule are money-raising bills, which according to the Constitution must start in the House, and appropriations (spending) bills, which by custom also begin there. Approximately 20,000 bills are introduced in Congress each year. (See Figure 4.2.) They may be part of the president's program and with Obama heading a majority party in both houses laws are likely to follow White House priorities. But laws may be drafted and amended by individual members or by committees, or they may be the result of alliances between Congress and the executive bureaucracy or lobbyists.

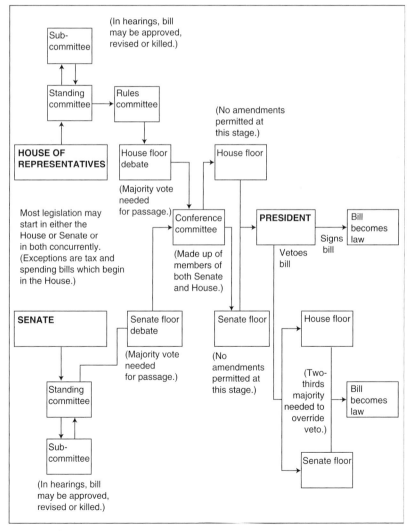

FIGURE 4.2
How a Bill (Rarely) Becomes a Law.

Further complicating matters is that the Senate and the House act separately and may amend or revise bills as they see fit. For any bill to become law, it must ultimately be passed by both houses of Congress in identical language and approved by the president or passed over his veto. Only 5 percent of the bills introduced survive to become law.

Congress operates by division of labor—in committees. House committees may have anywhere from 20 to 50 representatives; Senate committees usually have 10 to 20 senators. If they did not separate into committees, the Senate and House would move even more slowly and deal with far fewer issues because they could consider only one subject at a time. It is difficult to imagine Congress without the committee system.

When a piece of legislation is introduced in either the Senate or the House, it is assigned to a committee. The committee (or, often, one of its subcommittees) reviews the bill and decides whether to recommend it to the whole House or Senate. Between 80 and 90 percent of the bills introduced in Congress die in committee. The committee system is central to how Congress actually operates.

The Committee System

The *Washington Post* reported that on the last week of April 2004, the House of Representatives was in session for two days and one night, an average workweek. On one day they renamed a post office in Rhode Island and supported "Financial Literacy Month." On another they renamed a Miami courthouse and extended the popular repeal of the tax code's "marriage penalty." That same week, 35 U.S. servicemen died in Iraq and CBS showed shocking pictures of Americans abusing Iraqi prisoners.

This view of the House floor is a reminder that this is not the whole story. Floor sessions are often little more than a formality designed to make a public record. At the same time, many of the committee rooms would be buzzing with activity.

How Committees Work

"Congress in session is Congress on exhibition, whilst Congress in its committee rooms is Congress at work."

—*Woodrow Wilson*

There are three types of committees in Congress: standing, select, and joint. (A *conference committee* is set up in the final stages of legislation to reconcile differences between the two houses in passing a bill. (See below, p. 114.) *Standing committees* are the basic working units of

Congress. They were started early in the nation's history because Congress found it could do more work faster if it broke down into smaller, specialized groups. There are 20 standing committees in the House and 16 in the Senate, most focusing on one or two general subjects. Representatives serve on one or two standing committees; senators on three or four. Usually these committees break down into subcommittees for a further division of labor. In the 111th Congress, the House had 104 subcommittees and the Senate had 70. (see Figure 4.3)

Senate	House of Representatives
Agriculture, Nutrition, and Forestry	Agriculture
Appropriations	Appropriations
Armed Services	Armed Services
Banking, Housing, and Urban Affairs	Banking and Financial Services
Budget	Budget
Commerce, Science, and Transportation	Commerce
Energy and Natural Resources	Education and the Workforce
Environment and Public Works	Government Reform
Finance	Homeland Security
Foreign Relations	House Administration
Health, Education, Labor, and Pensions	International Relations
Homeland Security and Governmental Affairs	Judiciary
Judiciary	Resources
Rules and Administration	Rules
Small Business and Entrepreneurship	Science
Veterans' Affairs	Small Business
	Standards of Official Conduct
	Transportation and Infrastructure
	Veterans Affairs
	Ways and Means

FIGURE 4.3
Standing Committees of the 111th Congress.

Before any bill can be sent to the floor for consideration by the entire Senate or House, it must be approved by a majority vote in the standing committee to which it is assigned. A committee's examination of a proposed bill may include holding public hearings in which interested groups, including the executive bureaucracies and lobbyists, are invited to testify. Often the actual work on a bill assigned to a standing committee goes on in one of its subcommittees. If the full committee then approves the bill, it will be sent to the floor of the Senate or House with a report describing the committee's findings and the reasons the committee thinks the bill should be passed. If the bill is not supported by the committee, it will be killed. The bill's sponsors may resubmit it in a later Congress, but if the committee involved continues to reject it, it will fail again.

Select or *special committees* are temporary panels set up to do specific jobs and usually dissolved after they have completed them. Typically select committees do not have legislative authority and can only study, investigate, and recommend. For example, the Select Bipartisan Committee to Investigate the Preparation for and Response to Hurricane Katrina was set up in September 2005 to report back in February 2006 and then go out of business, which the committee did.

Joint committees are permanent bodies including both senators and representatives, usually set up to coordinate policy on routine matters. There are currently four joint committees; the most important is the Joint Economic Committee, which reports on the president's annual economic report. The jealousy of the two houses of Congress over their separate powers makes joint committees rare.

Committee Chairs and the Seniority System

By the unwritten rule of *seniority,* the chair of any committee is typically the majority party member who has served longest (consecutively) on the committee. While the current congressional leadership usually follows seniority, acceptance of the party's legislative agenda is also part of the job requirements for any committee chairman, making the OK of party leaders key to chairs being appointed.

The important power of the majority party was apparent in 2007 when the Democrats again outnumbered Republicans in the Senate, allowing them to have a majority on each committee and to appoint all the chairs. This meant control of the Senate agenda—the issues it would consider and those it would ignore. For example, when Republicans ruled the Senate, the Armed Services Committee generally supported controversial Bush administration policies in Iraq. But under a Democratic chairman, Carl M. Levin of Michigan, the committee investigated whether terrorism suspects were being tortured, and called for a "phased redeployment" of troops in Iraq. With Obama in the White House the committee was more supportive of the executive but showed its independence by voting to fund F-22 jets despite a veto threat, and pushed a reluctant administration to investigate Bush-era interrogation policies.

Chairs hire majority party committee staff, schedule committee meetings and agenda items, and have a say in the appointment of new members to their committees. Unless there is strong pressure from party leaders, chairs usually can kill legislation they oppose. Even when a majority of committee members supports legislation, the chair can refuse to schedule a bill for hearings. That stops a bill from moving forward. A chairman's blocking power is stronger in the House than in the Senate.

The tradition of appointing chairs based on seniority is not written down in the rules of the House or Senate, and yet for most of the twentieth century the custom was almost never broken. Then, starting in the mid-1970s, things changed. A combination of scandals and of junior Democrats vying for a "piece of the action" led to several committee chairs being ousted and an increase in the power of the party caucus.

When the Republicans took power in the House in 1994, party leadership was strengthened at the expense of the committees. The House Republican Conference imposed six-year term limits on chairs, leading to some early retirements by committee chairs in 2000. GOP leaders centralized power and rewarded loyal allies with important committee positions, with some weight given to seniority. Loyalty to the party and the White House was critical to winning the approval of the House Republican leadership. Nancy Pelosi at the beginning of the 111th Congress ignored seniority by allowing her party's caucus to replace the chairman of the House Energy and Commerce Committee, despite his seniority.

While the majority party leaders in the Senate exercise control over committees, these leaders—both Democrats and Republicans—nearly always defer to the seniority rankings in determining who heads a committee or subcommittee. Hence, seniority is more important in the Senate than the House.

The seniority system—mocked as the *senility system*—lives on. Attacked as undemocratic, it has allowed members who are reelected to accumulate national power. It has allowed minorities in the Democratic party and moderate Republicans to gain positions of power. Seniority ensures that an experienced person will become chairman, and has provided a predictable system of succession without constant fights over control of the chair. But party leaders of Congress, as they have gained in strength, have no longer felt the need to automatically follow a custom that limits their own influence.

Specialization and Reciprocity

Though weakened, two other informal rules support the power of committees in Congress. The first, *specialization,* is closely related to the second, *reciprocity.* Specialization means that once assigned to a committee or subcommittee, a member of Congress is expected to specialize in its work and become an expert in that area. Particularly in the House, members are not expected to follow all legislation in Congress equally, or to speak out on widely varying issues. The result is that committee members become experts in their own work but may not know much about other areas.

This potential problem is resolved through the practice of reciprocity. Here members look for guidance in voting on legislation outside their committee's field to members of committees that do specialize in it. Legislators tend to vote the way that their party's representatives on the most closely concerned committee tell them to vote. They assume that those on the committee know most about the legislation and because the members want the same support when their committee's business is involved. Specialization and reciprocity, then, are two sides of the same coin. You develop expertise in an area and other members follow your lead in that area. You, in turn, follow the lead of others more knowledgeable than you in areas outside your expertise. Because senators commonly serve on more committees—usually four—their areas of specialization are more varied and less intense.

Assignment to a committee or subcommittee is vital to a legislator's power. These patterns of influence tend to keep committees stable and discourage "hopping" from one to another. Once members of Congress have been assigned to a committee, they will not be removed against their wishes unless the ratio between the parties should shift, including a change in the majority party as happened when the Democrats won control of both houses in 2006.

Major Committees in the House

Power in the House is now concentrated in the leaders of the majority party and the senior majority party members of a few elite committees. With the GOP takeover in 1994, party leaders increasingly directed the shape of legislation in the committees. When the Democrats became the majority party they followed this Republican lead. The key committees in the House are usually those dealing with the budget. These are Budget, Rules, Ways and Means, and Appropriations.

Almost all legislation approved by committees in the House must pass through the Rules Committee before reaching the House floor. The Rules Committee's name comes from its function: If the committee approves a bill for transmission to the House floor, it assigns a "rule" to that bill, setting the terms of a debate. The Rules Committee can, for example, assign a "closed rule," which forbids any amendments and forces the House into a "take it or leave it" position. Thus the Rules Committee acts as a traffic cop. It has the power to delay or even stop legislation; it can amend bills or send them back to committee for revision; and it can decide where two committees have bills on the same subject, which one gets sent to the floor. In recent congresses this powerful committee has been largely controlled by the majority party leadership.

The Ways and Means Committee deals with tax legislation, or the raising of revenue for the government. One former chairman called it "the Cadillac of committees." Because all money-raising bills begin in the House, any tax legislation goes first to Ways and Means, making this committee a central power in Congress. The committee was key in moving much of the Bush administration's tax cut legislation through the House and has been central in health care reform.

While Ways and Means raises money, the Appropriations Committee deals with how government spends that money. When the federal budget is presented to Congress by the president each year, it is first sent to the House Appropriations Committee and its 11 subcommittees. Because the power to tax and spend is the power to make or break programs, industries, and interest groups, and because specialization and reciprocity nudge Congress to follow the lead of its committees, the importance of Ways and Means and Appropriations is clear. While Appropriations is limited by the budget process on its overall spending, it can still decide where it will spend money or make cuts. Traditionally Appropriations was the place for doing favors for other members, such as passing their *pork-barrel bills*—legislation designed to produce visible local benefits, like highways and post offices. Under an aggressive chairman, Democrat Dave Obey of Wisconsin, it has begun to scrutinize spending requests with a new zeal. (See "The Prince of Pork.")

Major Committees in the Senate

The most important committees in the Senate (besides Budget) are Appropriations, Finance, Judiciary, and Foreign Relations. The Senate Appropriations Committee receives spending bills after they have been passed by the House. The Senate committee acts as a "court of appeals," adding money to or subtracting it from the amounts granted by the House. If passed by the House, tax legislation then goes to the Senate Finance Committee, the Senate's equivalent to Ways and Means in the House.

The Prince of Pork

On reelection night the senior senator declared, "West Virginia has always had four friends: God Almighty, Sears Roebuck, Carter's Liver pills and Robert C. Byrd." Years earlier Senator Byrd had happily set his goal: "I want to be West Virginia's billion-dollar industry." In delivering pork to his poor state in the form of federally funded projects, the senator has accomplished his goal and earned the title, "Prince of Pork."

These "Byrd Droppings" fill the state, often with the senator's name attached. There is the Robert C. Byrd Locks and Dam project and the Byrd Green Bank Telescope, both with statues of the senator to greet visitors. There are two Robert C. Byrd U.S. courthouses, four Byrd stretches of highways, the Robert C. Byrd Bridge, and two Robert C. Byrd interchanges. The senator's name graces a Lifelong Learning Center, Hardwood Technology Center, Health and Wellness Center, and an Institute for Advanced Flexible Manufacturing. One newspaper counted more than 30 projects named for the senator and far more that he brought to the state without his name. One critic surmised, "What next—West Byrdinia?"

As chairman of the Senate Appropriations Committee the Democratic senator brought home 10 times the national average of legislative pork, or $236 per resident. In 2006 Byrd won a ninth term and became the longest-serving senator in American history, having arrived in the Senate in 1959.

The Judiciary Committee is one of the Senate's oldest and most important committees. Currently chaired by Patrick Leahy, Democrat of Vermont, the committee has broad jurisdiction over federal laws, including the review of proposed constitutional amendments. It also holds confirmation hearings for federal judges, of recent note the 2009 nomination of Sonia Sotomayor to the Supreme Court.

The Senate Foreign Relations Committee is a watchdog over the president's dominant position in foreign policy. Its importance comes from the Senate's role in confirming appointments of high-level State Department officials, including ambassadors, and approving treaties. It is a place for public dissent to administration policies such as pushing for cutting foreign aid (which is less than 1 percent of the federal budget) and for a more rapid withdrawal from Iraq. Foreign Relations membership has provided useful publicity for senators (including Barack Obama) aspiring to become president.

The Senate also has a Rules Committee, but it is much less important than its House counterpart. With fewer than one-fourth as many members as the House, the problem of coordination is not as great. So the Senate decided that it did not need a strong "traffic cop" to screen legislation. (See "Congressional Staff.")

Congressional Staff

Despite efforts to shrink staff, the U.S. Congress remains the most heavily staffed legislature in the world, with over 35,000 employees. Even junior members of Congress can have 18 full-time and 4 part-time staffers. By comparison, the 650 members of the British House of Commons get by with about 1,000 employees.

Congress finds it difficult to cut staff because, other than voting, a member's staff does everything he or she does. They organize hearings, negotiate agreements with other members' staffs, research proposals, speak with voters, and promote legislation. Staffers will often initiate policies and then "sell" them to their bosses. Lobbyists understand their importance and spend most of their time cultivating relationships with them. Because hired employees' influence is best exercised quietly, congressional staff remain the hidden power of the Hill.

On the Floor, and Beyond

Once a bill has been approved by committee (and in the House by the Rules Committee), it is sent to the House or Senate floor for debate. There it is placed on a calendar. *Calendars* are the schedules for business in Congress. Certain calendars are for routine or minor legislation; others, for more important bills. Although rarely employed, there is one in the House, the "discharge calendar," that can be used to force a bill out of committee against the committee's wishes.

In the House, floor debate is controlled by the Speaker. She schedules bills for consideration and then makes sure the committees deliver their bills in the correct form and at the right time. The Speaker has the right to preside over debate. House members are commonly restricted to a few minutes of talk. The Senate, being smaller, is able to operate more informally, and senators can speak longer. Power is more widely distributed in the Senate than in the House. Even junior (new) senators often chair subcommittees. The Senate majority leader schedules bills for debate, but his control of debate is less than the House Speaker.

When debate on a bill has ended, it is put to a vote. A majority of the legislators present is needed for passage. Whether a bill begins in the Senate or the House, sooner or later it must be submitted to the other chamber, where the whole procedure of committee review and floor action will be repeated. Then, any differences between the House and Senate versions of a bill must be eliminated before it can be sent to the president for his signature or veto.

When there are differences between the two houses on the same bill, a *conference committee* is set up. This is a temporary body including both senators and representatives, created solely to iron out the differences between House and Senate versions of one bill. These differences come about because of amendments attached to the bill by one chamber but not the other, or because the two houses have passed different bills dealing with the same subject, as was seen in the Health Care Reform passed late in Obama's first year. The huge reform measure needed to be passed in identical language by both houses.

The Speaker of the House and the Senate majority leader have the authority to appoint the members of conference committees. In practice they allow the chairs of the relevant standing committees to do this and typically appoint the senior members of these committees. The conference committee engages in bargaining and trade-offs to reach a compromise; once this job is finished, it is disbanded. When (and if) the conference committee reaches agreement, the new substitute bill is sent back to the House and Senate floors for a yea or nay vote. This bill cannot be amended; it must be accepted or rejected as is. Without this rule the bill might be amended again in different ways in the House and Senate, thereby requiring yet another conference committee, and so on.

Party identity is still the best single predictor for how members will vote, as seen in the two parties' division on most of President Obama's legislative agenda. Of course both in committees and on the floor of Congress, members of the same political party do not always vote together, and sometimes they vote across party lines. On measures such as the closing of military bases, regional coalitions of Republicans and Democrats have united to prevent the closing of their local bases. The most frequent division in Congress remains that between Republicans and Democrats. (See Table 4.1.)

TABLE 4.1 MAJOR DIFFERENCES BETWEEN THE HOUSE AND THE SENATE	
HOUSE	SENATE
Larger (435)	Smaller (100)
Shorter term of office (2 years)	Longer term of office (6 years)
More procedural restraints on members	Fewer procedural restraints on members
Narrower constituency	Broader, more varied constituency
Policy specialists	Policy generalists
Less media coverage	More media coverage
More powerful leaders	Less powerful leaders
Less prestigious	More prestigious
Briefer floor debates	Longer floor debates
Less reliant on staff	More reliant on staff
More partisan	Less partisan

In recent congresses, party loyalty has increased in both parties. The majority of the two parties oppose each other most often. Members now vote with their party about 80 percent of the time, whereas 25 years ago loyalty was only seen in 70 percent of the votes. Each party is more united and more different from the other. As the Democratic party loses conservative members from the South and the number of conservative Republicans increases, the parties have become more polarized—fewer liberal Republicans, fewer conservative Democrats. There are also fewer independent *mavericks* in both parties who show limited loyalty to their own party. The result: a harsher, more partisan congress. (See "Nastiness on Capitol Hill.")

Despite President Obama's call for a new era of bipartisanship, it is unlikely that this intense party division will end any time soon. For conservative Republicans the president's policies are decidedly left-leaning, and his image as a post-partisan leader is just rhetoric. They see any success that Obama has in confronting the country's economic problems as likely to cement Democrats in power. Democrats argue that despite the united Republican votes against their programs, there have been good-faith negotiations with the GOP. The president noted that the health care bill passed by one Senate committee contained "more than 160 Republican amendments—a hopeful sign of bipartisan support for the final product." Given the fierce opposition that the GOP inspired in the country to health care reform, the president's words turned out to be more hope than reality.

Nastiness on Capitol Hill

Thomas Jefferson recognized the importance of polite behavior in the legislature. He hoped the Senate would cool the passions of the more populist House and outlined rules to reduce personal attacks. Jefferson saw no reason that partisanship should undercut civility among legislators. But with Clinton's impeachment in late 1998, followed by the election crisis of 2000 and the intense culture wars escalated by competing cable TV programs, Congress has become increasingly nasty. By 2009, a Republican congressman could yell out "You lie" during President Obama's address to Congress on heath care.

The polarized politics on the Hill led to the decline of a bipartisan middle that might bridge the social and political distance between the parties. One leading political scientist, Burdett Loomis, remarked that this partisanship hurt good policymaking: "There seems to be almost no shame. Everyone is just completely righteous right now."

Filibuster

In the Senate, except under unusual circumstances, debate is unlimited. Senators may talk on a subject for as long as they wish without being cut off. Endless talk by one or a number of senators designed to delay or block action in the Senate is called a *filibuster.* The original filibuster was a type of pirate ship. Its current meaning probably comes from the image of a lone individual defying a majority. Senators engaged in a filibuster usually talk for several hours at a time (sometimes reading the Bible or the Washington phone directory) before giving up the floor to an ally. Former Senator Strom Thurmond of South Carolina set the individual filibuster record in 1957 by speaking against a civil rights act for 24 hours and 18 minutes nonstop.

Rule 22 (of the Senate Rules—a set of regulations governing Senate behavior) protects the filibuster unless three-fifths of the Senate (60 senators) votes for an end to debate. This is the only vote in Congress based on the total number of legislators. All other votes in both the Senate and House are based on the number of members who are present and voting. Voting to end debate is called *cloture.* Because many senators, especially those of the minority party, see advantages in having the filibuster available, cloture is difficult.

Filibusters are most effective late in a session of the Senate when legislation has piled up. Senators are eager to adjourn, and they feel the pressures of any delaying tactic. If 60 senators cannot be found to invoke cloture, the bill being filibustered is likely to die. In recent congresses the minority Republicans frequently used the threat of a filibuster to prevent majority actions, notably on healthcare reform. The majority Democrats hovered around controlling the magic number of 60 votes in the Senate in the 111th Congress. This need for a vote on cloture meant that having a majority in the Senate (51 votes) was no longer enough to pass major legislation.

Because the House of Representatives is larger and harder to manage, it has decided it cannot afford the luxury of unlimited debate. Hence, filibusters are not allowed in the House.

Presidential Veto

Even after approval by both the House and Senate, a bill may still be killed by a presidential veto. The president may veto any legislation he wishes. The threat of a veto is important because it allows a president to bargain with congressional leaders while legislation is still being drafted.

A president may not veto only part of a bill. He must veto it all or accept it all. But of course, Congress has the last word: If Congress *overrides* a veto, the bill becomes law. To override a veto requires two-thirds approval of each house of Congress. Vetoes are rarely overridden. They are also rare when a president's party runs Congress. Before the Democrats took control of Congress President Bush had only used the veto once in six years—on stem cell research. In his two years in office after the 2006 elections Bush exercised the veto 11 more times.

The president must act on a bill within 10 working days. If he does not sign it within that period while Congress remains in session, the bill becomes law without his signature. If Congress adjourns before the 10 days are up and the president does not sign the bill, it does not become law—this is called a *pocket veto*.

Because the item veto was declared unconstitutional by the Supreme Court in 1998, Congress retains the advantage of *riders* in any confrontation with the president. A rider is a piece of legislation attached as an amendment to another bill, which may deal with a totally different issue. Commonly, the rider contains provisions that the president does not like, whereas the "parent" bill to which the rider is attached is favored by the president. Either the president vetoes the rider and thus also the main bill or he accepts the unwanted rider in order to get the rest of the bill. These riders helped increase government spending. (See "The White House Trades for China Trade.")

Finally, passing legislation does not automatically make anything happen. If money is needed for the government's wishes (as expressed in a bill) to be carried out, the entire legislative process must be gone

The White House Trades for China Trade

To get members of Congress to agree with the White House often requires appealing to the interests of their district. In 2000 a bill to allow free trade with China came before Congress. It was strongly backed by the Clinton administration and eventually passed both houses. But before that could happen, the White House had to offer local deals for this national issue.

House Democrats, who generally opposed the trade agreement, were swayed by other considerations. Democrat Robert E. "Bud" Cramer voted "yes" after the Commerce Department promised to reconsider closing a weather station in his tornado-prone Alabama district. Martin Frost, a Texas Democrat, supported the bill when Northrop Grumman Corp., a major defense contractor, decided to stay in Dallas after reaching an agreement with the Navy. And three other Texas congressmen supported the administration when EPA promised to quickly complete its required environmental review that was holding up the opening of a gas pipeline across southern Texas.

Source: CQ Weekly, May 27, 2000, p. 1250.

through *twice*—once to pass a bill *authorizing* the activity and a second time to pass a bill *appropriating* the money to do it. The goals of the authorizing bill will not come into effect if the appropriations process does not provide the funds. This brings us to the budget process.

The Budget Process

The "power of the purse" is a basic constitutional power of Congress. Historically, the *authority* to control government spending and taxes has not meant the *ability* to control them. Congress has traditionally not acted coherently on the budget. The numerous committees and decentralized power bases in Congress has meant that overall spending (expenditures) was seldom related to taxes (revenues), and neither fit into a national economic policy. The responsibility for putting together a comprehensive government budget and national economic policy thus fell to the president. Congress has struggled to change this.

In 1974 Congress passed the Budget Act (the Congressional Budget and Impoundment Control Act), which allowed Congress to propose an alternative to the president's budget. Congress could now examine all spending and tax measures, and evaluate them in terms of the overall needs of the economy. The Budget Act did this in several ways.

The act set up House and Senate Budget committees. The House Budget Committee members are drawn mainly from the Ways and Means and Appropriations committees, with one member from each of

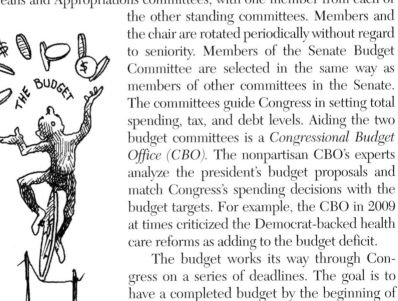

the other standing committees. Members and the chair are rotated periodically without regard to seniority. Members of the Senate Budget Committee are selected in the same way as members of other committees in the Senate. The committees guide Congress in setting total spending, tax, and debt levels. Aiding the two budget committees is a *Congressional Budget Office (CBO)*. The nonpartisan CBO's experts analyze the president's budget proposals and match Congress's spending decisions with the budget targets. For example, the CBO in 2009 at times criticized the Democrat-backed health care reforms as adding to the budget deficit.

The budget works its way through Congress on a series of deadlines. The goal is to have a completed budget by the beginning of the government's fiscal year, October 1. The process starts when the president submits his budget to Congress in January. All the committees in Congress then submit their estimates and views of the budget to the budget committees, which gather them in a first resolution. Congress must vote on this resolution, which sets overall spending and tax levels, by April 15. The various parts of this first resolution then go back to the standing committees concerned with the particular subject or program. By mid-June the standing committees' recommendations have gone back to the budget committees, which draw up a reconciliation bill that is then voted on by Congress. This part of the process is called *reconciliation* because it attempts to balance the separate standing committees' decisions with the targets set by the first resolution.

Throughout the 1980s the budget deficit skyrocketed into the hundreds of billions while various congressional efforts to control it failed miserably. In 1993 President Clinton introduced an ambitious deficit-reduction package that promised to reduce the deficit by $500 billion. The White House claimed that half of the reduction would come from tax increases (mostly on the wealthy) and half from cutting government spending. Republican opponents charged the bill's numbers were suspect and that it was too "tax heavy." After considerable debate and changes by Congress, and with no Republican support, the bill was passed.

In 1994 when Republican majorities took power in both houses, balancing the budget became a shared political goal. Failed attempts to pass a balanced budget constitutional amendment moved Republican leaders to the practical task of actually balancing the budget. The Republicans did what the Democrats charged they could never do—spell out their cuts in government spending. President Clinton's own balanced budget called for fewer tax cuts and fewer reductions in popular programs like Medicare. Disagreements over the budget between the president and Congress led to a government shutdown in late 1995 and early 1996.

The prosperity of the late 1990s increased tax revenues beyond all predictions and aided in producing balanced budgets in 1998, 1999, 2000, and 2001. It had been 50 years since the U.S. government had this many consecutive years of national debt reduction. It did not last. President George W. Bush pushed through a $1.35 trillion tax cut that slashed government revenues, the stock market cratered, the recession continued, and the war on terrorism and Iraq led to increased spending for defense. In 2003 the deficit climbed to $378 billion, in 2004 it reached $412 billion, and in 2005 it then receded to $319 billion. In 2006, the Bush administration was estimating that the year's federal deficit would hit over $400 billion because of spending on hurricane relief and on the war in Iraq. It was a blunt contrast with the *surplus* of $236 billion in fiscal 2000.

By August 2009 the Obama administration was estimating the budget deficit that year at $1.5 *trillion*, down from its earlier estimate of $1.8 trillion. The 2010 deficit was projected to be $1.25 trillion. (Keep in mind that the budget is an estimate, with Congress required to pass appropriations throughout the year using it as a blueprint.) President Obama set a goal of cutting the deficit by more than half to $533 billion by 2013. He plans to do that by allowing the Bush tax cuts to expire after 2010 and by predicting higher levels of economic growth in coming years, which produce higher tax revenues. His deficit-reduction goals are complicated by a health care reform bill that could cost the government $1 trillion over 10 years and his pledge not to raise taxes on individuals who earn less than $250,000 a year.

Other Powers of Congress

Besides these legislative powers, Congress also has several nonlegislative powers. Among them are *oversight* of the executive branch and *investigation.* With Congress and the Executive controlled by the same party the political advantages of these powers is clearly reduced. Still, Congress created the executive agencies and departments and specified their duties. It can oversee them in any ways it wants. For example, in providing bailout funds for banks in the Troubled Asset Relief Program (TARP) the legislation set up a bipartisan panel of outside experts to review the Treasury Department's management and report their findings to Congress every 30 days.

Congress appropriates the funds government agencies need to perform their jobs. These powers give Congress an interest in what the executive branch is doing and the means to find out. Congress, for example, can decide who will and will not receive food stamps, and judge who will be allowed to use federal lands. In short, the annual appropriations process gives Congress the chance to ask what the bureaucracies are doing, tell them what they ought to be doing, and give money for what Congress wants and withhold money for what it does not want.

The *General Accountability Office (GAO)* is an agency created by Congress to help with its oversight function. Congress uses the GAO to examine certain government programs or departments. Many of the stories about scandals in government that appear on shows like *60 Minutes* start life as GAO reports.

In addition, Congress has the power to investigate. If Congress, or a committee (or a committee chair), decides that something is not being done properly, an investigation may be launched. The subject might be the abuse of prisoners in Iraq, bankers' salaries, or illegal campaign contributions. In other words, Congress can investigate whatever it wishes.

Congressional investigations are not welcomed by the executive. On June 4, 2002, the House and Senate Intelligence committees began joint hearings to investigate "why the Intelligence Community did not learn of the September 11th attacks in advance." To divert attention from Congress's action, President Bush announced in a televised speech his proposal to create a cabinet-level Department of Homeland Security. Only later in the year did the president reluctantly agree to such a probe, and still later, and even more reluctantly, agree to testify before the 9/11 commission.

Congressional investigations have sometimes proven dangerous to civil liberties. In the 1950s, Republican Senator Joseph McCarthy's Permanent Investigations Subcommittee and the House Un-American Activities Committee ruined the reputations of many innocent people, forced able people out of government service, and whipped up fear throughout the country with charges of disloyalty and communist sympathies.

The Senate also has the power to approve or reject most presidential appointments, including ambassadors, cabinet members, and military officers. Most presidential appointments are routine, and there is a tendency in the Senate to agree that the president has a right to have the people he wishes to work with him. Still, the "behind-the-scenes" pressure of Senate dissatisfaction undoubtedly causes presidents not to make certain nominations in the first place. The Senate takes a more active role in presidential appointments to the independent regulatory commissions and the Supreme Court, as shown by the 68–31 Senate vote to confirm Sonia Sotomayor as a justice.

Congress has certain judicial functions. The House of Representatives can *impeach* (bring charges against) a federal official by a simple majority vote. Then, the Senate holds a trial on these charges. In the case of impeachment of the president, the chief justice of the Supreme Court presides. If two-thirds of the Senate votes to uphold the charges and to convict the official, that official is removed from office.

Impeachment is difficult, slow, and cumbersome. Several federal judges have been impeached and convicted in the past. Only two presidents were ever impeached, Andrew Johnson in 1868 and Bill Clinton in 1998. Neither was convicted by the Senate. Richard Nixon resigned the presidency in 1974 (the only president ever to do so) in the face of almost certain impeachment by the House and conviction by the Senate.

The failed 1998–1999 attempt to remove President Clinton illustrated the political and constitutional obstacles to impeachment. Acting on the report of Independent Counsel Kenneth Starr, the House of Representatives in the fall of 1998 took up the question of whether the president should be impeached. Accused of perjury for lying to a grand jury about his affair with Monica Lewinsky and then of obstructing justice by trying to cover it up, the president benefited from personal popularity and economic prosperity throughout the scandal. Voting on party lines, a majority of the House impeached the president. But on February 12, 1999, the GOP, lacking Democratic support, could not get a two-thirds vote for conviction in the Senate. His accusers could never quite convince either Democrats or the public that the president's sleazy behavior rose to the level of the "high crimes and misdemeanors" that the Constitution requires for impeachment.

Despite its difficulty, impeachment remains an ultimate check over the executive in the hands of the legislature.

CASE STUDY

Controlling Global Warming—The House Climate Bill

After years of denial Washington seemed ready in 2009 to tackle global warming. The evidence was clear. More than 2,000 scientists on the Nobel Prize–winning international Panel on Climate Change declared that carbon from burning fossil fuels was warming the planet, causing drought, rising sea levels, and disease. U.S. government agencies predicted that if nothing was done to cut these greenhouse gases the Southwest would become another Dust Bowl, and Florida would flood. Key West would be under water in the next century. The Environmental Protection Agency declared carbon dioxide a pollutant, and polls showed that three-quarters of Americans thought the government should regulate the release of greenhouse gases. With Democratic majorities in both houses and a new president making the issue a top priority, the push for legislation reflected this shift in political opinion.

But that didn't mean that the politically possible matched the planet's needs. Scientists thought that carbon emissions had to be reduced by 50 to 80 percent to prevent an environmental disaster. No country could do this alone, and developing giants like China and India were refusing to accept any limits, positions similar to that of the United States under George W. Bush. With an international conference on climate in Copenhagen scheduled for the end of 2009, it was hoped that American leadership on the issue would break the impasse.

The most straightforward way of limiting carbon would be a tax on emissions, which would make polluters pay. But for American politicians a new tax on consumers for every activity that burns carbon-based fuels would be a nightmare. The so-called cap-and-trade system seemed more doable.

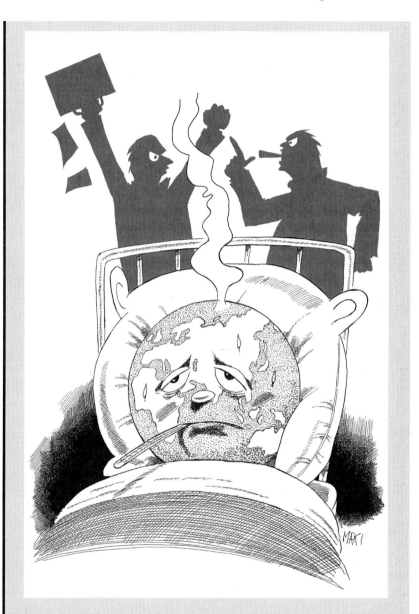

Cap and Trade: Let the Market Figure it Out

Under cap and trade the government would set a yearly limit on carbon emissions and gradually tighten it. It would then issue "permission slips to pollute," giving companies permits for each ton of carbon they burned. These permits could be bought and sold. The intention was to create a market that would put a price on allowable emissions. Supply and demand would determine how much these permits cost. Tougher standards year by year and fewer available permits would lead to higher prices. Companies would buy permits from each other as long as that was cheaper to do than making the technological changes needed to eliminate their use of carbon. They would pass along the increasing cost of the permits in their prices and presumably consumers would respond by cutting back on carbon-using products. Europe has had a similar system in place for years with mixed results.

The results of all this were vigorously debated. The Congressional Budget Office estimated that the costs to a typical family of reducing carbon by 15 percent would be $1,600 a year. Conservative groups did their own studies that found the costs many times more, plus a considerable loss of jobs. Because emissions are a global problem these reductions by the United States would only reduce the world's total emissions by about 3 percent. Advocates pointed out that this was just a start and that the legislation passed by the House would require reductions of 42 percent by 2030 and 83 percent by 2050. It would also encourage new technologies that would make it cheaper to use alternative energy like wind or sun or clean coal.

THE WAXMAN-MARKEY BILL

The legislation in the House attempting to set this up was called Waxman-Markey, after Henry Waxman of California, Democratic chairman of the Energy and Commerce Committee, and Edward J. Markey, a Democrat from Massachusetts. The bill, which would win approval from Waxman's committee, also had to go through the Ways and Means and Agriculture committees. After months of negotiations the bill was passed by the House in June by 219–212. Only eight Republicans voted for it, and the GOP denounced it as a national energy tax. President Obama, who actively lobbied for the bill, called it a "bold and necessary step." The bill itself had expanded to over 1,300 pages and even supporters called it a "patchwork of compromises."

The bill required a 17 percent cut in greenhouse gases by 2020, mostly through the cap-and-trade system. By then 20 percent of electricity had to come from renewable sources and energy efficiency. In accomplishing these goals the bill gave utilities, coal plants, manufacturers, farmers, oil refiners, and other industries special protections to help them in the transition to new ways of doing business. Originally in President Obama's proposal all allowances to emit greenhouse gases would have been auctioned off by the government. The money from this would have been used for tax breaks and energy assistance for the poor. Instead Waxman-Markey gave away free permits to polluting businesses during a transition period of 10 to 20 years.

The bill also depended heavily on carbon offsets. These were official certificates given for greenhouse gases that *might* have been emitted but were not. U.S. polluters could buy them and pay someone else to reduce emissions instead of doing it themselves. For example, foreign companies might be able to reduce their carbon emissions more cheaply than U.S. firms by planting several acres of trees or building solar power generators. This would provide an equal benefit to the climate at a lower cost. But whether such offsets actually happen overseas, whether they can be verified, or whether they would have happened anyway remains debatable.

There were other parts of the complex bill. New coal-fired power plants were required to produce 50 percent less carbon than existing plants. A tariff would be imposed after 2020 for goods from countries that refused to limit their carbon pollution. Concessions were made to farm groups that included involving the Agriculture Department in regulating parts of the program because it would be more favorable to these interests than the Environmental Protection Agency. Still, 44 Democrats, mostly from conservative and rural districts, voted against the measure.

WHEELING AND DEALING

To get the votes needed for passage the bill changed *who* pays the costs of cutting greenhouse gases. To satisfy Democrats from coal-mining states, allowances were given to coal-based electric utilities, energy-intensive manufacturers, oil refiners, and the auto industry. Instead of auctioning off these permits the government gave them away, costing the Treasury some $713 billion in the program's first 10 years. Coal-based electric companies would get 35 percent or more of the allowances. Energy-intensive manufacturers such as aluminum, glass, or steel would get up to 15 percent of allowances.

Members representing interests affected by the bill battled for concessions. Congressman Gene Green, a Democrat from Houston, Texas, demanded 5 percent of the permits be given to oil refiners to deal with the costs of carbon controls. He won 2 percent of the allowances. Colin Peterson of Minnesota got the list of farming activities that would qualify as offsets expanded, bringing a potential windfall to farmers. He then supported the bill. Members of Congress from Georgia, North Carolina, and Tennessee tried to protect utilities from their region by weakening the requirements for renewable energy. The original bill had called for 25 percent of electricity to come from renewable sources like wind, solar, or hydro by 2025. This was weakened to 15 percent by 2020 to gain their votes. Even liberal Democrats got a piece of the action. Bobby Rush of Chicago withheld his support until a last-minute agreement to provide $1 billion for energy-related jobs for low income workers.

In the months of horse-trading, the bill's targets for carbon use were weakened, its requirements for renewable electricity were reduced, and the incentives for industries were sweetened. While some environmentalists backed the final bill, others like Greenpeace and Friends of the Earth opposed it. Industry was split. The Chamber of Commerce opposed it while some of the nation's biggest corporations including Dow Chemical, Starbucks, and Ford backed it. President Obama welcomed House passage, though he admitted, "I think that finding the right balance between providing new incentives to businesses, but not giving away the store, is always an art . . ."

CONCLUSION

The process of passing the climate bill showed Congress at its best and worse. Polluting industries using coal and fossil fuels won considerable compromises. They limited the overall targets, were richly compensated to make necessary changes in their energy use, and got the costs of the permits passed on to consumers. But the bill did demonstrate that the United States was willing to do something about global warming and would no longer be "preaching temperance from a bar stool" on the environment. Under committed leaders the House of Representatives could pass far-reaching laws to transform the nation's use of energy. Of course for anything to really affect the world's climate, an international agreement needed to be signed, an agreement that would require concessions from countries such as China, India, and Brazil. And even in the United States any limits on fossil fuels still needed to pass the Senate.

Meanwhile a new M.I.T. study suggested that the planet was warming much faster than previously thought; melting Arctic Sea ice was releasing even more greenhouse gases in feedback loops that amplified the effects. But this was as former vice president Al Gore (who backed the bill) put it, "an inconvenient truth" for many political and economic interests. The climate bill skillfully managed to protect American regions and industries. Whether the same could be said about the world's population and environment was not as clear. As one scientist noted, "the laws of physics don't compromise."

Sources: John Broder, "Adding Something for Everyone . . ." The New York Times, July 1, 2009; David Fahrenthold, "Caps, Trades and Offsets," The Washington Post, May 26, 2009; Coral Davenport, et al., "Carbon, From the Ground Up," CQ Weekly, August 3, 2009.

WRAP-UP

The U.S. Congress consists of two houses, the Senate and the House of Representatives. Two senators are selected from each state, and they serve for six years. Representatives are allocated to districts in states according to population; they serve for two years. The Senate, with 100 members, is smaller, more informal, and more prestigious than the House, with its 435 members. The House, because it is larger, is more tightly controlled by the majority party leadership. Since the 2006 elections, Democrats have been the majority party in both houses of Congress.

The House and Senate operate separately, but before any legislation can be sent to the president for signing, it must be passed in identical language by both. In the House floor debate, the agenda for legislation, and even committee priorities, are controlled by the leadership elected by the majority party. The Speaker of the House works closely with the majority leader and whips. The Senate has no speaker; floor debate is managed by the Senate majority leader. Each branch also has minority leaders and minority whips.

While much of the work of the House and Senate goes on in committees and subcommittees, party leadership has generally become more important than committee chairs. The committee chairs (who are always from the majority party) do exercise considerable power. Despite some exceptions, they are usually chosen on the basis of seniority—longest consecutive service on the committee. The majority leadership in the House has become influential in this decision, but the leaders in the Senate defer to seniority. The focus on the budget, the rising deficit and the recent financial crises combined with members following specialization and reciprocity has raised the importance of the taxing and spending committees.

All legislation, other than revenue-raising and appropriations bills (which must start in the House), can be introduced in either the House or the Senate. Bills are then assigned to the relevant committee for review. If approved by committee, a bill is sent to the floor of the House or Senate (going through the Rules Committee in the House). When approved there, the bill goes to the other chamber for a similar process. If the House and Senate pass different versions, they will be ironed out by a conference committee. When both branches of Congress have approved the same bill, it is sent to the president. The president may sign it, veto it, pocket veto it, or allow it to become law without his signature. If he vetoes it, Congress may try to override the bill by a two-thirds vote in each house. The difficulty of passing any legislation, especially major legislation like the 2009 House climate Bill, should be clear from even this brief review.

Congressional procedures seem complex and confusing because they *are* complex and confusing. Congress has been criticized for being slow, unresponsive, and even unrepresentative. Certainly its procedures involve time-consuming duplication. The seniority system, the filibuster in the Senate, and the overall fragmentation of power into committees and subcommittees sometimes frustrate majority wishes. But they have not stopped Congress from quickly acting in an emergency, as seen in the weeks that followed the banking panic in the fall of 2008. Congressional complexity also doesn't stop voters from changing who leads Congress, as seen in the 2006 midterm elections.

If Congress is slow to solve national problems, it may be because the country's leaders do not agree on the nature of the problem or the way to fix it. If Congress bogs down in angry party disputes or struggles to reach a watered-down compromise, it may be because a country as large as the United States includes strongly opposing opinions that the Congress reflects. If special interests receive special treatment this may simply be an accurate reflection of these players' political power.

Congress was not set up to make government more efficient. It was designed to represent the wishes of the people governed, to be the political game's democratic centerpiece. Congress acts best not when it acts least, but when it reflects the public support on which America's government rests.

THOUGHT QUESTIONS

1. How can Congress be made more effective in responding to pressing national problems? Does the increased party leaders' control in Congress make the legislature more likely to bog down in partisan bickering, or more likely to act more coherently?

2. Think about the "unwritten rules" of seniority, specialization, and reciprocity. How do these rules help Congress to operate? What are their drawbacks?

3. Congress is generally unpopular, whereas individual members are popular and usually reelected. Why does the institution suffer while incumbents shine?

4. How does Congress know what to do? Did the 2008 elections give the Democratic majority in Congress direction for policy changes? Or did it just reflect a dislike for what the previous administration was doing?

5. Does the case history of the climate bill in the House illustrate the strength of a representative legislature or its weakness?

SUGGESTED READINGS

Caro, Robert A. *Master of the Senate: The Years of Lyndon Johnson.* New York: Alfred A. Knopf, 2002.
  The third volume of this masterful biography of Lyndon Johnson dissects the U.S. Senate in the 1950s and LBJ's powerful presence. The first 100 pages is an excellent history of the Senate.

Fenno, Richard E., Jr. *Home Style: House Members in Their Districts.* Boston: Little, Brown, 1978.
  Still the classic study of how representatives act in front of their most important audience—the folks back home.

Johnson, Haynes, and David S. Broder. *The System.* Boston: Little, Brown, 1997. Pb.
  Two top political reporters dissect what happened to Clinton's health reform proposals, with some striking conclusions about politics.

Kennedy, John F. *Profiles in Courage.* New York: Harper & Row, 1956. Pb.
  The future president wrote these prize-winning profiles of members of Congress
  who stood up to the popular pressures of their time and sacrificed their careers to
  do what was right.
Mann, Thomas E., and Norman J. Ornstein. *The Broken Branch.* New York:
  Oxford University Press, 2006.
  Two legislative experts write an alarming critique of what the Republican majority
  brought to Congress.
Mayhew, David R. *America's Congress.* New Haven, Conn.: Yale University,
  2000.
  A leading scholar of Congress takes an historical look at the importance of individual
  congressional members to our system of government.

CHAPTER 5

The Judicial Branch:
The Supreme Court and
the Federal Court System

Thehe Constitution gets right to the point in Article III: "The judicial Power of the United States shall be vested in one Supreme Court, and in such inferior courts as the Congress may from time to time ordain and establish." Whenever a new justice is appointed—as happened in 2009 with the Court's first Hispanic woman, Sonia Sotomayor, taking the bench—we are reminded of the Supreme Court's central importance to constitutional government. The public attention given to this change in leadership reflects the pressing political issues revolving around civil liberties, federalism and presidential power that the judicial player is called on to resolve.

Following the lead of the Constitution, Congress set up two major levels of federal courts below the Supreme Court—federal district courts and courts of appeals. It also established several special federal courts as the need for them has arisen. The federal court system is responsible for judging cases involving the U.S. Constitution and federal laws.

Paralleling the federal court system are the state courts. Each state has its own judicial system to try cases that come under state law (though it may also deal with cases under the U.S. Constitution and laws). Issues involving the Constitution may be appealed to the U.S. Supreme Court. In this chapter we will focus on the federal court system and particularly the Supreme Court; state courts are set up in much the same way.

Federal Court System

U.S. District Courts

At the base of the federal system are the courts of *original jurisdiction*—the *U.S. district courts*. Except in a few special instances, all cases involving federal law are tried first in district courts. There are 89 district courts in the United States and another 5 in the U.S. territories, with at least 1 federal district court in each state. The larger, more populous states have more district courts. New York, for example, has 4 district courts. Each district has between 1 and 28 judges, for a total of 678 district judges in the country. These judges preside over most federal cases, including civil rights cases, controversies involving more than $10,000, antitrust suits, and counterfeiting cases. The large volume of cases they handle (over 250,000 annually) has led to long delays in administering justice. At one time, it took four years to complete a civil case in the Southern District of New York.

Courts of Appeals

Above the district courts are the *courts of appeals* (sometimes called by their old name, *circuit courts of appeals*). These courts have only *appellate jurisdiction;* that is, they hear *appeals* from the district courts and from important regulatory commissions, like the Federal Trade Commission. If you took a civil rights case to your district court and lost, you could appeal the decision and have the case brought before a court of appeals. The United States is divided into 13 courts of appeals. There are 12 geographic *circuits* (11 plus 1 in Washington, D.C.), and 1 U.S. Court of Appeals for the Federal Circuit dealing with appeals from special federal courts like the U.S. Claims Court. Each of the 13 appeals courts has between 6 and 28 judges, depending on the volume of work. Usually 3 judges hear each case. One hundred and seventy-nine circuit court judges handle almost 55,000 cases a year. These are the final courts of appeal for most cases, but less than a hundred cases each year are appealed further to the Supreme Court. (See Figure 5.1.)

Special Federal Courts

Special federal courts have been created by Congress to handle certain cases. The *U.S. Claims Court* deals with people's claims against government seizure of property. The *U.S. Court of Military Appeals*

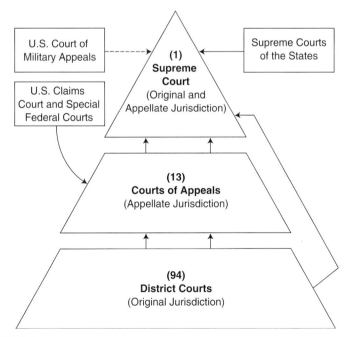

FIGURE 5.1
Federal Court Structure and the Flow of Cases to the Supreme Court.

(often called the *GI Supreme Court*), composed of three civilians, is the final judge of court-martial convictions. The U.S. Supreme Court can review only certain types of military cases.

The Judges

All federal judges, including Supreme Court justices, are nominated to the bench by the president and must be confirmed by the Senate. Un-der the Constitution, federal judges hold office for life "during good behavior" and are removed only by impeachment. This has rarely happened. However, in October 1989, the Senate impeached a Florida judge (who is now a Florida congressman), Alcee Hastings, in a controversial bribery case. To further protect them from political pressures, judges' salaries cannot be reduced while they're in office.

Despite these protections, the appointment of judges is a very political matter. Judges almost always are selected on a party basis, usually as a reward for their political services. One commentator called the judiciary "the place to put political workhorses out to pasture." In this partisan spirit, 87 percent of Bill Clinton's appointments to federal judgeships were Democrats, while 89 percent of George Bush Sr.'s were Republicans. This partisan spirit carries over to the Senate where the majority party may prove reluctant to confirm federal judges appointed by a president of the opposing party. In the past this has led to a "vacancy crisis" in the federal courts as the Senate delayed acting on presidents' nominees to the bench.

Adding to a president's problems is that many of these nominees need the consent of their home-state senators. This custom, *senatorial courtesy,* is followed by the Senate in confirming federal judges below the Supreme Court. By this practice, senators will not vote for nominees unacceptable to the senator from the state concerned. This gives the Senate the whip hand in appointing federal judges and makes sure local opinion is heard in the selection process. How the two senators of each state divide up their choices for nominees is left up to them. In the 1960s and 1970s, when the federal courts took the lead in enforcing racial integration, senatorial courtesy made the appointment of liberal federal judges in the South difficult for a president.

The president's power to influence the makeup of one of the three major branches of the government is extremely important, though it may be restricted in practice. By the end of his second term Clinton had appointed 373 federal judges, including 65 of the 179 appellate judges. Similarly, George W. Bush finished his eight years in office having appointed a total of 324 judges, 261 to district courts, 61 on courts of appeals, and 2 Supreme Court justices. Some scholars have argued that Democrats like Clinton stressed diversity over ideology, often picking minority and female judges that didn't necessarily reflect the president's own political philosophy. On the other hand, Republican presidents are more ideological, with conservative credentials given priority over diversity in filling judicial vacancies. In appointing Justice Sotomayor, who was not the most liberal choice among the candidates on his short list, Barack Obama seems to be continuing this Democratic pattern.

A majority of Supreme Court justices have been appointed by Republican presidents. In 2005 President Bush had the unusual opportunity to appoint two justices to the Court, John G. Roberts as chief justice and Samuel A. Alito Jr. as an associate justice. Both replaced Republican-appointed justices. Alito took the seat of Sandra Day O'Connor who, in 1981, became the first woman on the Supreme Court. Roberts replaced Chief Justice William Rehnquist who had been elevated to that post from his seat on the Court when Warren Burger resigned in 1986. At that same time President Ronald Reagan nominated an equally conservative Antonin Scalia to be the first justice of Italian descent. Reagan's 1988 selection of Anthony Kennedy, after the Senate had rejected Robert Bork, was aimed at pointing the Court in a conservative direction. President Bush's 1990 appointment of a moderate New Hampshire judge, David Souter, was later considered a mistake by conservatives.

Three justices have been chosen by Democratic presidents. Bill Clinton selected Ruth Bader Ginsburg in 1993 and Stephen G. Breyer in 1994, while Barack Obama appointed Sonia Sotomayor in 2009 to replace David Souter, who resigned. All these Democratic-appointed justices have been considered moderates when they were appointed and have generally voted as part of the Court's liberal wing. Justice Ginsburg, for example, has focused on gender issues. She and Justice Breyer vigorously dissented from the Court's decision to stop the vote recount in the 2000 Florida presidential election.

Senate confirmation of justices, once a fairly gentlemanly affair, turned nasty in the late 1980s. President Reagan's 1987 nomination of Robert Bork set off fierce opposition from liberal groups offended by his views on civil rights, abortion, and privacy. After a flurry of personal attacks (now called "borking" by conservatives), Bork was rejected by the Democratic Senate. This unusually public politicizing of the confirmation process continued with President Bush's nomination of conservative Clarence Thomas in 1991. Unlike Bork, Thomas had fewer

Presidents and the Court

Less than 6 months after taking office the new president had a chance to nominate Judge Sonia Sotomayor to the Supreme Court. The popular enthusiasm for the first Latin woman justice may have obscured her record as a moderate who was probably not as liberal as Barack Obama. Justices do have a way of disappointing the president appointing them.

Theodore Roosevelt said of famed justice Oliver Wendell Holmes: "He has the backbone of a banana." President Eisenhower was so angered at Chief Justice Earl Warren's rulings that he called Warren's appointment "the biggest damn-fool mistake I ever made." The controversy set off by the Warren Court's activism led President Nixon to appoint Warren Burger as chief justice to replace Earl Warren when he retired in 1969. Nixon hoped that the four justices he had appointed, including Burger, would inspire greater restraint in the Court. However, the Burger Court, in *U.S.* v. *Nixon* (1974), ruled that President Nixon had to surrender to the special Watergate prosecutor the White House tapes of his conversations about illegal activities. The president, who resigned shortly afterward, was certainly not pleased by this example of the Court's independence.

qualifications, which ironically gave opponents less of a "paper trail" to criticize. Despite the dramatic televised testimony of Anita Hill (accusing him of sexual harassment), Thomas was confirmed, though by the smallest margin of approval (52–48) in more than 100 years.

The confirmation hearings in 2005 and 2006 of Chief Justice Roberts and Justice Alito looked mild by comparison. Although partisan in their questioning of the nominees, Democratic senators seemed relieved that the appointees were not as conservative as other potential candidates. Although most Republican senators opposed Justice Sotomayor in 2009 her hearings were also restrained, perhaps because a Democratic majority made her confirmation a given. Recent appointees have also been better briefed on how to deal with televised Senate hearings than they were in the past. On hot-button issues, like abortion, the nominees duck and weave repeated questions without firmly expressing a position. This tends to produce Senate confirmations of less substance and more ritual. (See "Presidents and the Court.")

Jurisdiction

Jurisdiction refers to the matters over which a court may exercise its authority. The jurisdiction of the federal courts falls into two broad categories: In the first group, it depends on the *subject of the case;* in the second, on the *parties to the case,* no matter what the subject. The federal courts have jurisdiction over all subjects related to the Constitution and over treaties of the United States. (Admiralty and maritime cases involving international law are also included.) Jurisdiction determined by parties includes cases involving ambassadors and other foreign representatives, controversies in which the United States is a party, and controversies between two or more states or between a state or citizen of the United States and a foreign citizen or state. The federal court system's last and largest source of cases is suits between citizens of different states.

This definition does not mean that the federal courts have the *only* jurisdiction over such cases. Federal courts have *exclusive jurisdiction* in some cases, such as cases involving crimes against the laws of the United States. However, in other cases, they have *concurrent jurisdiction,* shared with state courts. For example, some suits between citizens of different states may be heard by both federal and state courts.

U.S. Supreme Court

Composed of a chief justice and eight associate justices, the *Supreme Court of the United States* sits on the summit of the federal court system. (See Table 5.1.) Although Congress is allowed to set the number of justices on the Supreme Court, the number has remained at nine justices since 1869. The Supreme Court has some *original jurisdiction* (cases that can be presented first to the court), but most of the cases it hears are appeals of lower court decisions, which involve its *appellate jurisdiction.* If your civil rights case lost in both the district court and the court of appeals, you could be heard by the Supreme Court.

TABLE 5.1 THE SUPREME COURT, 2010

JUSTICE APPOINTED	DATE OF BIRTH	APPOINTED BY	DATE
John J. Roberts Jr. (chief justice)	1955	Bush II	2005
John Paul Stevens	1920	Ford	1975
Antonin Scalia	1936	Reagan	1986
Anthony Kennedy	1936	Reagan	1988
Clarence Thomas	1946	Bush	1991
Ruth Bader Ginsburg	1933	Clinton	1993
Stephen G. Breyer	1938	Clinton	1994
Samuel A. Alito Jr.	1950	Bush II	2006
Sonia Sotomayor	1954	Obama	2009

Actually very few cases reach the Supreme Court. Of more than 10 million cases tried every year in American courts (federal and state), some 7,400 petitions for review are taken to the Supreme Court. In the 2007–2008 term the Court issued signed opinions in only 67 cases, a reduction from the case load of previous years. The other petitions are affirmed or reversed by written *memorandum orders.* The majority of the cases that come to the Court do so in the form of petitions (written requests) for a *writ of certiorari* (*certiorari* means to be informed of something). A writ of certiorari is an order to the lower court to send the entire record of the case to the higher court for review. If you lost your civil rights case in a lower court, you could petition for this writ. It is granted when four justices of the Supreme Court feel that the issues raised are important enough to merit a review. Many of these involve constitutional issues. The Court denies almost 90 percent of these applications. This procedure rests control over the appeal process in the hands of the Supreme Court, keeping a maximum number of decisions in the lower courts.

The Final Authority?

The prominence of the Supreme Court in American history rests on its "final" authority over what the Constitution means. Yet a ruling of the Court has not always been the final word. The Court itself has reversed its decisions. (See "Separate but Equal?") If the Court interprets a law in a way Congress does not like, Congress can simply rewrite the law. In 1990 Congress passed the Civil Rights Restoration Act, which extended civil rights protection to all programs of colleges accepting federal aid. The act overturned a court ruling that limited this protection. Amendments to the Constitution also have reversed decisions by the Court. An 1895 Court decision striking down the federal income tax was overturned by the Sixteenth Amendment in 1913, which allowed income taxes.

The strength of the Court's "final" authority is also tempered by the other branches of government and by public opinion. Despite the Court's popularity, the public's acceptance of a decision is not always guaranteed. In civil rights cases like racial profiling, where police indiscriminately stop black motorists, and in civil liberties cases like Christmas displays in public buildings, local communities have ignored the Court's interpretation of the Constitution. Congress and the president have taken their turn in interpreting vague parts of the Constitution to meet the demands of the time and the needs of those in power. The president's right to involve the country in the Vietnam and Iraq wars, without a formal declaration of war, would seem to fly in the face of the war-making powers given to Congress by the Constitution. Yet without a challenge by Congress, the president's interpretation of the Constitution stood.

Despite this shared role in changing the Constitution, the Supreme Court, through its rulings, constantly explains and applies the Constitution, breathing life into 200-year-old words. A brief history of the Court will show how.

Early Years of the Court

In its first years the Supreme Court was neglected. It did not start life as the powerful player we know today. No cases at all were brought to the Court in its first three years. Many leaders, such as Patrick Henry and Alexander Hamilton, refused appointments to the Court; court sessions were held in basement apartments. When Washington, D.C., was first planned, the Court was overlooked, with no building provided to house it.

Under the leadership of John Marshall, 1801–1835, the Court's influence greatly increased. Two landmark decisions marked this growth in power. The first announced the Court's *judicial review,* the power not only to declare acts and laws of any state and local government unconstitutional but also to strike down acts of any branch of the federal government. The second major decision established the principle of *national supremacy,* that the U.S. laws and Constitution are the supreme law of the land and that state laws that are in conflict with federal laws cannot stand. (See "Chief Justice John Marshall.")

Judicial Review and National Supremacy

Marbury v. *Madison* (1803) clearly established the principle of judicial review. In this case the Supreme Court, for the first time, struck down an act of Congress. The case shows Chief Justice John Marshall as a shrewd politician.

Shortly before leaving office, President John Adams (who had nominated Marshall to the court) appointed a number of minor judicial officials in order to maintain the influence of his party in the coming administration of his opponent, Thomas Jefferson. When Jefferson took office, he discovered that the commission of William Marbury had not actually been delivered. Jefferson ordered Secretary of State James Madison to hold it up. Under a section of the Judiciary Act of 1789, Marbury sued in the Supreme Court to compel delivery of the commission. Marshall was then confronted with deciding a case between his political allies and his enemy, Jefferson, who as president was determined to weaken the power of the conservative Supreme Court.

Chief Justice John Marshall

"Marshall found the Constitution paper and he made it power."
—President James A. Garfield

John Marshall served as the fourth, and arguably greatest, chief justice. He applied his genius to a single mission: building the government of a united nation. Raising the limited prestige and power of the Supreme Court was necessary so that it could serve that mission. Marshall shaped constitutional law so that it too could propel a strong central government into an unlimited future. For Marshall, the Constitution must serve its goal of creating a lasting union. Thus his famous phrase, "We must never forget that it is a *constitution* that we are expounding."

Marshall acted more like a statesman than a judge. In his major decisions on judicial review and national supremacy, he was not strictly interpreting and applying the law. Marshall was establishing principles for an infant nation. Interestingly, his lack of legal education—less than three months of law classes, and poorly attended at that—may have helped him. Rather than deciding cases legalistically, he acted like a legislator breaking with the past. His experience in General Washington's army at Valley Forge may have provided his most important lesson, reminding him of the price of disunity.

When Marshall died in Philadelphia, citizens rang the Liberty Bell in his honor. It cracked and has never been rung again.

What Marshall did was to dismiss Marbury's case, ruling that the section of the Judiciary Act under which he had sued was unconstitutional (the act allowed the Supreme Court original jurisdiction in a case not mentioned by the Constitution). By doing so he clearly asserted that the Supreme Court, on the basis of *its* interpretation of the Constitution, could limit the actions of Congress. At the same time, the Court supported Jefferson's argument that he did not have to deliver the commission. How could the president object?

Another early decision established that states could not interfere with the functioning of the federal government. In this case, *McCulloch* v. *Maryland* (1819), the state of Maryland attempted to tax the Baltimore branch of the unpopular Bank of the United States, established by the federal government. Chief Justice Marshall, speaking for a unanimous court, ruled that the federal government, "though limited in its powers, is supreme within its sphere of action." Marshall also found that although the Constitution did not specifically allow Congress to create a bank, Article I, Section 8 gave Congress the power to make all laws "necessary and proper" for carrying out its authority.

Implied powers based on this clause were used later in broadly expanding the duties that Congress could undertake.

In 1857 came the famous *Dred Scott* case (*Dred Scott* v. *Sandford*). Here, the Court ruled that a slave (Dred Scott) was not automatically free just because his owner had taken him to a state not allowing slavery. Congress, the Court said, had no right to interfere with property rights guaranteed by the Constitution. The Court went on to say that the Missouri Compromise (1820), which had attempted to resolve the slavery issue by dividing the new western territories into slave and free parts, was invalid. In terms of constitutional development, this unpopular decision supporting slavery was the first time an act of Congress of great importance was struck down by the courts. As such, the *Dred Scott* case marked a critical expansion of judicial powers. Had the Court gone too far?

The Court after the Civil War

The end of the Civil War signaled the end of the major political conflict dominating the first 75 years of the Republic—*states' rights* versus *federal powers*. With federal unity achieved, rapid national growth began. The resulting economic expansion and the unrestrained growth of giant monopolies created a new demand for government regulation of the economy. The Supreme Court became more active, and judicial power was greatly enlarged. In just 9 years (1864–1873), 10 acts of Congress were struck down, compared with only 2 acts in the previous 74 years.

Not only was the Court more active, it also was more conservative. Many liberals viewed the Court as an instrument for protecting the property rights of the rich and ignoring popular demands for government regulation.

This trend continued into the twentieth century, when the Court found itself up against the growing power of the executive branch. The presidency was widely felt to be the most effective place in the government to regulate the social and economic changes brought about by the post-Civil War industrialization. But the Supreme Court continued to resist the expansion of government's regulatory power, even though much of the legislation it struck down (such as minimum wage and child labor laws) was widely popular. Between 1890 and 1936, the Court declared 46 laws unconstitutional in full or in part.

It was President Franklin D. Roosevelt who caused the Court's policy to change. He fought the Court's opposition to his New Deal measures by threatening to expand the Court with new judges of his own choosing, the so-called *court-packing* bill. Although Roosevelt's plan was unsuccessful and aroused a storm of public and congressional opposition, it may have accomplished FDR's purposes. In 1937 the Court backed down—the famous "switch in time that saved nine"—and turned away from economic policymaking.

Modern Courts

Beginning in 1937, Supreme Court decisions have shown three major trends. These trends peaked in the decisions of the Warren Court (led by Chief Justice Earl Warren) in the 1950s and 1960s, and have been eroded in the decisions of more recent, more conservative courts.

First, the Court invalidated much less federal legislation than it had in the 50 years before the New Deal. Generally only a few federal laws were held unconstitutional, and in most of these cases the legislation struck down was not very significant. In a second area, the Court avoided protecting private property rights. The Court, until recently, has not been greatly concerned with guarding economic interests from government policymaking.

The Court has shown more positive interest in a third area—increased judicial protection for civil liberties. While reducing property rights in importance, the Court has sought to preserve and protect the rights of individuals against the increased powers of an expanding government. First Amendment freedoms of speech, press, religion, and assembly have been developed and extended by modern Supreme Courts. With Earl Warren as chief justice (1953–1969), the Supreme Court moved to liberalize reapportionment, racial discrimination, and the rights of defendants in criminal cases.

In decisions dealing with reapportionment, beginning with *Baker* v. *Carr* (1962), the Warren Court established the principle of "one man, one vote" for election districts. The Court ruled that districts must contain roughly equal population, while still allowing partisan advantage in drawing their boundaries. In moving to eliminate racial discrimination, the Court led the nation in cutting away racism in schooling, voting, housing, and the use of public facilities.

Another major interest of the Warren Court, the rights of criminal defendants, saw the Court throw the protection of the Bill of Rights around people accused of crimes by state and federal authorities. The Court insisted on an impoverished defendant's basic right to a lawyer, declared that illegally seized evidence cannot be used in state criminal trials, and held that suspects must be advised of their constitutional right to silence and to have a lawyer before questioning. This last area, summed up as *Miranda* (*Miranda* v. *Arizona*, 1966), is familiar to all fans of TV detective series. (See "Miranda: Pop Culture and the Court.")

Miranda: Pop Culture and the Court

"You have the right to remain silent" is how the *Miranda* warning begins. It was also how Chief Justice Rehnquist began his decision upholding *Miranda*. The chief justice was reflecting the fact that TV had made *Miranda* a part of pop culture. Detective shows starting with Sergeant Joe Friday in *Dragnet* had repeated this warning endlessly. It was delivered so frequently that these by-the-book TV cops made it a bit of a joke.

When the Supreme Court had to rule on Congress's effort to overturn *Miranda* v. *Arizona (1967)*, it had to deal with a warning that had become part of the nation's culture. In *Dickerson* v. *United States* (2000), Chief Justice Rehnquist, speaking for a 7 to 2 majority, ruled that Miranda "announced a constitutional rule," which Congress was not free to replace with a case-by-case test. The Court noted that *Miranda* had become an accepted national norm for making an arrest legitimate. It had become difficult for the justices to overturn both the Constitution and the culture.

The Supreme Court under Warren Burger (1969–1986) was not as liberal as the Warren Court, but not as conservative as his supporters had hoped. On the liberal side, the Burger Court legalized abortions except in the last 10 weeks of pregnancy, declined to stop publication of the Pentagon Papers (official papers on the government's planning for the Vietnam War unofficially leaked to the press), and drastically limited capital punishment.

In more conservative directions, the Burger Court allowed local communities, within limits, to define obscenity and ban those works considered pornographic. (See "The Court Examines Porn.") Perhaps the most important changes the Burger Court made were in the rights of the accused. Here the Court allowed the police broader powers in searching without a warrant—deciding, for example, that people detained on minor charges (like traffic violations) may be searched for evidence of more serious crimes (like possession of drugs). The Court also permitted illegally obtained information to be used at a trial and allowed the police to continue their questioning after a suspect claimed the right to silence. However, the Burger Court left the *Miranda* decision in place.

The Rehnquist Court (1986–2005)

When Chief Justice William Rehnquist died at the age of 80 in the summer of 2005 he had served on the Supreme Court for 33 years and as its chief since 1986. His appointment as chief justice came from President Ronald Reagan's hopes for a more conservative, more restrained court.

The Court Examines Porn

The following is an account of how the Burger Court researched a decision on pornography:

The Justices take their obligation to research opinions so seriously that in one area of law—obscenity—the result has led to a lot of snickering both on and off the bench. Since 1957, the Court has tried repeatedly to define obscenity. The subject has become so familiar at the Supreme Court building that a screening room has been set up in the basement for the justices and their clerks to watch the movies submitted as exhibits in obscenity cases. Justice Douglas never goes to the dirty movies because he thinks all expression—obscene or not—is protected by the First Amendment. And Chief Justice Burger rarely, if ever, goes because he is offended by the stuff. But everyone else shows up from time to time.

Justice Blackmun watches in what clerks describe as "a near-catatonic state." Justice Marshall usually laughs his way through it all. The late Justice Harlan used to dutifully attend the Court's porno flicks even though he was virtually blind; Justice Stewart would sit next to Harlan and narrate for him, explaining what was going on in each scene. Once every few minutes, Harlan would exclaim in his proper way, "By George, extraordinary!"

Source: From Nina Totenberg, "Behind the Marble, Beneath the Robes," *The New York Times Magazine,* March 16, 1975. Copyright © 1975 by The New York Times Company. Reprinted by permission.

These hopes were only partly fulfilled. While Rehnquist was a skillful leader noted for his wit and informality, he never was able to create a "Rehnquist Court" in the same defining way that there had been a "Warren Court." He was often in the minority, positioned firmly to the right of the Court's majority, on issues like affirmative action, abortion, religion, property rights, and campaign finance. The courts he presided over were deeply split. Both the independent-minded jurists (described as "nine scorpions in a bottle") and the polarized nation they served made it hard for Rehnquist to win converts to his conservative philosophy.

Consequently the Rehnquist Court, lacking a conservative majority, did not dramatically break with past Court rulings. In some areas, like civil liberties, the Court zigged and zagged with little of the clear direction that Rehnquist's Republican backers had hoped for. In its abortion rulings, for example, the Court placed few limits on the practice while affirming it as a woman's basic right. In major decisions affecting race and religion, the Court was cautiously conservative. In three 5–4 decisions, the Court narrowed the use of race in hiring for government programs, in attracting suburban students into city schools, and in drawing boundaries for congressional districts. Its landmark 2003 decision on affirmative action at the University of Michigan upheld the practice in college admissions. (See Chapter 7, Case Study: "University of Michigan and Affirmative Action.")

The Rehnquist Court's activism was most apparent in its rulings on federalism. Here the Court seemed willing to overturn laws of Congress and decisions by executive agencies in order to guard the rights of the states. The Court's modest revolution over federalism limited the power of Congress while protecting the rights of the states. In *United States* v. *Lopez* (1995) the Court ruled that Congress had exceeded its authority to regulate interstate commerce by passing a law intended to keep guns out of schools. This marked the first time in 60 years that the Court had limited Congress's power to regulate interstate commerce. By a 5–4 decision in the 2000 term, the Court threw out a congressional law that allowed victims of violence to sue in federal court against their assailants. In this case (*United States* v. *Morrison*), the Court found the matter so clearly noncommercial that it remained a state issue that Congress lacked the power to punish. Previous courts for most of the nineteenth century and since the New Deal had used the Commerce Clause to expand federal power. The Rehnquist Court reversed this course and restrained the federal government.

Many of these decisions reflected a thin 5–4 majority in which two moderate justices, O'Connor and Kennedy, swung to either a conservative or liberal core of justices to produce a majority. The Court also showed a pragmatic ability, as one law professor put it, "to split the difference and avoid drawing bright lines." This led varying majorities in the Court to overturn student-led prayers at public high school football games, yet to allow partial-birth abortions because they are the most medically appropriate way of terminating some pregnancies. Arguably the Court's most memorable ruling was in *Bush* v. *Gore* in 2000, where the Court split on partisan lines, stopped a vote count, and made George W. Bush president. Their decision may have avoided a national crisis as Rehnquist suggested, but the weakness of the majority's legal arguments have also stained the Rehnquist legacy. (See "*Bush* v. *Gore*.")

The Court under Rehnquist spoke on issues where it was most interested. These were less in the areas of race and individual rights, where modern Courts have historically been assertive. Instead Rehnquist focused on a federal government—including Congress—that his Court viewed as too big, too powerful, and too out of control. Whether this emphasis is extended or modified will depend on his successor as chief justice, John Roberts, and the jurists appointed to serve with him.

Bush v. Gore

The reaction was almost as extraordinary as the decision itself. "Judicial lawlessness," said a writer in the *Washington Post*; "Comparable to Dred Scott," thundered both Alan Dershowitz of Harvard Law and Jesse Jackson. A Columbia law professor predicted increased cynicism about the courts. What the Supreme Court had done in their December 12, 2000, decision, *Bush* v. *Gore*, was to decide the outcome of the presidential election. Five Republican-appointed justices decided that Republican George W. Bush would be the next president of the United States.

By a 5–4 decision the Supreme Court, in a reversal of their usual federalist support of state rulings, overturned the Florida Supreme Court and halted further counting of the state's disputed presidential votes. This effectively ended 35 days of arguments in the nation's closest presidential election, which had focused on whether to allow hand recounts of Florida's vote. Bush, who had narrowly won the state votes, resisted further counts. Al Gore, who had won the nation's popular vote, thought recounting votes overlooked by machines would give him Florida's electoral votes and the election. The legal fights in the lower courts had brought the case to the Supreme Court.

The majority ruled that the different standards in Florida counties for counting punch-card ballots created problems of due process and equal protection of the law. In other words, a valid vote in one county wouldn't necessarily be valid in another one. Some of the dissenting justices agreed that there were problems but thought they could be corrected and the counting resumed. The majority recognized the limits in their opinion when they added that it would only apply in this case. The dissent by Justice John Paul Stevens criticized the Court for serving partisan interests: "Although we may never know with complete certainty the identity of the winner of this year's presidential election, the identity of the loser is perfectly clear. It is the nation's confidence in the judge as an impartial guardian of the rule of law."

The Roberts Court (2005–)

At first the Roberts Court seemed in transition. Its new chief justice, John J. Roberts Jr. was in charge, but not in control. Even when President Bush appointed Samuel Alito in 2006 to replace a more moderate justice, Sandra Day O'Connor, the Court only gradually changed. The Roberts Court was divided but clearly led by a smart, canny strategist as chief justice. As a result it took small incremental steps in the major cases before it.

Early in his tenure the Roberts Court limited presidential power in *Hamdan* v. *Rumsfeld* (2006) by not allowing the president to try Guantanamo detainees without conforming to various judicial protections and congressional authorization. In this case, the chief justice did not vote because he had earlier, as an appeals court judge, supported the president's position.

Issues of race brought out the chief justice's skepticism about government efforts to promote equality. In *Lulac* v. *Perry* the Court ordered one Latino district redrawn because it violated the Voting Rights Act designed to increase minority representation. Roberts dissented, declaring, "It is a sordid business, this divvying us up by race." *Community Schools* v. *Seattle School District* (2007) saw Roberts in a 5–4 majority limiting the use of race to promote diversity in school. In his most-quoted phrase he wrote: "The way to stop discrimination on the basis of race is to stop discriminating on the basis of race." Similarly in *Ricci* v. *DeStefano* (2009) involving reverse discrimination in New Haven, Connecticut, the Roberts Court sought to restrict affirmative action by supporting the results of exams even when the results were racially unbalanced. In speaking of a group of white firefighters who were denied promotion despite high exam scores, Roberts asked, "Now, why is this not intentional discrimination?"

In areas of voting rights, criminal justice and campaign finance the Court moved resolutely in conservative directions. It showed a new boldness by overturning previous Courts' precedents and congressional reforms in *Citizens United vs. Federal Election Commission* (2010) which removed almost all restraints on corporations' spending to influence elections. While labels like 'conservative' risk simplifying complex judicial decisions, legal observers mostly agreed with Jeffrey Toobin writing in 2009 that, "In every major case since he became the nation's seventeenth Chief Justice, Roberts has sided with the prosecution over the defendant, the state over the condemned, the executive branch over the legislative, and the corporate defendant over the individual plaintiff."

The chief justice has spoken of his judicial philosophy as one of "modesty and humility." But he and the Court's majority are more conservative than he publically admits. Despite the recent appointment of Sonia Sotomayor and the expectation that Obama will be nominating more justices, most of the coming retirements are likely to be from the aging liberal side of the Court. That means the majority of the future Court will remain on the right while the elected part of the federal government is on the left. The Roberts Court may be George W. Bush's most lasting legacy. (See "The Chief Umpire: John Roberts.")

The Chief Umpire: John Roberts

"And I will remember that it's my job to call balls and strikes, and not to pitch or bat."
—John G. Roberts Jr. September 13, 2005

"It's hard to see home plate from right field."
—Senator Richard J. Durbin (D-Illinois), July 13, 2009

From the time he surfaced as a nominee for the Supreme Court, John Roberts embraced modest goals for a judge. He stressed at his Senate confirmation hearings that a judge was to be an umpire, not a player. "Umpires don't make the rules. They apply them." And he emphasized his limited role: "Nobody ever went to a ballgame to see the umpire." His stated lack of a judicial philosophy ("I am not an ideologue") and a respect for precedents set by previous Supreme Courts left the expectation of a restrained, articulate new leader of the Court. But that seems to be only half the story.

Appointed at age 50, Roberts was considerably younger than his colleagues and was expected to serve for decades. Well-known in Court circles, he served as a young law clerk of Chief Justice Rehnquist and as a private lawyer representing corporate clients before the Court. Roberts's early career included service in the Reagan administration, where he wrote strong defenses for conservative positions. His conservative credentials were enough to secure the support of President Bush. After Roberts's public bow to moderation during Senate hearings, he ended up as a strict conservative in most of the major cases before the Court. When Barack Obama was a senator he opposed Robert's nomination, saying at the time, "It is my personal estimation that he has far more often used his formidable skills on behalf of the strong in opposition to the weak."

"The Least Dangerous Branch of Government?"

Despite its great power of judicial review, the Supreme Court is the weakest of the three branches, as Alexander Hamilton predicted in his famous quote. The Court must depend on the other parts of the government to enforce its opinions. Its authority to cancel actions of the rest of the federal government is in fact seldom used and strictly limited. These limits are found both within the Court and within the political system.

Internal Limits on the Court

Most of the limits on the power of the Supreme Court are found in the traditional practices within the Court. For one thing, a long-held interpretation of the Constitution requires that an actual case be presented to the Court for it to exercise judicial review. The Court cannot take the lead in declaring laws unconstitutional. It cannot give advisory opinions. Justices must wait for a real controversy brought by someone actually injured by the law to make its way through the lower courts. Years may pass after a law is put on the books before the Court can rule on it. (The Supreme Court's *Dred Scott* decision struck down a law— the Missouri Compromise—passed 37 years before.)

Its refusal to resolve political questions is another important restraint on the Court. A *political question* is an issue on which the Constitution or laws give final say to another branch of government, or one the Court feels it lacks the capability to solve. Political questions often crop up in foreign relations. The justices of the Court lack important secret information, they are not experts in diplomacy, and they recognize the president's dominance over foreign affairs. Consequently, a federal court in December 1990 used the doctrine of political questions to avoid deciding whether President Bush Sr. could use force against Iraq without congressional approval. Similarly, a dozen years later the courts were equally reluctant to interfere with his son's decision to attack Iraq.

The Supreme Court has narrowed or expanded its definition of a political question at various times. For many years, the Court used this doctrine of political questions to refuse to consider reapportionment of state legislatures and congressional districts. In 1962 the Court reversed its position forcing state legislatures to draw boundaries to create districts with more nearly equal populations (*Baker* v. *Carr*). In the 2000 presidential election, the Court could have avoided deciding *Bush* v. *Gore* by declaring that it was more appropriate for state courts or Congress to resolve—a position consistent with the Court's support for federalism—but it did not. A political question, then, is an issue the Supreme Court wants to avoid.

Just as the Supreme Court avoids political questions, so too it avoids *constitutional issues.* The Court will not decide a case on the basis of a constitutional question unless there is no other way to dispose of the case. The Court will not declare a law unconstitutional unless it clearly violates the Constitution. It will assume that a law is valid unless proved otherwise. Although we have stressed the role of the Court in applying the Constitution, the vast majority of its cases deal with interpretations of less important federal and state laws.

A final internal limit on the Supreme Court is that of *precedent* or *stare decisis* ("to stand by the decision"). Justices generally follow previous court decisions in cases involving the same issue. Recent abortion cases have illustrated the reluctance of the Court to reverse precedents, in this instance, *Roe* v. *Wade* (1973), which legalized abortion. Yet as the conservative majority on recent opinions has shown, at times the Court will not follow precedent if they feel the prior cases did not follow the Constitution or the justices' own leanings. The Court likes to appear consistent with precedent even when changing the law.

What these limits on its power mean is that the Supreme Court avoids most of the constitutional questions pressed upon it. "Delay" is the Court's favorite tactic when, for both political and legal reasons, the Court wants to duck an issue that is too controversial, on which the law is uncertain, or where there is no political consensus. The Court may simply not hear the case, or may decide it for reasons other than the major issue involved. An example of this judicial avoidance occurred in June 2004 when the Supreme Court refused to rule on the constitutionality of the phrase "under God" in the Pledge of Allegiance. The Court cited procedural reasons for not deciding on this inflammatory issue in an election year. Knowing the difficulty of enforcing a ruling against strong public opinion, the Court generally avoids such a confrontation.

This self-imposed restraint may make the use of judicial review scattered and long delayed, but the Court has maintained its great authority of judicial review by refusing in most instances to use it.

External Limits on the Court

The Supreme Court's external limits come from the duties the Constitution gives to other parts of the government, especially to Congress. Congress has the right to set when and how often the Court will meet, to establish the number of justices, and to restrict the Court's jurisdiction. This last power has been used to keep the Court out of areas in which Congress wished to avoid judicial involvement. For example, in passing the 2006 Detainee Bill allowing the president to lock up terrorist suspects without various constitutional rights—including indefinite detention without a trial—Congress stripped the courts of jurisdiction over these cases. Nevertheless, such legislation can still be challenged in court.

Congress may also pass legislation so detailed that it limits the Court's scope in interpreting the law. The Senate has the duty of approving or rejecting the president's nominations to the bench, and Congress has the seldom-used power to impeach Supreme Court justices.

These limits on the Court underscore the weakness of that body. With no army or bureaucracy to enforce its decisions, the Supreme Court must depend on the rest of the government to accept and carry out its decisions. (President Andrew Jackson, angrily disagreeing with a Supreme Court decision, once remarked: "John Marshall has rendered his decision; now let him enforce it!") Yet with few exceptions, the Court's decisions have been accepted and enforced. When opposed, this semi-isolated branch of government has overcome resistance. Why?

Strengths of the Court

The Supreme Court relies on three major supports: (1) its enormous prestige, (2) the fragmented nature of the American constitutional structure, and (3) the American legal profession, which acts as the Court's constituency.

The Court's *prestige* is unquestionable. Despite public dissent to many of its decisions in areas like civil liberties and abortion, the Court retains its high public standing. Opinion polls have shown that the position of a judge is one of the nation's most respected. This is due not only to the quality of the people who become judges but also to the public image of an elevated judicial process. Anyone who has watched criminal trials, even televised ones, is familiar with the qualities of theater in the legal process: the judge sitting on a raised platform dressed in robes, the formal speeches addressed to "your honor," the use of Latin phrases, and the oath on the Bible.

These customs creating a somber impression of dignity mask the fact that a judge is simply an administrator resolving public controversies. The Supreme Court, which presides over this judicial system, has added prestige because it is seen as the guardian of the Constitution and often is equated with that document in people's eyes. Nor does the Supreme Court have to actively shape its public relations. After the controversial 2000 Florida election decision, no justice felt the need to explain the opinion in the press, and yet the Court's popularity remained high. (See "The Court's Supreme Popularity.")

Another strength of the Court lies in the *fragmented nature of the American system of government*. With powers separated among the three branches of the federal government, and federalism dividing power between the states and federal government, conflict is inevitable. This division of power creates a need for a referee; the Supreme Court fills that role.

In acting as a referee, the Court is hardly neutral. Its decisions may reflect the justices' partisan loyalties. They are certainly political in determining who gets what, when, and how, and to enforce them the Supreme Court needs political support. The other players might not give this support to decisions they strongly disagree with. Consequently, the Court's rulings generally reflect the practices and values of the country's dominant political forces. As a referee, the Court enforces the constitutional rules of the game as practiced by the political game's most powerful players, of which it is one.

A final source of support for the Court is the *legal profession*. There are more than 1 million active lawyers in the United States. Lawyers occupy all the major judicial positions, and more lawyers than any other

The Court's Supreme Popularity

One of the ironies of American democracy is that the least democratic branch is also the most popular. Other than the president's popularity following 9/11 and Obama's first months in office, people usually show more confidence in the Supreme Court than in the two elected branches of government. One explanation for this lies in the very invisibility of the Court's activities. As a scholar of the Court remarked, the public likes its politics done quietly and without an appearance of partisanship. The Court generally does this. Other reasons lie in the popular view that the Court carries out its duties in a disinterested way, that the justices are people of wisdom, and that the Court both protects and reflects the Constitution. (See Figure 5.2.)

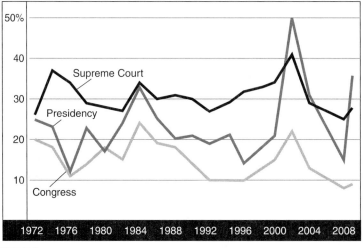

FIGURE 5.2
Public Confidence in the Supreme Court. A higher percentage of the public has consistently said it has a "great deal of confidence" in the Supreme Court, greater than in the presidency or Congress.
Source: The Harris Poll, *http://www.harrisinteractive.com*; Compiled from Harris Poll data by John R. Hibbing and James T. Smith for their article "What the American Public Wants Congress to Be" in *Congress Reconsidered*, seventh edition, Lawrence Dodd and Bruce I. Oppenheimer, eds. (Washington: Congressional Quarterly Press, 2001).

occupational group hold offices in national, state, and city governments. The American Bar Association (ABA), with about half the lawyers in the country as members, reviews nominees to the bench, and its comments on candidates' fitness influence whether they are appointed. Because of their own commitment to law, as well as some similarity in educational and social backgrounds, lawyers generally back the Court.

In 2007 there were over 45,000 lawyers in Washington, D.C. Perhaps the number of lawyers explains why so many political conflicts, including sex scandals and presidential elections, end up as legal issues. Other countries manage with far fewer lawyers and far fewer issues winding up in court. Some scholars argue that lawyers use their domination of elected offices to pass laws and regulations that create new demands for their skills.

The Court as a Political Player

In applying the Constitution and laws to the cases before it, the Court clearly makes political choices. In arriving at decisions on controversial questions of national policy, the Supreme Court is a player in the political game. The procedures may be legal and the decisions may be phrased in lawyers' language, but to view the court solely as a legal institution is to ignore its important political role.

"We are under the Constitution, but the Constitution is what the judges say it is," declared former Chief Justice Charles Evans Hughes. In interpreting the meaning of the Constitution, each Supreme Court must operate within the political climate of its time. Judges not only read the Constitution, they read the newspaper as well. The Court must rely on others, especially the executive branch, to enforce its rulings. The Court cannot ignore the reactions to its decisions in Congress or in the nation because its influence ultimately rests on the acceptance of these decisions by the other players and the public. Generally, the Court's opinions are not long out of line with the dominant views in the legislative and executive branches. (See "The Court Waits for an Election.")

Judicial Activism vs. Judicial Restraint

The question of how the political and legal power of the Supreme Court should be applied has centered on whether judicial authority should be active or restrained. How far should the Court go in shaping policy when it may conflict with other branches of the government? The two sides of this debate are reflected in the competing practices of *judicial restraint* and *judicial activism*.

Judicial restraint is the idea that the Court should not impose its views on other branches of the government or on the states unless there is a clear violation of the Constitution. Judicial restraint (often labeled *strict constructionism*) calls for a limited role in which the Court lets the elected branches of the government lead the way in setting controversial policies. The Constitution is constructed or interpreted as close to the intent of the framers as possible and practical. The

The Court Waits for an Election

Civil rights decisions have never been far removed from politics. Here is an example of the Court keeping an eye on the political arena in a landmark case:

"Why doesn't the Supreme Court pass the school desegregation case?" asked one of Chief Justice Vinson's law clerks in 1952. *Brown v. Board of Education of Topeka, Kansas,* had arrived on the Court's docket in 1951, but it was carried over for oral argument the next term and then consolidated with four other cases and reargued in December 1953. The landmark ruling did not come down until May 17, 1954.

"Well," Justice Frankfurter explained, "we're holding it for the election"—1952 was a presidential election year.

"You're holding it for the election?" the clerk persisted in disbelief. "I thought the Supreme Court was supposed to decide cases without regard to elections."

"When you have a major social political issue of this magnitude, timing and public reactions are important considerations, and," Frankfurter continued, "we do not think this is the time to decide it."

Source: David M. O'Brien, *Storm Center: The Supreme Court in American Politics.* New York: W.W. Norton, 1993.

Supreme Court intervenes in political conflicts only with great reluctance. Felix Frankfurter and Oliver Wendell Holmes Jr. are two famous justices of the Supreme Court identified with judicial restraint. Frankfurter argued that social improvement should be left to elected officials of the federal and state governments. The Court, he declared, should avoid conflicts with the other branches of the federal government whenever possible.

Judicial activism is the view that the Supreme Court should be a creative partner with the legislative and executive branches in shaping government policy. Judicial activists seek to apply the Court's authority to solving economic and political problems ignored by other parts of the government. In this view, the Court is more than an umpire of the American political game: It is an active participant. The Supreme Court under Earl Warren practiced judicial activism. In its rulings on reapportionment, school desegregation, and the right to counsel, the Warren Court boldly changed national policy.

It is important not to confuse judicial activism versus restraint with liberal versus conservative. Although twentieth-century activist justices, such as Earl Warren and Thurgood Marshall, took liberal positions on issues like race and dissent, this was not always so. John Marshall's court was both activist, in establishing judicial review, and conservative, in protecting private property rights. The conservative Supreme Court during the 1930s attempted to strike down most of Franklin D. Roosevelt's New Deal program as unconstitutional. On the restraint side, justices Frankfurter and Holmes were political liberals, yet both believed it was not wise for the Court to dive into political battles to support positions they may have personally backed.

In recent times judicial restraint and conservatism have overlapped. Conservative jurists, under the banner of *strict constructionism*, have viewed modern courts as stretching the Constitution for liberal ends, and thereby ignoring the intentions of the framers. This is most apparent in the vast expansion of federal power to regulate the economy, which liberal courts have ruled acceptable under flexible interpretations of the Constitution. However, when the Burger Court found abortion to be constitutional in *Roe* v. *Wade*, it heated this legal debate to a boil.

Critics of the decision point out that in most countries elected representatives have legalized abortion. But in America this change in policy was done by unelected judges who found a right to abortion in constitutional phrases, hidden for centuries, ". . . completely unknown to the drafters . . ." as Rehnquist put it. One reason why the debate over abortion may have turned more bitter in this country than elsewhere is because many Americans believe that the courts are "legislating from the bench."

But the conservative judges now in an uneasy majority in the courts also face a dilemma. Abortion has become a legally accepted practice; a precedent embedded in decades of court rulings and legislation. For any court to ban abortion based on a strict reading of the written Constitution would hardly be an act of judicial restraint.

American Apartheid

In the South during the late nineteenth and early twentieth centuries, *Jim Crow laws* (taking their name from a blackface minstrel song) were passed to prohibit blacks from using the same public facilities as whites. These state laws required segregated schools, hospitals, prisons, restaurants, toilets, railways, and waiting rooms. Some communities passed "sundown ordinances" that prohibited blacks from staying in town overnight. Blacks and whites could not even be buried in the same cemeteries.

There seemed to be no limit to the absurdity of segregation. New Orleans required separate districts for black and white prostitutes. In Oklahoma, blacks and whites could not use the same telephone booths. In North Carolina and Florida, school textbooks used by black children had to be stored separately from those used by white children. In Birmingham, Alabama, the races were specifically prohibited from playing checkers together.

CASE STUDY

Separate but Equal?

The evolution of "separate but equal" offers a window into the political role played by the Supreme Court. By first approving racial segregation late in the nineteenth century and later abolishing it in the mid-twentieth century, the Court was central in establishing a national policy that governed relations between the races. The changing but always powerful position of the judiciary in the history of racial segregation demonstrates the influence of the Supreme Court in national politics.

POLITICAL BACKGROUND OF SEGREGATION

The end of the Civil War and the emancipation of the slaves did not offer black people the full rights of citizenship, nor did the passing of the Thirteenth Amendment in 1865 (which outlawed slavery), the Fourteenth Amendment in 1868 (which extended "equal protection of the laws" to all citizens), or the Fifteenth Amendment in 1870 (which guaranteed the right to vote to all male citizens regardless of "race, color, or previous condition of servitude").

Between 1866 and 1877, the "radical Republicans" controlled Congress. Despite becoming a bad memory in the white South, *Reconstruction* was a time when blacks won political rights. In 1875 Congress passed a civil rights act designed to prevent any public form of discrimination—in theaters, restaurants, transportation, and the like—against blacks. Congress's right to forbid a *state* to act contrary to the Constitution was unquestioned. But this law, based on the Fourteenth Amendment, assumed that Congress could also prevent racial discrimination by private individuals.

The Supreme Court disagreed. In 1883 it declared the Civil Rights Act of 1875 unconstitutional. The majority of the Court ruled that Congress could pass legislation only to correct *states'* violations of the Fourteenth Amendment. Congress had no power to enact "primary and direct" legislation on individuals—that was left to the states. This decision meant the federal government could not lawfully protect blacks against most forms of discrimination. In other words, white supremacy was beyond federal control.

With this blessing from the Supreme Court, the southern states passed a series of laws legitimizing segregation. These laws included all-white primary elections, elaborate tests to qualify for voting, and other racial restrictions. (See "American Apartheid.")

SEPARATE BUT EQUAL

Segregation was given judicial approval in the landmark case of *Plessy* v. *Ferguson* (1896). Here, the Supreme Court upheld a Louisiana law requiring railroads to provide separate cars for the two races. The Court declared that segregation had nothing to do with the superiority of the white race, and that segregation was not contrary to the Fourteenth Amendment as long as the facilities were equal. The doctrine of "separate but equal" in *Plessy* v. *Ferguson* became the law of the land in those states maintaining segregation.

HEAR   SPEAK   SEE
NO   NO   NO
EVIL   EVIL   EVIL

In approving segregation and establishing the "separate but equal" doctrine, the Court was undoubtedly reflecting white attitudes of the time. To restore the South to the Union, the new congresses were willing to undo the radicals' efforts to protect blacks. It was the southern black who paid the price—exile halfway between slavery and freedom. Just as the Court was unwilling to prevent these violations of civil rights, so too were the executive and legislative branches.

Plessy v. *Ferguson* helped racial segregation continue as a southern tradition. For some 40 years, the "separate but equal" doctrine was not seriously challenged. "Separate" was strictly enforced; "equal" was not. Schools, government services, and other public facilities for blacks were clearly separate from tax-supported white facilities but just as clearly inferior to them. The Supreme Court did not even support its own doctrine during this period.

By the late 1930s, the Court began to look more closely at the "equal" part of these separate facilities. In *Missouri ex. rel. Gaines* v. *Canada* (1938), the Court held that because Missouri did not have a law school for blacks, it must admit them to the white law school. In *Sweatt* v. *Painter* (1950), a black (Sweatt) was denied admission to the University of Texas Law School on the grounds that Texas was building a law school for blacks. The Court examined the new school carefully, found that it would in no way be equal to the white one, and ordered Sweatt admitted to the existing school.

Thus the *Plessy* doctrine of "separate but equal" was increasingly weakened by judicial decisions. By stressing the "equal" part of the doctrine, the Supreme Court was making the doctrine impractical. (Texas was not likely to build a law school for blacks equal to its white one.) These decisions also reflected the Court's change in emphasis after 1937 from making economic policy to protecting individual rights.

Still, the Court did not overrule *Plessy*. The Court was following precedent. Paralleling the rulings of the Supreme Court were the actions of the executive branch and some northern states that were increasingly critical of racial segregation. In 1941 Roosevelt issued an executive order forbidding discrimination in government employment. And Truman abolished segregation in the army in 1948. Congress, however, dominated by a conservative seniority system and blocked by southern filibusters in the Senate, was unable to pass civil rights measures. Nonetheless, public attitudes toward segregation were changing, and the Supreme Court's rulings were reflecting that change.

THE END OF SEPARATE BUT EQUAL

In 1954 the Supreme Court finally reversed *Plessy* v. *Ferguson* in *Brown* v. *Board of Education*, even while denying it was overturning the precedent. The Court held that segregated public schools violated the "equal protection of the laws" guaranteed in the Fourteenth Amendment. "Separate but equal" had no place in public education, the Supreme Court declared. Drawing on sociological and psychological studies of the harm done to black children by segregation, the Warren Court's unanimous decision stated that, in fact, separate was "inherently unequal." This finding was the beginning of the end of *legal segregation*.

The Court backed up its new equal protection stand in areas other than education. In the years following the *Brown* decision, it outlawed segregation in interstate transportation, upheld legislation guaranteeing voting rights for blacks, reversed convictions of civil rights leaders, and protected civil rights demonstrations by court order. These decisions, though they stirred up opposition to the Court (including demands to impeach Earl Warren), helped a political movement apply pressures to wipe out racial discrimination. Civil rights groups were active in these cases, which shows how results can be gotten from one part of government (the courts) if another part (the Congress) is unwilling to act.

Congress finally joined in by passing Civil Rights Acts in 1957, 1960, and 1964. Both political parties had gained a heightened appreciation for the black voter, especially the large numbers who voted in northern cities. The 1964 act, coming after continuing agitation by civil rights activists, was the first comprehensive legislation of its kind since 1875. The act prohibited discrimination in public accommodations (such as hotels, restaurants, and gas stations) involved in interstate commerce and in most businesses, and enforced equal voting rights for blacks.

The Court encouraged all levels of the government—federal, state, and local—as well as the private sector to move toward full equality. The Supreme Court's support of busing to end the segregation of schools caused by housing patterns aroused opposition in northern cities like Boston. By the 1980s President Reagan was calling *affirmative action* "reverse discrimination" against white males. Yet affirmative action expanded beyond remedies for discrimination to include goals of cultural diversity and racial "balance." It was also applied to groups from the Middle East and Latin America, with little historical claim to its benefits. Judicial and public support for affirmative action waxed and waned. In recent decisions the Supreme Court has both narrowed and upheld affirmative action programs. The current chief justice has declared that the time has come to restrict broad government remedies for racial discrimination. (See "University of Michigan and Affirmative Action," Chapter 6.)

Still, racism remains. And for this, the Supreme Court as well as the rest of the political system must share responsibility. The Supreme Court struck down Civil Rights Acts of the Reconstruction Era and failed to protect the rights of African Americans between 1883 and 1937 when they were most trampled on. And it was the Court that made "separate but equal" the legal justification for white supremacy. Even today the Court has viewed housing patterns—a major cause of segregated public schools—as largely beyond its authority. The Court's effort to put equal rights before the eyes of the nation was in many ways merely undoing its own past mistakes.

Throughout this history of "separate but equal," the Court has acted politically as well as legally and morally. At times the Supreme Court held back efforts at reform, at other times it confused them, and at still others it forced political and social changes more rapidly than many preferred. Yet as the history of "separate but equal" makes clear, the Court is seldom removed too far or for too long from the positions dominating the political game.

WRAP-UP

The federal court system consists of U.S. district courts, courts of appeals, special federal courts, and the U.S. Supreme Court. Although very few of the cases tried in the United States ever reach the Supreme Court, it retains its position as the "final authority" over what the Constitution means. Nevertheless, the Court's decisions have changed over the years, usually at the hands of the Court itself, in part reflecting the changing political climate. Our brief history showed this, as did the case study of "separate but equal," where the Court first allowed racial segregation and then gradually reversed its position.

The practices of judicial activism and judicial restraint are two sides of the debate over how far judicial review and the political involvement of the Court should go. The Supreme Court is limited by a number of its own practices and by its dependence on other parts of the government to enforce its decisions. The Court's respect for these limits, as well as its own great prestige, has given it the strength to overcome most resistance. Recent criticism of its decisions, from both conservatives and liberals, on issues like abortion, religion, and protection of minorities has run up against solid support for the Court.

Secure within its limits and resting on public respect, the Supreme Court of the United States remains a unique political player. No other government can boast a long-held tradition that gives "nine old men" (and women, now)—nonelected and serving for life—the duty of overturning the acts of popularly elected officials. Through this power of judicial review, the Court is deeply involved in setting national policy, limiting how the political game is played, and bringing pressing social issues to the attention of the people and their leaders. Whether the Supreme Court protects individual liberties or partisan interests depends on who are the justices, how they interpret the law, and which political forces prevail in the nation.

THOUGHT QUESTIONS

1. How did the Supreme Court become so important to our system of government? Would John Marshall be pleased or surprised?
2. Are Supreme Court justices influenced too much by their own partisan philosophies? Give some examples.
3. Why did the courts take the lead on civil rights for minorities? Isn't this issue more appropriate for the elected officials of the government?
4. Do judges deserve to be more popular and more respected than other government officials? Why or why not?
5. Why have recent chief justices had so much trouble gaining a clear direction from the Supreme Courts they led? Does this reflect broader political trends?

SUGGESTED READINGS

Branch, Taylor. *Parting the Waters: America in the King Years, 1954–1963.* New York: Simon & Schuster, 1988.
   The Pulitzer Prize–winning account of the civil rights movement with a focus on Martin Luther King Jr.
Burns, James MacGregor. *Packing the Court: The Rise of Judicial Power and the Coming Crisis of the Supreme Court.* New York: The Penguin Press, 2009.
   A warning by an eminent historian that the power of judicial review has often been used against "the progress of history."

Lewis, Anthony. *Gideon's Trumpet.* New York: Vintage Books, 1966. Pb.
  A short story that traces the development of a case from a Florida jail to the U.S. Supreme Court.
Rosen, Jeffrey. *The Supreme Court: The Personalities and Rivalries that Defined America.* New York: Holt Paperback, 2007.
  A law professor writes a lively history of four personal rivalries that defined the court decisions of their time.
Toobin, Jeffrey. *Nine: Inside the Secret World of the Supreme Court.* New York: Anchor Books, 2007, Pb.
  A revealing look at the politics, personalities, and rivalries that make the current Court's decisions more than just legal scholarship.

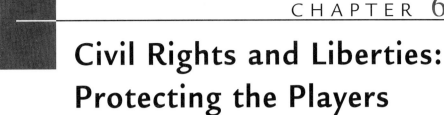

CHAPTER 6

Civil Rights and Liberties:
Protecting the Players

Civil Rights and Liberties

C ivil rights and liberties protect the political players, as well as the American people. They restrain government, for example by requiring officials to follow due process of law, and describe some of the goals of the republic, such as allowing the greatest possible freedom of speech. They guard citizens against discrimination because of their gender, age, sexual preference, and race; protections that people didn't have a half century ago. The Constitution defines certain rules that govern the relationships between people and their government, and other rules that govern the relationships between groups of citizens. These rules rest on two principles: The government must not violate the civil rights and liberties of the people; the government must protect people from those who would violate their rights.

This chapter focuses on how the courts and other players protect civil rights and liberties. We will see what these rights and liberties are, and how the protections in the Bill of Rights have expanded down through American history. We will discuss the different players involved in applying these protections. A case study of an accused terrorist and due process will show these civil liberties under pressure today.

The Politics of Civil Liberties and Rights

Civil liberties are protections against government restrictions on freedom of expression. Civil liberties are those First Amendment rights of freedom of speech, petition, assembly, and press that protect people against government actions that would interfere with their participation in democratic politics. This definition includes Fifth Amendment and Fourteenth Amendment guarantees of due process of law in courtrooms and government agencies. The underlying principle here is that ours is a government of laws rather than of arbitrary action.

Civil rights are protections for some groups that because of their race, religion, ethnicity, or gender may be discriminated against by others. Civil rights include the protections of the Fourteenth Amendment to the Constitution, recognizing that all citizens are entitled to be treated equally under the law. No members of a racial, religious, or economic group may claim or receive privileged treatment because of group membership, nor may any group be discriminated against by others or by officials.

Our daily lives are full of issues of civil rights and liberties. Civil liberties involve your rights as a college student: Can school authorities suspend a student for making critical remarks about homosexuals? Establish a "civility" code barring "hate speech"? How about your right as a citizen to be informed: Can the government prevent a newspaper from publishing a story on "national security" grounds? Can it require reporters to reveal their sources to prosecutors investigating a crime? Can the government restrict information on making bombs sent over the Internet? Or can corporations spy on their employees or obtain private phone records? (See "Cartoons and Colleges in a Delicate Time.")

Everyone is affected by civil rights issues: Will you, as a woman, receive equal pay for equal work? As a Mexican American, will you be discriminated against in hiring and promotion? Will affirmative action programs designed to make up for past discrimination against minorities and women lead to "reverse discrimination" against you as a white male?

These debates have inflamed our national politics. In presidential elections a woman's right to an abortion, a gay couple's right to marry, and a gun owner's Second Amendment right to defy local gun control laws have become sources of conflict. Congress regularly grapples with civil rights issues: proposals to bar discrimination against the disabled, bills to limit federal funding for abortions in public hospitals, and

 ## Cartoons and Colleges in a Delicate Time

In March 2006, a student group at New York University planned to hold a panel discussion called "Free Speech and the Danish Cartoons" to debate the controversial Danish cartoons of Mohammed, which after publication in Europe had sparked protests and rioting in Muslim countries. Shortly before the meeting, the NYU administration (which had just negotiated to build a new campus in the Muslim country of Abu Dhabi) ordered the group either to not display the cartoons or to not allow anyone from off campus to attend. Their meeting was held in front of a row of blank easels.

At Century College in Minnesota, a geography teacher posted the cartoons on a public bulletin board and had them repeatedly torn down, until college administrators asked her not to post them again. She followed her employers' request but asked, "If we can't talk about this controversy at a college, where are we supposed to talk about it?"

The *Daily Illini*, the student newspaper at the University of Illinois at Urbana-Champagne printed several of the cartoons. The two editors responsible were dismissed for not consulting other editors, and representatives for the newspaper apologized. Other newspapers at the University of Wisconsin, University of North Carolina at Chapel Hill, and Harvard printed the cartoons without censoring.

Nat Hentoff, a writer on First Amendment issues, quoted Justice Oliver Wendell Holmes as a challenge to universities: "If there is any principle of the Constitution that more imperatively calls for attachment than any other, it is the principle of free thought—not free thought for those who agree with us, but freedom for the thought that we hate."

measures making it easier to prove discrimination against women in employment. To understand these current issues, let's look at how some of them developed in the past.

Expanding the Bill of Rights

The Bill of Rights applied only to the national government when it was added to the Constitution in 1791. The Congress that passed the Bill of Rights had no intention of restricting state governments or any private individual or group. Since the early twentieth century, however, the protections of the Bill of Rights have gradually been extended to cover actions of state and local officials as well as individuals and organizations. To do this, the federal courts have relied on the *Fourteenth Amendment*. That amendment, ratified in 1868, reads in part: ". . . nor shall any State deprive any person of life, liberty or property, without due process of law, nor deny to any person within its jurisdiction the equal protection of the laws." The two key, if vague, phrases are "due process" and "equal protection."

The *equal protection* clause has been used to prevent state officials from discriminating based on race or sex. It has also prevented discrimination by private individuals when that action (1) is aided by state action, such as a law; (2) furthers a state activity such as an election, or the activities of a political party; or (3) involves a fundamental state interest such as education or public safety. Therefore, the equal protection clause has been used to strike down state laws segregating students by race in public schools. It has been used to put an end to the "whites only" primaries that the Democratic parties of southern states used prior to the general elections. It was even used to halt the hand recounting of votes in Florida in the 2000 election when the Supreme Court declared that different methods for counting votes would deprive citizens of equal protection. Though individuals may practice racial, religious, or gender discrimination in inviting guests to their homes, they cannot discriminate in private schools because education involves a fundamental state interest. And private clubs that serve the public are now considered public places. If they discriminate in selecting members on the basis of race or gender, they may lose certain tax advantages.

The *due process* clause of the Fourteenth Amendment applies the standards of fair procedures to the activities of state and local governments. But to what extent should the Bill of Rights protections be "incorporated" into the language of the Fourteenth Amendment and thus apply to the states? On one side of the debate over due process are the *partial incorporationists*. They believe that only some of the Bill of

Rights should be included in the meaning of "due process" in the Fourteenth Amendment, mainly those procedures guaranteeing fair criminal trials and First Amendment freedoms of religion, speech, and press. Which rights are to be incorporated? Those that are considered *preferred freedoms*—that is, the liberties necessary for a democracy to function—which, in the words of Justice Louis Brandeis, form the essence of "a scheme of ordered liberty." But not everything in the Bill of Rights is considered fundamental by partial incorporationists.

On the other side of the debate are the *complete incorporationists.* They believe that the entire Bill of Rights was incorporated into the Fourteenth Amendment. Thus, there is no need to consider which rights to apply. When a case comes before them, they incorporate the entire Bill of Rights and use it as a limit against state action.

Consider the case of a prisoner held in a state penitentiary who sues the warden in federal court. The prisoner argues that two months of solitary confinement for a mess hall riot is a violation of the Eighth Amendment prohibition against "cruel and unusual punishment." Partial incorporationists first must decide whether or not the Eighth Amendment should be incorporated into the Fourteenth Amendment as a limit on state prison officials. They might argue that it applies only to criminal trials in state courts and that prison discipline does not involve any "fundamental rights." Full incorporationists would automatically incorporate the Eighth Amendment into the Fourteenth Amendment: There would be no question that the amendment applied to state prison officials. The judge would decide only the question of whether two months of solitary confinement qualified as "cruel and unusual punishment."

Full incorporation has never been embraced by the Supreme Court. Yet, in the past 90 years, the effect of numerous federal court decisions has been to incorporate almost all of the Bill of Rights into the Fourteenth Amendment. There are some exceptions, such as the Second Amendment, which organizations representing gun owners claim should be used to restrict states and localities' gun control laws. While states may still ignore a few parts of the Bill of Rights, such as a jury trial in civil cases, most of the rights not incorporated are not very important.

Civil Liberties: Protecting People from Government

For the framers of the Constitution, the greatest danger to citizens lay in the abuse of government power. For this reason, the most important civil liberties are those that protect citizens from their government.

Most of these "preferred freedoms" are found in the *First Amendment,* which states:

> Congress shall make no law respecting an establishment of religion, or prohibiting the free exercise thereof; or abridging the freedom of speech, or of the press, or the right of the people peaceably to assemble, and to petition the Government for a redress of grievances.

The First Amendment's "rules of the game" are essential for democracy to work. They enable people to keep informed, to communicate with each other and with their government without fear. Remove these protections, and it would be difficult for political players to function. The press, interest groups, and even members of Congress would find their ability to "go public" and organize to change government policies restricted. The political party that lost an election might be prevented from getting out its message, making it impossible to contest the next election. The Bill of Rights, along with separation of powers and checks and balances, are designed to protect a people who historically have had a healthy fear of governmental power.

Supreme Court Justice Oliver Wendell Holmes once wrote that a democratic society needs competition among ideas as much as an economic marketplace needs competition among producers. "When men have realized that time has upset many fighting faiths," he wrote, "they come to believe . . . that the ultimate good desired is better reached by free trade in ideas—that the best truth is the power of the thought to get itself accepted in the competition of the marketplace." Put another way, how can you be sure your opinion is correct unless you are willing to test it against different opinions? And how can wrong opinions ever be changed, even when held by a majority, unless there is freedom for other opinions to be expressed?

Fundamental to Holmes's thinking is the belief that good ideas would drive bad ideas out of the market and that the public will reject the false in favor of the true. Given the awesome power of modern media, and the ignorance about politics shown by many Americans, these calculations may not always be true. Propaganda sometimes overwhelms reason; the demagogue may defeat the statesman. But it is hard to see how restricting speech can provide better safeguards for democracy, though other countries may disagree. (See "World Democracies Dissent on U.S. Freedoms")

A look at recent thinking about four of the most important civil liberties—freedom of speech, freedom of religion, the right to privacy, and due process of law—will help us to understand how the Bill of Rights is used to protect Americans.

World Democracies Dissent on U.S. Freedoms

- *England, South Africa, the Netherlands, Australia, and India have laws banning hate speech.*
- *In Canada and Germany it is a crime to deny the Holocaust.*
- *A French court fined an animal rights activist for criticizing a Muslim ceremony where sheep were slaughtered.*

In most democracies of the world, denouncing other races, displaying ethnic hatred, or urging discrimination against religious minorities will result in the speaker being fined or imprisoned. Not in the United States.

Under the First Amendment, even false, provocative, or hateful speech about minorities and religions is protected. There is only one justification for making such speech a criminal offense—the likelihood of immediate violence. This high hurdle to suppressing speech in part reflects the nation's emphasis on the individual and Americans' historic fear of allowing the government to decide what speech is acceptable. Other countries like Canada, Germany, South Africa, India, and Israel use the law to promote social harmony. These are all democracies separated from America by their own histories, which give pause to any criticism from one nation to another over banning, or allowing, hate speech.

Source: From Adam Liptak, "Unlike Others, U.S. Defends Freedom to Offend in Speech," The *New York Times*, June 12, 2008.

Freedom of Speech

The First Amendment guarantee of freedom of speech has been widened to apply to state governments under the Fourteenth Amendment. "Speech" has also been deepened by court decisions to include not only speaking but also gesturing, wearing armbands, raising signs, and leafleting passersby. The Supreme Court has upheld laws that make conspiracy to overthrow the government by force a crime. But it has struck down convictions of Communists based on their membership in the Communist party because the government was infringing on their freedom of association. Just believing in the violent overthrow of the government, or even giving a speech about revolution, is not a crime, nor is membership in an organization that believes in the violent overthrow of the government. The courts insist that if the government puts terrorists in prison, it first must prove that they took concrete action to commit violence.

The First Amendment not only protects your right to say what you believe but it also prohibits the government from forcing you to say what you do not believe. In 1943, during World War II, schoolchildren who were Jehovah's Witnesses refused to say the Pledge of Allegiance on the grounds that they would be worshipping "graven images" (the flag) against the beliefs of their religion. The Supreme Court overturned their suspension from school by state officials, and Justice Robert Jackson wrote, "No official, high or petty, can prescribe what shall be orthodox in politics, nationalism, religion, or other matters of opinion, or force citizens to confess by word or act their faith therein." As Americans, we have the freedom to refuse to say what we do not believe.

The Supreme Court has protected what is called *speech plus*. This involves symbolic actions, such as wearing buttons or even burning flags. In one case, an antiwar student who entered a courthouse with the words "Fuck the Draft" written on the back of his jacket was held in contempt by a local judge. The decision was reversed by the Supreme Court. As one justice pointed out, "While the particular four-letter word being litigated here is perhaps more distasteful than most others of its genre, it nevertheless is often true that one man's vulgarity is another's lyric." (See "Conservative Bake Sales.")

The First Amendment provides no protection to speech that directly leads to illegal conduct or that might be illegal conduct by itself. Shouting "fire" in a crowded theater (when there is no fire) is not

Conservative Bake Sales

On a pleasant fall day a few years ago, conservative student organizations held "affirmative action bake sales" on college campuses across the country. Brownies were sold at varying prices: black and Hispanic students were charged less than Asian and white students. Supporters described the sales as satire designed to draw attention to the discrimination involved in affirmative action. Many university administrators were not amused.

At William and Mary, for example, the president denounced the bake sale there as "inexcusably hurtful" and "abusive." The sale was halted because it "did not meet the administrative requirements we routinely impose on such activities." A lawyer for the student group remarked, "One can hardly imagine such tactics being used to shut down a protest that administrators found more to their liking politically." At other campuses, like the University of Washington, the College Republicans holding the sales were attacked by other students.

Elsewhere, universities defended the sales. An Indiana University administrator remarked, "It is exactly the kind of dialogue that should be encouraged on college campuses." Back at William and Mary, after press coverage, a second bake sale was allowed two months after the previous one was halted.

considered speech, but rather a reckless action that the state may punish. Writing or speaking damaging lies about a person (libel and slander) is not protected, and you can be sued. Making or selling child pornography is not protected speech and does not involve freedom of expression, and you go to jail for it. When an individual directs abuse or "fighting words" at someone, particularly a police officer, convictions for disorderly conduct will be upheld by the courts.

Schools can limit speech that would be allowed in other settings. In 2007, in a 5–4 split decision *(Morse* v. *Frederick)*, the Supreme Court permitted schools to punish a student for speech that promotes illegal drug use. The Alaskan high school student had unfurled a banner that read "Bong Hits 4 Jesus" at a gathering to watch the Olympic torch pass in front of his high school. The student wanted to make a statement about his First Amendment rights in front of TV cameras. Though the banner was "cryptic," both his principal and a majority of the Supreme Court saw it as promoting drugs. As such schools had the right "to safeguard those entrusted to their care from speech that can reasonably be regarded as encouraging illegal drug use," according to Chief Justice Roberts.

Internet communications have been a fertile field of conflict over questions of free speech. At the urging of religious groups a few years ago, several senators downloaded pornography from the Internet. The result has been a back-and-forth debate between the elected branches and the Supreme Court over what can be allowed online. The Communications Decency Act of 1996 punished making "indecent" or "patently offensive" material available to minors over the Internet. But in 1997 the Supreme Court struck down the act as overly vague *(Reno et al.* v. *ACLU et al.)*, ruling that free speech protections apply just as much to online systems as they do to books and newspapers. Congress tried again in 1998 in the Child Online Protection Act, which penalized Internet material posted for "commercial purposes" that was "harmful to minors." A 5–4 Supreme Court didn't like this law any better *(ACLU* v. *Ashcroft, 2002)*. Justice Kennedy wrote for the majority, "There is potential for extraordinary harm and a serious chill upon protected speech."

Since the Court's rulings, as well as the 9/11 attacks, the Justice Department has asked Internet companies to keep records on their e-mail users. Whether it is for child pornography or terrorism or general law enforcement this has led to an obligation to retain all information on all customers for all purposes. Paralleling this expansion of government interest in online communications is the development by computer companies of technological tools to filter information on the Web. Depending on your viewpoint, this filtering technology is either a parent's tool for controlling their children without government involvement or a censoring device limiting this democratic communications media.

Freedom of Religion

The Constitution provides that there will be no religious test for office, and the First Amendment allows the "free exercise of religion" and prohibits the establishment of an official religion by Congress. Yet there has never been a complete "wall of separation" between church and state in the United States. The armed forces have chaplains paid for by Congress; the Supreme Court chambers have a mural of Moses giving the Ten Commandments; the dollar bill states "In God We Trust." This involvement with religion was extended by President George W. Bush, who supported giving government funds to faith-based groups for their charitable work.

The question of freedom of religion inevitably gets mixed up in the constitutional prohibition against the establishment of religion. To allow students to pray in school, a position favored by a large majority of Americans, may seem to be simply an issue of free exercise of religion. But if most children in the class are Protestant, should the prayer be from a Protestant denomination? And if so, which one? Will other children feel like outcasts, even if they are excused from saying the prayer? Administrations have tried to clarify the legal limits of religion in public schools and to distinguish between what teachers cannot do and what students can do. (See "Dos and Don'ts on Religion in Public Schools.")

While Americans strongly support freedom of religion, most believe that the government must not favor one religion over another. Balancing these competing values is difficult, and the courts have

 ## Dos and Don'ts on Religion in Public Schools

Department of Education guidelines on religious activity in schools:

Permitted:

- Student prayer by individuals or groups
- Student-initiated discussions on religions
- Reading the Bible
- Saying grace before meals
- Wearing religious clothing or symbols
- Religious activities before or after school

Forbidden:

- Prayer endorsed or organized by teachers or administrators
- "Harassing" invitations to participate in prayer
- Teaching or encouraging a particular religion, rather than teaching about religion
- Denying school rooms to religious groups

become less rigid in separating government from religious practices. In 1995 the Supreme Court ruled against the University of Virginia for refusing to fund a student publication because it had a Christian orientation. In 2002 the Catholic Church argued—unsuccessfully—in court that it was shielded from suits against priests for child abuse by the First Amendment protection of religious freedom. In 2003 the Alabama chief justice placed a two-ton granite monument to the Ten Commandments in his state building. A federal district court found he had violated the separation of religion and government and ordered the monument removed. A Gallup poll found that 77 percent of the public disagreed with the decision to remove the monument.

How to recognize the religious feelings of the people, while not hindering religious freedom or favoring one group over another, is a delicate matter. In many states religious facilities are exempt from property taxes, religious employers do not have to obey labor laws protecting employees, and religious day care centers and drug-treatment clinics do not have to be licensed by the state. Abuses have been reported. Some groups argue that the constitutional wall separating church and state is needlessly high by, for example, forbidding Christmas displays on public property. Perhaps. But former New York Governor Mario Cuomo observed, "I protect my right to be Catholic by preserving your right to be a Jew, or a Protestant, or a nonbeliever, or anything else you choose."

Right of Privacy

". . . the right to be let alone—the most comprehensive of rights and the right most valued by civilized men."

—*Justice Louis Brandeis*

Do citizens have privacy rights against intruding government officials? Though nowhere mentioned in the Constitution, the First, Fourth, and Ninth Amendments are sometimes read by the courts as creating a "zone of privacy" that shields individuals from government monitoring of their phones and computers, homes and bedrooms.

In late 2005 the *New York Times* revealed a secret effort by the National Security Agency to monitor phone calls and e-mails by Americans without a court-approved warrant normally required for domestic spying. This antiterrorist tactic was begun shortly after the 9/11 attacks to track overseas links with Al Qaeda. After asking newspapers not to reveal this spying to the public, the Bush administration justified it in two ways. First, it was part of a president's inherent constitutional authority to protect the national security and, second, when Congress authorized the president to use "all necessary and appropriate military force" against those responsible for the attacks, it included these sort of modern military methods.

These policies have evolved over time. The Bush Administration eventually sought and got Congress's approval for its surveillance without court warrants, a 2008 bill that then-Senator Obama voted for. While the new administration has continued many of these antiterrorist measures, they have shown greater respect for Congress's role, and insisted on strict adherence to antitorture rules. Civil liberties critics charge that this is window-dressing, and that by ratifying the surveillance and detention policies he inherited, Obama has given them bipartisan acceptance. Formerly controversial executive practices have now become entrenched features in all of the federal government. (See "Privacy on the Internet.")

Some recent privacy issues have centered on sexual conduct. The states, according to the Supreme Court, cannot prevent couples from using contraceptive devices, nor can states forbid abortions in the first trimester of pregnancy. However, state regulations have been upheld that make it difficult for women to use abortion services without informing their spouses or waiting 24 hours after "family counseling."

Privacy on the Internet

The courts have tried to balance individuals' privacy with the government's interest in public safety. With telephone and mail the courts have been pretty clear what is out of bounds for government snooping. For example, a detective can look at an envelope but cannot read a letter without a search warrant signed by a judge. These distinctions are difficult to apply online. Three characteristics of the Internet have confounded government monitoring:

- *It's global:* On the Internet, a computer across the world can be reached as easily as one across the room. How do you enforce national laws in this environment? In 2006 Congress attempted to stop gambling on the Internet that used computers located outside the United States. The law did this by preventing credit card companies from transferring funds for online gambling. Gambling continued.
- *It's anonymous:* Disguising your name on the Internet is easy. An occasional contributor to a pornography newsgroup identifies himself as "George W. Bush," although the assumption is it is not really the former president.
- *It's huge:* Terabytes, or trillions of bytes, of data are circulating on the Internet at any given moment. As one commentator put it, "Trying to locate illegal or offensive data on the net would be harder than trying to isolate two paired words in all the world's telephone conversations and television transmissions at once."

The 1996 Defense of Marriage Act, signed by President Clinton, defined marriage as exclusively between one man and one woman, and said that states could not be forced to recognize same-sex marriages authorized in another state. In early 2004, President Bush endorsed a constitutional amendment that would restrict marriage to two people of the opposite sex, but the difficulty of the amendment process made the proposal more of a partisan campaign issue than a likely constitutional change. Since then six U.S. states have legalized same-sex marriage. Although President Obama does not support same-sex marriage, he has endorsed civil unions along with federal benefits for them, and supported repeal of the Defense of Marriage Act.

Due Process Rights

The Fifth Amendment and the Fourteenth Amendment can be called on to prevent national and state governments from depriving individuals of their lives, liberty, or property without due process of law. Due process guarantees involve fundamental procedural fairness and impartial rulings by government officials, especially in (but not limited to) criminal courtrooms. In criminal trials, the right to due process includes the right to free counsel if you cannot afford a lawyer; the right to have your lawyer present at any police questioning; the right to reasonable bail after being charged; the right to a speedy trial; the right to confront and cross-examine your accuser and witnesses testifying against you; the right to remain silent; the right to an impartial judge and a jury of your peers, selected without racial bias; and the right to appeal the decision to a higher court, if you believe legal errors were committed by the judge.

These rights were granted in federal criminal trials under the Fifth Amendment and the Sixth Amendment. As a result of Supreme Court decisions over the years, these rights also have been established for state criminal trials. In the 1970s the federal courts began to require some of these procedures in noncriminal settings. Students could not be suspended from high schools or public universities without certain kinds of hearings. People on welfare could not be purged from the rolls without receiving "fair hearings." Whether these rights extend to wartime situations and people accused of terrorism is now an ongoing debate. (See "Fighting Terror, Guarding Liberties.")

Consider the case of a student who has participated in a disruptive campus demonstration against the war in Afghanistan. She is told by university officials that she has violated rules and will be suspended for a semester. Surely she would want all the due process guarantees she could obtain in order to prove to these officials that they are wrong. Obtaining one due process right often leads to obtaining others. Once the college decides that students are entitled to a hearing, students may demand the right to an attorney. The attorney will insist on written transcripts and an appeals process. The very existence of a fair hearing procedure and the presence of lawyers can encourage informal settlements without a hearing.

These due process rights support First Amendment political freedoms. It does little good to give people the right to protest if officials can retaliate by cutting off essential services to protesters. Students or workers who are politically involved need legal protection from unfair action by school administrators or employers. Due process protects them. It also protects officials. By requiring them to meet standards of fairness and procedure, authorities gain legitimacy for their decisions.

Civil Rights: Protecting People from People

Protecting people against state action is only half the game. Civil rights involve the national government in the protection of minorities (or women, who are a majority) against actions by state and local governments or private individuals and organizations.

Civil rights issues involve discrimination based on race, religion, gender, age, sexual preference, or national origin. A group that believes it is being discriminated against may try to obtain satisfaction from elected officials, or it may turn to the judiciary. African Americans may find it difficult to rent apartments because landlords discriminate against them. To combat this, many states and the national government have passed fair housing laws, which make such discrimination illegal. Presidents have signed executive orders banning racial discrimination in public housing and in private housing financed through federal mortgage programs.

Civil rights issues are not always clear-cut. Free speech advocates may find that exercising that right runs up against minority groups perceiving harassment. (See "Conservative Bake Sales," p. 168). Affirmative action programs sometimes have placed groups in opposition to one another. The woman who supports affirmative action in order to get a job may be in conflict with the African American who believes that these programs were designed primarily to redress wrongs committed against blacks. As the late civil rights leader Dr. Kenneth Clark remarked, if women, blacks, Latinos, and Asians are all given affirmative action preferences, almost three-quarters of the population would be protected. These programs have fueled charges of "reverse discrimination" by white men not covered.

However valid their arguments, critics who deplore the racial nature of these programs often fail to support non-racial government programs that address poverty, illiteracy and unemployment wherever they exist. If greater resources were given to inner-city public schools, fewer programs giving advantages to these schools' graduates might be needed. But even if non-racially based programs evolved that reme-died these social ills, the courts still would play a role.

Which People Need Protection? Suspect Classifications

The Fourteenth Amendment declares the right to "equal protection of the laws." However, the government may pass laws applying to some citizens and not to others, or applying different criteria to different classes of people. For example, working people with low incomes may receive money from the government—in the form of the earned-income tax credit—and pay taxes at a lower rate, at least in theory. Up-per income groups provide the government with most of its money by paying taxes at higher rates than others.

What limits are placed on government classifications of people? Hardly any if the classifications involve wealth and income. The laws dealing with economic issues are routinely approved by the judiciary, under the doctrine of *presumptive legislative rationality.* Courts as-sume that the lawmakers know what they are doing when they make such classifications. On the other hand, if lawmakers apply racial, reli-gious, or national origin classifications, the courts subject these to "close scrutiny," because these are *"suspect" classifications.* Here the burden of proof is on the government to demonstrate that the classifi-cation is not, on its face, unconstitutional.

Governments must, when the law or action touches a "suspect class," prove a compelling state interest for their action. The courts begin their scrutiny with the assumption that the action violates the equal protection guarantee, and it is up to the lawmakers to prove otherwise. Racial classifications always are considered sus-pect, and almost always are struck down. Gender classifications are not suspect. To them the court applies a "middle test,"  stricter than standards for wealth and income but looser than standards for race. While courts have struck down many gender classifications, they have upheld some: Women are not registered for the military and, because they give birth, may get different medical benefits than men.

Race as a Suspect Classification

In 1896 the Supreme Court supported state actions that segregated the races. We saw that *Plessy* v. *Ferguson* upheld Louisiana's right to re-quire racial segregation in railway cars. "Equal protection of the law" was misshapen into the doctrine of "separate but equal": After all the African American, Plessy, would travel in a separate railway car, but would reach his destination at the same time and on the same train as a white person. Then in the 1954 landmark case *Brown v. Board of Education,* the Supreme Court held that schools segregated by race were unequal and violated the Fourteenth Amendment. After *Brown,* courts struck down most laws based on racial categories and made race a suspect classification.

But do racial classifications always violate the Fourteenth Amendment? Are there circumstances in which classification by race is a valid use of governmental power? Courts have upheld racial classifications when used to eliminate prior state-sponsored segregation. In devising plans to desegregate schools, for instance, administrators took into account the race of students attending schools, as well as their teachers. To make desegregation work, blacks would have to attend schools that had previously been all white.

Affirmative action programs permit racial classifications. An affirmative action program in schools allows admissions officers to take race and ethnicity into account in awarding places in the entering class. An affirmative action program in employment usually requires employers to make efforts to match the racial and gender numbers in their workforce with the pool of qualified workers in their areas. In 1978, in *University of California Regents v. Bakke,* the Supreme Court upheld the principle of affirmative action, holding that it was a "state interest" to provide for diversity among medical students at the University of California. At the same time, the Court held that the use of numerical quotas for minorities was a violation of the equal protection clause.

The Supreme Court has grown more skeptical of affirmative action programs. As we saw in the last chapter, Chief Justice Roberts has been reluctant to approve programs to promote racial balance, declaring himself "more faithful to the heritage of *Brown v. Board of Education,*" which he sees as banning assigning schools by race. While not declaring all affirmative action programs unconstitutional, past courts have made it clear that there had to be a "compelling interest" to relieve a specific case of discrimination and that the remedy had to be "narrowly tailored." In the 2003 University of Michigan case, the Supreme Court allowed such narrow affirmative action programs in university admissions to promote educational diversity. (See "University of Michigan and Affirmative Action.")

Recent administrations have been lukewarm toward affirmative action. The Clinton administration's Justice Department issued guidelines for federal agencies that led to reducing or eliminating 17 affirmative action programs. President Bush publicly opposed affirmative action and supported the cases against the University of Michigan. One member of

University of Michigan and Affirmative Action

In *Grutter* v. *Bollinger* (and a parallel case in the college), the Rehnquist Supreme Court heard arguments about the University of Michigan's admission policies to its law school intended to boost minority enrollments. A white student argued that because less-qualified minorities were admitted, she was denied a place. The university said that race-conscious admissions were a constitutional and limited way of ensuring "educational diversity." Opponents, including the Bush administration, argued that this was in fact a racial quota and that diversity could be reached through other methods. Using race violated white students' constitutional right to equal treatment under the law.

On June 23, 2003, the Court supported the law school's affirmative action program as a flexible, narrow way of promoting diversity in their student body. At the same time they rejected the undergraduate admissions program that awarded points based on race, regardless of individual merits. The Supreme Court supported the *Bakke* decision (1978) that race could be a factor in admissions, but worried that what was once a temporary "catch-up" remedy to discrimination was becoming permanent.

The 5–4 majority looked beyond Michigan to the 78 briefs filed by the country's leading corporations, law schools, and foundations stressing their need for affirmative action programs. One of the most influential was from U.S. military leaders who, with the war in Iraq raging, pointed to their need for a multiethnic officer corps. The irony of the government arguing against racial preferences that they supported in their own military academies was not lost on the Court.

his administration denounced affirmative action as "a corrupt system of preferences, set-asides and quotas." Even the first president who actually benefited from these programs only gingerly supported them. President Obama declared that affirmative action "hasn't been as potent a force for racial progress as advocates will claim and it hasn't been as bad on white students seeking admissions or seeking a job as its critics say."

Public opinion, which was negative toward the programs a few years ago, seems more mixed today. Polling data are unreliable because the results depend on the wording of the questions. In one CBS poll, support for affirmative action programs stood at 53 percent. However, when mention is made of "preferential treatment" for minorities, support dropped by half. Yet the consequences of eliminating affirmative action also concern the public. The banning in California of the use of race in college admissions led to a drastic 57 percent drop in black applicants and a 40 percent decline in Hispanic high school seniors accepted for admission to Berkeley. This led some opponents of affirmative action to question their criticisms and puzzle over these "unintended consequences." In other arenas, like the military and corporations, affirmative action programs appear to be a permanent fixture, whatever their popularity.

Is Sex Suspect?

In the nineteenth century, women and children were widely exploited. They worked 14-hour days in factories, seven days a week, for low wages in unsafe conditions (as did male workers). In the late nineteenth century, a coalition of women's rights advocates, labor organizers, and public health professionals demanded that government protect women and children through wage and hour regulations. Some states passed these laws, known as *protective legislation*. The Supreme Court, which opposed state efforts to regulate industry, held many of them to be unconstitutional.

But protective legislation did not stop with factory conditions. State legislatures further "protected" women by restricting their opportunities to enter professions. In 1873 the Supreme Court upheld a decision by the Illinois courts that prevented Myra Bradwell from becoming a lawyer. "The natural and proper timidity and delicacy which belongs to the female sex," a justice wrote, "evidently unfits it for many of the occupations of civil life." Under this reasoning, women were denied the right to enter businesses, serve on juries, sign contracts, or work at all if they were pregnant. Former Supreme Court Justice William Brennan observed that this "romantic paternalism" put women "not on a pedestal, but in a cage."

Throughout the twentieth century, these restrictions on women were chipped away. By the 1970s, women's groups had attacked the remaining "protective" laws in federal courts, arguing that gender should be considered a suspect classification. The Supreme Court responded by striking down many laws involving gender, including professional and educational requirements that discriminate against women. It has ruled that men have an equal right to sue for alimony, that the drinking age must be the same for both sexes, and that unwed fathers have rights in deciding whether a baby is put up for adoption. But the Court has not held that gender classifications are suspect.

In fact the Supreme Court has allowed state laws granting certain tax benefits to widows but not widowers. It upheld a state law permitting men but not women to serve as guards in a maximum security prison. It let stand a lower-court decision permitting single-sex schools to continue to receive federal funds. The Court has also upheld gender classifications when used for approved purposes such as an affirmative action plan. No challenges to single-sex bathrooms have succeeded.

The federal courts do retain part of the protective movement, the one that involves sexual harassment. The Supreme Court has recognized a pattern of harassment that exists, which makes it difficult for women to work in a hostile environment. In a 1991 civil rights law, Congress gave women who have been harassed on the job the right to sue in federal court for damages. In 1998 the Court held employers liable for a supervisor's behavior even if it did not know of the misconduct. In another case the same year, the Supreme Court declared that the law included sexual harassment even if both parties were men or the same sex (*Oncale* v. *Sundowner*).

Despite these cross-currents, it is likely that more sex-based classifications will fall as a result of present standards applied by the courts.

Actors in Civil Liberties and Rights

Many players in the political game act on civil liberties and rights. Within the government, the courts have been the most important, although Congress's laws and the president's executive acts affect these issues. Outside the government many organizations champion the rights of particular groups, pressuring officials with tactics like lobbying, publicity, and boycotts. The politics of civil liberties and rights involves struggles of group against group, as well as group against government, in ongoing attempts to strike a balance among competing claims.

Judges

Judges have taken the lead in protecting and expanding civil rights and liberties. Activist judges, who along with other supporters of civil liberties are called *civil libertarians,* issue decisions in *class action suits* in which lawyers bring a case to court not only for their individual clients but also on behalf of everyone in a similar situation—perhaps millions of people. Judges may rely on court-appointed experts to do the research needed to resolve complicated social issues. To decide a case, they may use not only previous cases and laws but also the equity powers of the judiciary.

Equity is used to prevent permanent damage in situations not covered by existing law. Suppose my neighbor, Jones, decides to cut down a tree in his yard. I see that the tree will crash into my house. My legal remedy is to sue Jones after my house is damaged. My equitable remedy is to obtain a court injunction that prevents Jones from cutting down the tree in the first place. Activist judges use equity powers to shape remedies that overcome the effects of discrimination. Take a school district that has been segregated by race. Requiring that the system ignore race may not have any effect if housing segregation exists so that schools will, in fact, remain segregated. Some federal judges have applied equitable remedies: They have required that the school districts take into account racial imbalances and come up with plans to overcome these imbalances.

Other judges show greater restraint in civil liberties and civil rights cases. They follow past decisions rather than expand constitutional protections. They place great weight on the policies of Congress, the president, and state legislatures, even when these restrict civil rights and liberties. These judges will presume that elected officials are acting lawfully unless proven otherwise. Because elected officials are directly accountable to voters, these unelected judges hesitate to impose their own views. (See Chapter 5, pp. 151–53 for more on activist and restrained judges.)

The Justice Department

Historically the Department of Justice has played a key role in protecting civil rights and liberties. Its lawyers in the U.S. attorney's offices in each judicial district may prosecute individuals, including state or federal officials, accused of violating people's civil rights. Under Republican presidents since Ronald Reagan the Justice Department pulled back from support of civil rights groups. The department opposed busing plans to overcome segregation of schools, opposed some affirmative action hiring plans, and argued that job discrimination cases should be limited to the individuals involved and not cover broad patterns of employment.

President Clinton entered office calling for civil rights enforcement. He appointed the first female attorney general, Janet Reno, as well as liberal judges and U.S. attorneys. Nevertheless the Republican takeover of Congress in 1994 and the unpopularity of affirmative action programs led to a more lukewarm stance. George W. Bush, elected with little black support, steered a conservative course toward civil rights. He opposed affirmative action, which he equated with racial quotas. He did support "affirmative access" such as the Texas 10 percent plan, where students graduating in the top 10 percent of their high school class were automatically admitted to a state university. The Bush Justice Department brought only a single case of employment discrimination—and that was for reverse discrimination against whites—and no cases of voter discrimination on behalf of African Americans.

Barack Obama appointed a black attorney general, Eric Holder, and pledged to "reinvigorate federal civil rights enforcement," particularly voting discrimination against African Americans. Issues like racial profiling and police abuse are likely to receive more government attention. In his first budget Obama included an 18-percent boost in funding for the Civil Rights Division.

"Private Attorneys General"

Various organizations have been created to support the rights of individuals and groups. These are called *private attorneys general* because they act not for the government, but for groups bringing court cases against the government or against other groups. They are funded by foundations, wealthy donors, and members' dues.

The largest of these groups is the *American Civil Liberties Union* (ACLU). The ACLU has a national staff and 50 state chapters handling more than 6,000 cases each year. The ACLU was organized in the 1920s to defend against the hysteria of "red scares" (a period when socialists were persecuted) and has fought against wiretapping, surveillance, and "dirty tricks" by law enforcement agencies. It is especially active in First Amendment freedom of speech, press, and religion issues. Recently it has opposed speech codes on campuses and has defended the due process rights of those swept up in the war on terrorism.

The NAACP's Legal Defense and Educational Fund, Inc. (LDF) began in 1939 with one lawyer, Thurgood Marshall, who later became the first black on the Supreme Court. In the past, the LDF concentrated on school desegregation, but today its dozens of lawyers focus on discrimination in employment and housing, and abuses in the judicial system. The largest legal organization for women is the National Organization for Women (NOW) Legal Defense and Education Fund, which works for women's employment rights and against discriminating legislation.

The foundation for Individual Rights in Education (FIRE) is a conservative/libertarian nonprofit that defends students and faculty confronting restraints on their freedom of speech on college campuses. The Council on American-Islamic Relations (CAIR) is the major Muslim organization involved in civil liberties cases of people accused of terrorism, and in encouraging a greater Muslim presence in the media and government.

Legal Strategies

These organizations use a range of legal tactics. Their research attempts to find a pattern of discrimination for a large class of people. They offer their services to individuals whose rights have been violated. Such people cannot afford the hundreds of thousands of dollars it takes to pursue a case to the Supreme Court, so the assistance of the "private attorneys general," almost always provided *pro bono* (free), is crucial. Civil liberties lawyers can choose, from a large number of complaints, a *test case* for their arguments. Such a case offers the group its best shot because the violation is so obvious, the damage so great, and the person making the case so appealing. The white student challenging the University of Michigan Affirmative Action admission program was represented by a law firm, *pro bono*.

These groups hope that their case eventually will wind up in the Supreme Court as a *landmark decision*—one that involves major changes in the definition of civil rights and liberties. Often similar cases will be filed in different courts, hoping for conflicting constitutional interpretations that will "force" the Supreme Court to rule on the issue. Such a decision creates a new precedent, such as the right to counsel in a state trial, which is then enforced by lower federal and state courts. After the landmark case is announced by the high court, the lawyers from these organizations then must bring dozens of cases in federal district courts to make sure that rights affirmed by the Supreme Court are followed by government officials. (An example of a landmark case is, *Brown v. Board of Education,* p.156.)

Obeying the Courts

These private organizations ask judges to do several things. First, they want a law or executive order to be declared unconstitutional, or that actions of private individuals be found to violate the law or the Constitution. Second, they may ask that a right be protected by judicial action. Of these, the most important are the *injunction,* which prevents someone from taking an action to violate someone else's rights, and the *order,* which requires someone to take a specified action to ensure another's rights.

In the event of noncompliance with a judicial injunction or order, the judges may issue a citation for contempt of court. Civil contempt involves the refusal to obey a court order granted to a party in a case and can lead to imprisonment. The court also may find someone in criminal contempt of court for disrupting or showing disrespect for the court's enforcement powers. This too may lead to prison or a stiff fine.

The orders of a federal court are enforced by federal marshals, backed up by the state's National Guard (which may be brought into federal service by the president) or by federal troops under the orders of the president. In 1957, for example, when Governor Orval Faubus of Arkansas refused to obey a federal court order to desegregate Little Rock Central High School, President Dwight Eisenhower took control of the Arkansas National Guard away from the governor. Federal troops were used to protect black students at the school.

In writing their orders, federal courts can act as administrators over state agencies. At one time in the 1970s, federal judges in Alabama were running the state highway patrol, the prison system, and the mental hospitals because the governor refused to obey federal court orders guaranteeing equal protection and due process of law by these agencies.

Sometimes state officials do not wish to comply with the spirit or letter of court orders. Consider the landmark decision of *Miranda* v. *Arizona* (1966), in which the Supreme Court held that once an investigation by police focused on an accused, that person had to receive the following warning:

> You have the right to remain silent.
> Anything you say may be used against you in a court of law.
> You have the right to be represented by an attorney of your choice.
> If you cannot afford an attorney, a public defender will be provided for you if you wish.

At first, there was only limited acceptance by police of the new rules of the "cops and robbers" game. After all, unless there was a federal judge in every patrol car, voluntary compliance was the only practical way such a rule could be implemented. Some departments ignored the order; others gave only part of the warning. The courts gained compliance through the *exclusionary rule:* They threw out evidence obtained illegally, including confessions where *Miranda* warnings had not been given. The Supreme Court, while continuing *Miranda,* has narrowed the exclusionary rule, allowing evidence if police officers "acted in good faith," even if they did not follow all due process rules. (See Chapter 5, Box: "Miranda: Pop Culture and the Court" on p. 141.)

Public Opinion and Civil Liberties

Public support for civil rights and liberties cannot be assumed. A majority of the public, for example, does not believe that evidence should be thrown out in state criminal trials on "legal technicalities," which is what *Miranda* requires. Five years after 9/11, when Americans were asked whether it was more important to investigate terrorist threats even if that intrudes on personal privacy, or for the federal government not to intrude on privacy even if that limits its ability to investigate these threats, 65 percent backed aggressive investigation. On whether to permit wiretapping overseas calls without a court warrant if needed to catch terrorists, 57 percent approved. Most Americans do not expect to need the Bill of Rights protections because they are not criminals or terrorists or illegal immigrants. While the American idea of freedom includes freedom from their government, this view does not easily apply when people are scared or in the midst of a national crisis or toward demonized groups.

But it is because the rights of politically unpopular groups have been violated that judicial protection becomes necessary. (See "Uncle Sam: Enemy of Civil Liberties?") Where support by local leaders does not exist and community sentiment runs against the decision, as with the ban on prayer in the public schools, compliance may be spotty. Often a Supreme Court ruling signals the beginning—not the end—of political debate. The Supreme Court decision affirming the right to abortion (*Roe* v. *Wade*) was followed by congressional and state laws cutting off public funding for abortions and requiring parental consent for teenagers.

The legitimacy of judicial action supporting civil liberties and rights never rests on its popularity. The federal judiciary is not elected and does not directly answer to the people. It is accountable to a constitution that attempts to secure the rights of the people against governmental action. The judiciary protects these rights. Low levels of approval for some of its decisions are to be expected. If anything, it is a sign that the system is working as a check on popular excesses.

Uncle Sam: Enemy of Civil Liberties?

Freedom as a slogan appears frequently in American leaders' speeches. But throughout U.S. history, there are uncomfortable reminders of government actions that violated the freedoms in the Bill of Rights.

Not many years after the ink had dried on the Constitution, Congress passed the *Alien and Sedition Acts* of 1798. Aimed at the opposition party, these acts promised heavy fines and imprisonment for those guilty of writing or speaking anything false, scandalous, or malicious against any government official. Such a broad prohibition today would put an end to most political campaigns. The slavery issue in 1840 led Congress to pass the "Gag Rule," preventing antislavery petitions from being received by Congress (thus violating a specific First Amendment right).

Violations of civil liberties continued into the twentieth century. Five months after the United States entered World War I, every leading socialist newspaper had been suspended from the mails at least once, some permanently. During World War II, Japanese Americans along the West Coast were forced into internment camps, based solely on their national origins. The Smith Act of 1940, which is still on the books, forbade teaching or advocating the violent overthrow of the government. In 1951, Communist party leaders were convicted under it for activities labeled "preparation for revolution." This "preparation" involved teaching works like the *Communist Manifesto,* which today can be found in any college library. Ten defendants were sentenced to five years in prison.

In more recent times, the FBI infiltrated the anti–Vietnam War movement, spied on civil rights leaders like Martin Luther King Jr., and got into a shoot-out with a right-wing family at Ruby Ridge, Idaho. After 9/11, the government denied American citizens labeled terrorists the right to a lawyer and the chance to challenge their detention before a judge—fundamental due process rights. To this day, Uncle Sam's respect for freedom remains a sometime thing.

Of course, for the courts to operate in the political game, and for their decisions to be enforced, they must function within the bounds of public opinion and the cooperation of other parts of the government. This is not automatically given, as shown in the following case of civil liberties in the years after a terrorist attack.

CASE STUDY

Fighting Terror, Guarding Liberties

The enemy has declared war on us. And we must not let foreign enemies use the forums of liberty to destroy liberty itself.

George W. Bush

They that can give up essential liberty to obtain a little temporary safety deserve neither liberty nor safety.

Benjamin Franklin

Two Asian men with box cutters were taken off an Amtrak train in Texas on September 12, 2001, and held in isolation for some three months without being brought before a court or being given a lawyer. Both were eventually cleared of any involvement with terrorism.

After 9/11, defending the country against terrorism and defending the Constitution's civil liberties seemed in conflict. President Bush, acting under his powers of commander-in-chief, took a number of aggressive actions. Without approval from Congress or the courts, the executive branch locked up over 1,200 people either for violating immigration laws or as material witnesses—though the real motive was to investigate them. (Bush's attorney general refused to release their names, claiming, without a trace of humor, that he was protecting their privacy.) Secret deportation hearings were ordered for suspected terrorists. The administration held to a firm position in terrorist-related cases: no judicial review, no right to counsel, no public disclosure, and no

open hearings. A federal appeals court later ruled these secret hearings "undemocratic" and "in complete opposition to the society envisioned by the Framers of our Constitution."

Past presidents fighting wars have found a way around civil liberties, and the Supreme Court usually goes along. George W. Bush's actions look mild compared with his predecessors: Abraham Lincoln detained thousands of rebel sympathizers, Woodrow Wilson banned antiwar publications during World War I, and Franklin D. Roosevelt interned tens of thousands of Japanese Americans in World War II. The courts avoided intervening in these presidential abridgements of civil liberties, and public opinion supported them.

The men who wrote the Constitution wanted a strong president for protection against foreign attacks. But whether wartime needs could override fundamental rights like representation by a lawyer and a chance to contest detention before a civilian judge raised profound questions. The Bush administration argued that these were military decisions that the Constitution gave to the executive branch alone. Yet terrorism was a criminal threat as much as a military one and, arguably, not quite the same danger to the republic as enemies like the Southern Confederacy or Nazi Germany.

A TALIBAN AND DUE PROCESS

In the years following the 9/11 terrorist attacks, the case *Hamdi* v. *Rumsfeld* (2004) brought up core civil liberties issues and the role of the courts in reviewing government actions.

Yaser Hamdi, a Saudi national, was captured in Afghanistan and, along with other prisoners, was taken to Guantanamo Bay in Cuba. When Hamdi said he was born in Louisiana and therefore an American citizen, he was declared an "enemy combatant," taken to Norfolk, and held incommunicado in a Navy jail. His father and a public defender tried to get access to him, but the government said that for reasons of national security he could not have visitors.

A federal district judge in Norfolk (an appointee of another Republican president, Ronald Reagan) ruled that Hamdi had a right to see a lawyer. The judge described the situation as "the first where an American citizen has been held incommunicado and subjected to an indefinite detention in the continental United States without charges, without any findings by a military tribunal, and without access to a lawyer." The Court of Appeals ruled against the judge, twice asking him to reconsider his decision, giving greater consideration to the executive branch's right to wage war. But the Court also questioned the administration's "sweeping proposition" that "any American citizen alleged to be an enemy combatant could be detained indefinitely without charges or counsel on the government's say-so."

The issue was not whether the government could detain an "enemy combatant." This had already been allowed under precedents from World War II. The issue was whether the executive could lock up U.S. citizens it *says* are enemy combatants and refuse them the opportunity to tell their side of the story to a court, to a lawyer, or to the public. Could they be held in solitary confinement for months or even years without a hearing? Does this accused citizen have the right to be heard?

The government responded to the appeals court by giving the district judge a two-page declaration of why Hamdi was an "unlawful enemy combatant" entitled to neither constitutional protections nor international prisoner-of-war status. The government refused to give the judge any further information. The federal judge was not impressed: "I do think that due process requires something other than a basic assertion that they have looked at some papers and therefore they have determined he should be held incommunicado. Is that what we're fighting for?"

In the summer of 2004 the U.S. Supreme Court ruled in the Hamdi case against the government's claim of sweeping executive power. The Court declared that an American citizen detained as an enemy combatant had a due process right to a hearing to challenge his detention. Many observers thought that the abuses by the American military revealed at Abu Ghraib prison in Iraq had shown that the executive branch could not be trusted with such an extensive claim to power. The reports of the torture of prisoners also produced a climate of public opinion that made it politically easier for the Supreme Court to limit presidential powers, even in wartime.

By the end of September 2004, after nearly three years in solitary confinement, Yaser Hamdi was released from custody and flown home to Saudi Arabia. He was required to renounce his American citizenship. The compelling national security concerns that led the executive branch to fight his release all the way to the Supreme Court were never revealed.

CONGRESS SHIFTS POWER TO THE PRESIDENT

Whether a president has the power to label people, including American citizens, enemy combatants and imprison them indefinitely without trial continued to be debated after Hamdi's release. In the past when such claims were made the war lasted a limited time. Now in a war with neither a definite beginning nor end, the concern was that these claims by the executive would shape civil liberties for the indefinite future. That is what worried a majority on the Supreme Court, as Justice O'Connor wrote, "A state of war is not a blank check for the president when it comes to the rights of the nation's citizens."

Congress resolved this debate in the fall of 2006 when it passed a bill that generally approved the president's power over terrorist suspects. It authorized the president to define enemy combatants and imprison and interrogate them indefinitely (including American citizens), and it stripped the courts of jurisdiction over challenges to his interpretation. This detainee bill banned the use of torture and answered complaints that the president was acting unilaterally without congressional approval. But the law clearly undermined Hamdi and a later case, *Hamdan* v. *Rumsfeld* (2006), which had disapproved of military commissions to try combatants. This law, as one professor put it, "further entrenches presidential power."

Critics accused the Obama administration of continuing Bush's detention policies. While there was a show of greater involvement of Congress, many of the practices themselves remained the same. Yet the decision in late 2009 to put five accused planners of the 9/11 attacks on trial in a civilian court in New York City was a clear break with the past. It also produced a political uproar with accusations that Obama was "extending legal protections to terrorists."

The Patriot Act

The Patriot Act passed quickly by Congress on October 25, 2001. It has been blamed by one side for things it does not do and overhyped by the other side as key to the antiterrorism war. (The attorney general at the time declared that repealing any part of it would "disarm" the United States.)

The act did strengthen law enforcement. It allowed the FBI and CIA to share evidence. It made it easier for the FBI to ask federal judges to force libraries and bookstores to turn over records, and to delay telling people that their homes and offices were being searched. It also allowed "roving" wiretaps, under court order, to listen to electronic devices.

But it did not include all that was alleged:

- When the Justice Department detained hundreds of Middle Eastern men after 9/11, it was done under immigration laws.
- When the government locked up 650 suspected terrorists as "enemy combatants" at Guantanamo Bay, Cuba, it was done under the president's war powers.
- When the president authorized military tribunals to try noncitizens, this was done under Defense Department rules (although none has been held so far).

On March 9, 2006, a renewed Patriot Bill was signed by the president, after being overwhelmingly passed by Congress. The question over what is included continues to be blurred in public.

WRAP-UP

Civil rights and liberties are constitutional protections granted to all citizens. They protect people against violations of their rights by other people or by the government. Civil liberties refer to rights—such as freedom of speech and religion and guarantees of due process of law—that allow people full participation in a democratic political system. Civil rights guard groups against discrimination by other groups. Historically, both sets of rights have been deepened as to what they cover and widened as to whom they cover.

Using the Fourteenth Amendment concepts of "equal protection of the laws" and "due process of law," the courts have applied the Bill of Rights to the states as well as the national government. Freedom of speech has expanded to include freedom of expression, including symbolic speech. Privacy rights now include protection for consenting adult sexual behavior, but not necessarily administration wiretapping. Due process rights cover bureaucracies as well as the state criminal justice system. Civil rights similarly have been widened with the use of suspect classifications to deal with racial prejudice. Although the strict scrutiny test does not apply to gender classifications, a large number of laws containing "protective" gender classifications have been removed from the books.

Helping the process along have been activist judges and private attorneys general, whose test cases have changed the law, sometimes dramatically and sometimes slowly. The case study of terrorism and civil liberties illustrates how difficult it is to support constitutional protections for unpopular individuals and groups in wartime.

Civil rights and liberties do not just protect individuals. They also defend our system of government. These well-tested values balance and restrain the drives and ambitions of leaders. They give us standards by which to judge the actions of these players. They underline the historical truth that majorities make mistakes, and that leaders can mislead. These rights may grant "freedom for the thoughts that we hate," but they also restrain the "tyranny of the majority."

Although the Bill of Rights is written in inspiring and absolute language— "Congress shall make no law"—these rights are seldom applied that way. Judges weighing civil liberties and rights (and students as well) are influenced by the political climate. First Amendment freedoms are easier to support when we agree with the voices speaking. Liberals may not be quite as upset by violations of free speech when police rough up protestors against health care reform. Conservatives may not see an issue of freedom of the press when newspapers publish classified leaks about secret government prisons. And few want to see terrorism flourish because of a blind commitment to due process. But each citizen's understanding and support for these freedoms is their most important defense. As Judge Learned Hand wrote, "Liberty lies in the hearts and minds of men and women; when it dies there, no constitution, no law, no court can save it."

THOUGHT QUESTIONS

1. How can individual citizens support civil liberties? Do they?
2. Some people believe that the Bill of Rights could not be passed in Congress today. Do you agree? Which of the ten amendments do you think would be the most controversial?
3. Should affirmative action be used just to remedy the effects of discrimination? Or should it be used for broader goals of a more diverse society? Should affirmative action programs be limited to African Americans?

4. Do you think that the threat of terrorism will cause a long-term decline in popular support for civil liberties in the United States? How would you prevent this from happening?

5. Will officials enforcing the law or guarding national security almost always try to avoid obeying civil liberties? How can this be changed?

SUGGESTED READINGS

Crier, Catherine. *The Case against Lawyers*. New York: Broadway Books, 2002.
A TV journalist tackles the American legal system—its complexity, unfairness, and expense.

Friendly, Fred W. *Minnesota Rag*. New York: Vintage Books, 1982.
A delightful account of a famous case of freedom of the press.

Goldsmith, Jack. *The Terror Presidency*. New York: W. W. Norton, 2009. Pb.
This former high legal official for the Bush administration finds his bosses sadly lacking respect for civil liberties.

Hentoff, Nat. *Living the Bill of Rights*. New York: HarperCollins, 1998.
Entertaining flesh-and-blood examples of how Americans from Justice William O. Douglas to an Alabama homecoming queen have fought for their civil liberties.

Leone, Richard C., et al. *The War on Our Freedoms: Civil Liberties in an Age of Terrorism*. New York: Public Affairs, 2003. Pb.
A collection of essays by experts worried about the current political climate and our freedoms at home.

Lewis, Anthony. *Freedom For the Thought that We Hate*. New York: Basic Books, 2008.
The former *New York Times* columnist writes a "biography of the First Amendment" with considerable praise for the brave judges who protect it.

Schlesinger, Arthur M., Jr. *The Disuniting of America*. New York: W. W. Norton, 1998.
The late eminent historian's brief, eloquent argument against the excesses of political correctness.

CHAPTER 7

Voters and Political Parties

T he institutions of government discussed so far are only half the game. Equally important are the players outside of government. Don't assume that they have less influence over issues than those within the government. That will be determined by their skills and resources, as well as the nature of the issue. The next two chapters will discuss four nongovernmental players—voters, political parties, interest groups, and the media—their power, and how they exercise it in American politics.

In this chapter, we will first look at voters—who they are and who they are not. What leads some to vote and participate in politics, and others to not do either? Our two political parties, whatever their shortcomings, are a critical link between voters and government. The history of the party system, its functions, and how well it performs its tasks today are the key topics. The case study at the end, on Barack Obama's use of the Internet in the 2008 campaign, shows how one candidate maximized his use of this technology and by doing so his chances of winning.

Voters

Who Votes?

"Who votes in America?" seems like an easy question. Citizens who are 18 and older (because of the Twenty-sixth Amendment lowering the voting age) and who have satisfied their states' residency requirements can vote. But in presidential elections almost 40 percent do not vote; in elections between presidential years some 60 percent of those eligible don't show up. The good news is that voting turnout seems to be improving.

In the 2008 election almost 62 percent of those eligible voted. At 131 million people, this was the highest turnout since 1968 when Richard Nixon beat Hubert Humphrey in the swirl of the controversies over the Vietnam War. 2008 was, however, only a slight increase from 2004 when 60 percent voted. Despite the Democrats' hype before the election of a tidal wave of new voters, a downturn in Republican voters going to the polls lowered the predicted turnout. The voting rates for blacks, Asians, and Hispanics each increased by about 4 percentage points, while whites saw their turnout rate decrease slightly. The youngest voters (18–24) were the only age group to show a significant increase in voting: 49 percent compared with 47 percent in 2004. But younger voters still had the lowest voting rate, while older citizens had the highest. Women had a higher voting rate (66 percent) than men (62 percent). Neither was statistically different from 2004. (See Figure 7.2.)

Voting rates have been much lower in nonpresidential elections. In 2006 just under 40 percent of eligible voters turned up at election

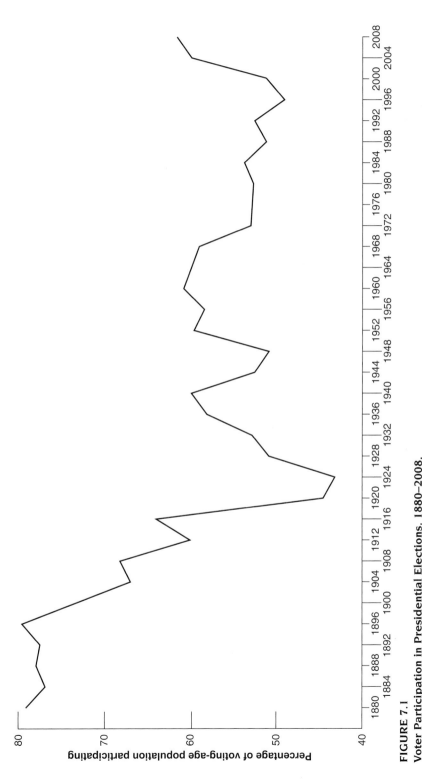

FIGURE 7.1
Voter Participation in Presidential Elections, 1880–2008.

Source: Figures for 1880 to 1916 reprinted with permission of The Free Press, a division of Macmillan Publishing, Inc., from *Political Life* by Robert E. Lane. Copyright © 1959 by the Free Press. Figures for 1920 to 1948 in U.S. Bureau of the Census, *Statistical Abstract of the United States,* 1969, p. 368. Data for 1952–1972 in U.S. Bureau of the Census, "Population Estimates and Projections," *Current Population Reports,* Series P-25, No. 626 (May 1976), p. 11. Later data in *Congressional Quarterly Weekly Reports,* 1977–2009.

booths, a figure that remained 20 percent lower than midterm elections in the 1960s. As seen in the chart (Figure 7.1), it is by no means certain that the long-term decline in voting has been reversed.

The questions grow. What leads some people to vote? What influences how they vote? And why do large numbers of people not vote?

Political Socialization

Political socialization helps explain how, or if, people participate in politics. *Political socialization* is the *process of learning political attitudes and behavior.* The gradual process of socialization takes place as we grow up, in settings like the family and schools. In the home, children learn about participating in family decisions—for example, the more noise they make, the better chance they have of staying up late. Kids also learn which party their parents favor, how they generally view politics and politicians, and what are their basic values and outlook toward their country. Children, of course, do not always copy their parents' political leanings, but they usually do. Most people stay with the party of their folks. Schools have a similar effect. Students salute the flag, take civics courses, participate in student politics, and learn that democracy (us) is good and dictatorship (them) is bad.

People's social characteristics also affect their participation in politics. Whether a person is male or female, religious or not, black or white, rich or poor, and a northerner or southerner will affect her or his political opinions and behavior. These views are reinforced by a person's peer group (friends and neighbors), and by the communities we live in that tend to echo and reinforce similar political beliefs.

The influence of religion and ethnic background can be seen today in the "politics of identity," where people find meaning in politics from participating as a member of a religion, or gender or ethnic group. These intensely felt loyalties have brought new voters to the polls and increased involvement in public affairs. But they have also tended to divide and at times polarize American politics. Activists opposing each other on issues like abortion or affirmative action or even health care reform see the other side not as political adversaries, but as wrong, even evil. The need to compromise, which is the hallmark of American pluralism, becomes an act of betrayal or weakness for the political leaders who attempt it.

Class and Voting

Class may be just as important in shaping people's political opinions and behavior. The term *social class* refers to a *group's occupation and income, and the awareness it produces of their relations to other groups or classes in the society.* In general we can speak of three broad, overlapping categories: a working class, a middle class, and an upper class. The *working class,* which almost always includes the majority of people in a society, receives the lowest incomes and fills "blue-collar" jobs in factories and farms, as well as "white-collar" positions like clerks and secretaries in offices. The *middle class* consists of most professionals (like teachers and engineers), small businesspeople, bureaucrats, and some skilled workers (say, those earning more than $50,000 a year). The *upper class* (often called the *elite* or *ruling class*) is composed of those who run our major economic and political institutions and receive the highest incomes for doing so.

At least as important as these "objective" categories that political scientists use is the "subjective" way in which people in these classes view their own position. Whether union members or teachers or housewives see themselves as members of the working class or the middle class will influence their political attitudes. An important fact about class in the United States is that class identification is quite weak. People either do not know what class they are in or do not think it is important. Most Americans see themselves as members of the middle class no matter what "objective" class they are placed in.

Class as reflected in education, income, and occupation, however, does influence people's attitudes on a variety of issues. Studies have shown that people in the working class tend to be liberal in wanting greater economic equality as well as more social and educational programs. This liberalism on economic issues contrasts strongly with their ideas on civil liberties. Here, people of lower income and education tend to be intolerant of dissenters and not supportive of minority views or different styles of behavior (such as homosexual rights). Members of the middle class are more conservative in their economic views and more liberal on issues such as free speech and respect for civil liberties. Class attitudes on political questions, then, are both liberal and conservative, depending on the type of issue.

Government policies and economic growth may also affect different classes differently. The prosperous 2001–2007 business cycle was the first ever in which the nation's middle-class families had less real income at the end than when they started. The medium real income for working-age middle-income families dropped $2,000 from $58,500 to $56,500, according to the U.S. Census Bureau. Income for the top

1 percent, in contrast, grew 204 percent since 1989, while the top 0.1 percent saw their income grow 425 percent. In 2006, the top 1 percent held the highest share of total U.S. income since 1928.

The problem with figuring out how characteristics of race, class, and religion influence a person's political behavior is that so many of them overlap. If we say that blacks are more likely to be nonvoters than whites, are we sure that race is the key category? We also know that poorer people, those with less education, and those who feel they have less effect on their government also are less likely to vote. All these categories have in the past included the majority of blacks. But we do not yet know which is more important in influencing behavior, and so even the historically "true" statement that blacks vote less may conceal as much as it reveals. We also have to examine whether blacks with more income or education (or a black presidential candidate to vote for) also vote less—which they do not. Further muddying the waters, in 2008 the historic gap between black and white voter participation virtually disappeared. In fact younger blacks voted in greater proportions than whites for the first time, and black women turned out at a higher rate than any other racial, ethnic, or gender group.

Who Doesn't Vote?

Pollster: *Do you think people don't vote because of ignorance or apathy?*
Nonvoter: *I don't know and I don't care.*

The difficulty of answering the question of why people do not vote ought to be clear. As the charts indicate, turnout depends on education, race, gender, and age, and it changes over time. Studies have shown that nonvoters most often are from the less educated, nonwhite, rural, southern, poor, blue-collar, and young segments of the American population. Voters most often come from the white, middle-aged, college-educated, urban or suburban, affluent, white-collar, and female groups. These are only broad tendencies, with a great many exceptions in each case. *Generally, people with the biggest stakes in society are the most likely to go to the polls:* older individuals and married couples, and people with more education, higher incomes, and good jobs.

There is other information, gathered from opinion polls, of which we are sure. First, Americans are poorly informed about politics. Surveys show that less than half the voters know the name of their representative in Congress, and only about one-fifth know how he or she has voted on any major bills. There is no doubt that the less income you have, the less likely you are to vote or participate in politics. During the

Voting Turnout, 2008 Elections

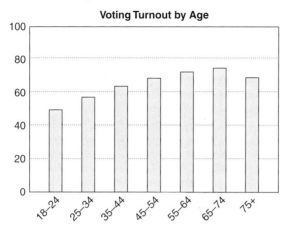

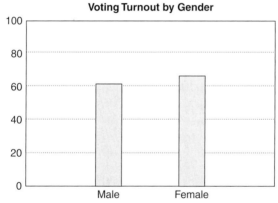

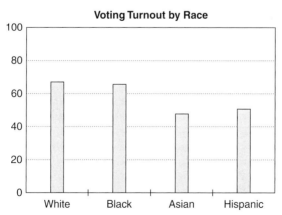

FIGURE 7.2
Presidential Voting Turnout of Eligible Voters by Age, Gender, Race, Education, Income and Marital Status, 2008.
Source: U.S. Census Bureau, Current Population Survey, November 2008.

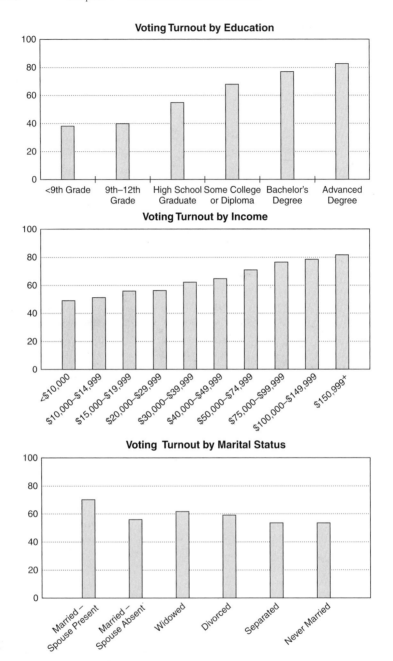

FIGURE 7.2 (continued)

lead-up to the 2008 primaries, 66 percent of those who said they were "having an easy time financially" said they were likely to participate in the primaries, compared with only 49 percent of those who said times were tough for them. Despite increased engagement, young people were still less likely to follow election news than older citizens.

A month before the 2008 election, less than 40 percent of voters under 35 claimed to be paying close attention to the election, compared with 53 percent of those 35–54 and 72 percent of those 70 and older.

Class differences in voting reflect differences in economic security. Low-income people who face immediate challenges like finding a job or paying bills may view politics as a luxury they can't afford. Class differences in political socialization also have an effect. Children of working-class parents, perhaps because of poor education, grow up believing that they can have little influence on politics ("You can't fight city hall"). At the same time, because of the disadvantaged reality they and their parents face, they tend to have a not-so-favorable image of political leaders. These children, then, end up being both more resentful and more passive toward politics. Middle- and upper-class children have a higher regard for political leaders and are taught in their schools to value participation in politics. They are encouraged to participate and are led to believe that the political system will respond favorably to their involvement. Of course, political leaders may be more likely to listen to people with a similar background and education as theirs—upper middle class.

Electoral barriers to voting also play a role in lower turnout. State registration laws—some that require 50 days of residency and periodic registration—make voting inconvenient. Making registration and voting two separate acts on different days clearly cuts out the "last-minute shoppers." As we learned in recently disputed elections, older voting machines in poor neighborhoods may lead to long lines at the polls, more votes being disqualified, and more people being discouraged from voting.

Until recently, the U.S. government stood virtually alone in not helping its citizens cope with voter registration. The so-called *motor voter* legislation made registration easier by allowing voters to register when they got drivers' licenses. The assumption behind the 1993 law was that the easier it was for people to register, the more likely they would be to vote. Yet in the first elections after the law passed there seemed to be little impact on either registration or voting. Fewer people registered to vote in 1996 and even fewer voted. It took until the 2004 election for both registration and voting numbers to surge, and then it was for partisan reasons (i.e., Hate Bush! Love Bush!); it had little to do with ease of registration. In the 2008 election the 10 million increase in people registering was not matched by a similar increase in voting.

Government can still make voting easier. Making election day a national holiday, as it is in many European countries, or letting people vote on Saturday, or by mail or online would help. Same-day registration—where any eligible citizen can roll out of bed on election day and register to vote at the polls—has seemed to work in Minnesota and Maine, which are two states ranking near the top in voting turnout. These states' 75 percent turnout may reflect their close-knit rural

communities, where personal communications among neighbors reinforce a traditional belief that they have a duty to vote.

Explanations

The objective categories describing nonvoters—younger, less educated,
lower incomes—may conceal as much as they reveal. The term *nonvoters*
after all covers more than half of the American population, and a great
deal of variety. (Note: This counts not just *eligible* voters.) For example,
surveys have shown that while nonvoters tend to be less affluent, 43 percent have incomes over $30,000. Nonvoters are significantly younger
than voters, but one-quarter of nonvoters are 45 years old or older. When
people who registered but did not vote were asked why, more than one in
five said they could not take time off work or were too busy. Time constraints are now the biggest single reason given for not voting. Apathy was
cited as a reason by 17 percent of registered nonvoters.

The ability to generalize about nonvoters gets cloudier in examin-
ing negative feelings toward government. While it is true that nonvoters feel alienated from government, this is also true for voters. In one
study of a recent election, about two-thirds of the population felt that
to some extent "most elected officials don't care what people like me
think." The percentage for nonvoters was exactly the same. Nonetheless, mistrust of government has grown in recent years parallel to the
growth of nonvoting. This has likely had a cumulative effect, especially
on the views of young people as they form their impressions of government and their role as citizens. In recent elections, however, young
people seem to be coming back to the polls. (See "Is The Vanishing
Young Voter Reappearing?")

 ## Is The Vanishing Young Voter Reappearing?

For years complaints were heard that young voters were invisible on
election day. They voted less, scholars said, because they moved more,
married and bought homes later in life, and had no strong identity to
either political party—all factors that erode the voting habit. While
young people are no more cynical than older ones about politics (equal
percentages believe most politicians are crooks), young cynics vote almost 40 percent less than older ones. Most young voters do not consider it a civic duty to vote, while those over 30 overwhelmingly do.

While they still vote less than the population as a whole, young people have increasingly been showing up in recent elections. In the 2008
elections nearly 53 percent of people under 30 voted in the election,
about 3.4 million more than voted in 2004, when almost 21 million
young voters went to the polls. This was up from 16 million votes in
2000. Though a historic high, it still means nearly half did not vote.

This lack of *political efficacy*—a sense that government will respond to people's needs—among both voters and nonvoters has several explanations. That people "don't think it makes any difference" in whether they participate may come in part from the way they were socialized or brought up. People may not consider politics relevant to their lives, identify with a political party, understand the political system, follow news about public affairs, or some combination of these. The less informed people are about politics, the less relevant it appears to their lives. And, in fact, government may not be responsive.

Lack of confidence in government has grown. In the early 1960s, three out of four Americans responded to survey questions by saying they trusted Washington all or most of the time. Today it is just the opposite: Three out of four no longer trust their government. There has been much debate over the causes of this lack of trust. In the 1960s, the government was remembered for having rescued people from the Great Depression and winning World War II. Since then the issues have gotten more complex and the victories fewer. Poverty, crime, discrimination, and terrorism are just some of the problems that government is now expected to solve—and has not. At the same time, institutions like the family, religion, and schools have all weakened in their ability to speak to many of society's ills. The media, with their blustering talk shows and skeptical reporting, have been blamed for turning people off politics. And, at least prior to 9/11 and the 2008 financial meltdown, the argument was heard that big issues like the Great Depression or Vietnam were not around to shock people into familiarizing themselves with political issues.

The government is not exactly blameless in this cycle of distrust. At least beginning with Vietnam and Watergate, leaders have misled. President Clinton, with half truths about his personal life from avoiding the Vietnam draft to not avoiding Monica Lewinsky, reinforced popular prejudices. The George W. Bush administration benefited from the initial patriotic rallying after 9/11. Then came the invasion of Iraq. Justifying the war with undiscovered weapons of mass destruction and nonexistent ties to Al Qaeda undermined popular confidence. The TV images of American leaders squirming to avoid responsibility for their lack of planning in occupying Iraq or for the abuse of prisoners of war or for painting an unrealistically rosy picture of the war all increased public disillusionment.

Presidential elections have traditionally been seen as a major vehicle for gaining public participation. In the past they have also been faulted for going on far too long and for focusing on only a dozen key states for intensive activities and advertising. Press coverage that is negative about candidates and absorbed with horse-race stories—stressing "who's ahead?"—may minimize issues and maximize cynicism. Many politicians in seeking high office go out of their way to denigrate and distance themselves from Washington, which doesn't help. Yet the candidacy of Barack Obama is a reminder that leaders can encourage participation. Obama attracted young people to his campaign and to voting, and they in turn made a difference in his being elected. Whether or not this will translate into their continuing involvement in elections and political issues is not yet clear.

Of course, voting is not the only way of participating in politics. Recent years have seen an increase in personal politics—on issues about gender, the environment, energy, food, health, and relationships. In the home, in dorms, and at work, politics flourishes among friends, parents and children, and everyone on e-mail. Individuals dip into politics by wearing a "Thank You for Not Smoking" button, by teaching younger relatives to read nutrition labels at the supermarket, or by trying to get their families to live "green" by turning down the thermostat or by eating less meat. Women and minorities may do politics just by showing up in jobs where they were rarely seen before. Teens use blogs to protest drug laws, march for more funding for breast cancer research, or join their church group in cleaning up a local park in a poor neighborhood.

Professor Michael Schudson has made the argument well: "The changes that have made the personal political have been profound, arguably more so than the slackening of voter turnout."

And isn't this politics—people influencing others on public issues?

Political Parties

A *political party* is an organization that runs candidates for public office under the party's name. Although the framers of the Constitution worried more about factions and interests, they were well aware that parties could soon develop. George Washington, in his famed farewell address, warned against "the baneful effects of the spirit of party." Despite his advice, parties soon arose, and for good reasons.

The national government, as we have seen, is based on a system of dividing or *decentralizing* power. Political parties, on the other hand, are a method of organizing or *centralizing* power. The Constitution decentralized power in separate branches and in a federal system of states partly to avoid the development of powerful factions that could take over the government. This decentralization of power, however, created the need for parties that could elect candidates who could work together and effectively govern.

For the rest of the chapter, we will ask and answer the following questions: What are the functions of parties? How have they historically developed? How are they organized? What are the consequences of our two-party system? How important are parties today? What about the future of our parties?

Party Functions

What do political parties do? Political parties throughout the world organize power in order to control the government. To do so, American parties (1) contest elections, (2) organize public opinion, (3) put together coalitions of different interests, and (4) adopt policy changes proposed by smaller political groups.

First, parties *contest elections.* They organize voters in order to compete with other parties for elected offices. Parties and their candidates recruit people into the political system to work on campaigns. Parties provide people with a basis for making choices. Most people vote for their party's candidate. Even in the supposedly "post-partisan" 2008 election, 89 percent of Democrats voted for Obama and 90 percent of Republicans chose McCain. (The other major motive behind a voter's choice is whether to favor or oppose the incumbent.) In addition, when parties contest elections, they express policy positions on important issues, which serve to *educate* voters. Most people are not ordinarily involved in politics. They rely on elections to keep themselves informed.

Second, parties *organize public opinion.* Despite the variety of views within them, parties give the public a limited channel of communication to express how they think government should operate. At the least, voters can approve the actions of the party that has been holding office by voting for it, or they can disapprove by voting for the opposition. The 2008 election gave voters the opportunity to show their disapproval of a president who was not even on the ballot.

Third is building *coalitions.* Parties put together, or *aggregate various interests.* The Democratic and Republican parties organize different regions, ethnic groups, and economic interests into large coalitions for the purpose of winning elections. When Barack Obama campaigned in the Ohio primary he promised to renegotiate a trade treaty, NAFTA, that he had previously favored. This was an effort to cement the support of union workers behind his candidacy. Gathering special interests under the broad umbrella of a party label is an important function of American parties. This can be seen clearly at the presidential level, where elected candidates often claim a *mandate,* or the widespread national support needed to govern.

Finally, the two major parties *adopt changes* or reforms proposed by third parties or social protest movements. If third parties or political movements show that they have considerable support, their programs are often incorporated, usually in more moderate form, by one of the major parties. George W. Bush saw that conservative religious groups were outraged at the spreading acceptance by state courts of gay marriages. The Republicans in 2004 incorporated in their party platform support for a constitutional amendment forbidding such marriages.

The Rise of Today's Parties

The *Federalists* and *Anti-Federalists*, the groups that supported and opposed the adoption of the Constitution, were not organized into actual political parties. They did not run candidates for office under party labels. There were, in fact, no political parties anywhere in the world at the time. At the time, what did exist were networks of communication and political activity struggling on opposite sides of a great dispute—ratification. The framers preached against political parties. Jefferson, who founded what would become the Democratic party, wrote a bit hypocritically that "if I could not go to heaven but with a party, I would not go there at all." Being called a "party man" was a stain against the political honor of this revolutionary generation. Yet as soon as these revolutionaries had to operate a national government, they ran into problems. They confronted separate executive and legislative branches, a complex brew of checks and balances, and a fragmented federal system of states. Not surprisingly, they reached out for parties to help organize this unwieldy divided government. Popularly based parties would evolve first in the United States. (See "Political Parties around the World.")

 Political Parties Around the World

One hundred years ago, political parties were confined to Europe and North America. Elsewhere they were weak or nonexistent. Now parties are found everywhere in the world. Generally they are better organized with far more members than in the early twentieth century.

In their spread worldwide, parties have adapted to their local societies. In Africa parties sometimes form around a tribe, with party leadership drawn from chiefs' families. In Asia membership in modern parties is often dominated by religious groups or by ritual brotherhoods. Many parties in less-developed countries are partly political, partly military.

The organization of parties mirrors their political system. In Great Britain, where Parliament acts as both the legislative and executive branches of government, parties are centralized and powerful. Members of Parliament choose the party leaders, and even if they should attain government position, they are dependent on party support. So in 2007 the British Labor Party pressured Prime Minister Tony Blair to resign. This was despite his leading his party to 3 general election victories, the latest in 2005. The party's officials essentially removed the head of government without any input from voters.

After the Constitution was ratified, the Federalist faction grew stronger and more like a political party. Led by Alexander Hamilton, secretary of the treasury under President Washington, the Federalists championed a strong national government to promote the financial interests of merchants and manufacturers. After Thomas Jefferson left Washington's cabinet in 1793, an opposition party formed under his leadership, due to the behind-the-scenes politicking skills of James Madison. The new *Democratic-Republican party* drew the support of small farmers, debtors, and others not benefiting from the financial programs of the Federalists. Under the Democratic-Republican label, Jefferson won the presidential election of 1800, which, because it was the first peaceful transition from one party to another, ranks as one of the most important elections in American history. Jefferson's party continued to control the presidency until 1828. The Federalists, without power or popular support, died out.

At the end of this 28-year period of Democratic-Republican control, the party splintered into factions. Two of these factions grew into new parties, the *Democrats* and the *Whigs* (first called the *National Republicans*). Thus the Democratic party, founded in 1828, is the oldest political party in the world. The early Democratic party was led by Andrew Jackson, who was elected president in 1828. Jackson spread power down into the party ranks by using a national convention (first created by a third party and then adopted by the Democrats) to nominate presidential candidates. Under Jackson, the Democrats became known as the party of the common people. The Whigs, like the old Federalists, were supported by the wealthier conservative groups in society: bankers, merchants, and big farmers.

In 1854, a *coalition* (a collection of interests that join together for a specific purpose) of Whigs, antislavery Democrats, and minor parties formed the *Republican party*. One of the unifying goals of this new party was to fight the expansion of slavery. The Republicans nominated a *dark horse* (a political unknown), Abraham Lincoln, on the third ballot for president in 1860. The Democrats were so deeply divided over the slavery issue that the southern and northern wings of the party each nominated a candidate. Against this divided opposition, as well as a fourth candidate, Lincoln won the election in the electoral college with less than a majority of the popular vote, but more than any other candidate—in other words, a *plurality* of the vote.

Maintaining, Deviating, and Realigning Elections

For 150 years, the Democratic and Republican parties have dominated American politics. Their relative strength and the groups supporting them have shifted back and forth. We can put this history into categories by looking at three types of presidential elections: maintaining, deviating, and realigning elections. *Maintaining elections* keep party strength and support as they are. *Deviating elections* show a temporary shift in popular support for the parties, usually caused by the exceptional popular appeal of a candidate of the minority party. *Realigning elections* reflect a permanent shift in the popular base of support of the parties, and a shift in the strength of the parties so that the minority party emerges as the majority party. The president who emerges from a realigning election, whether an Abraham Lincoln or a Franklin Roosevelt, has a fresh national coalition behind him, able to change the course of the nation's history.

Most presidential elections between 1860 and 1932 were maintaining elections. The Republicans (or GOP for *Grand Old Party*) kept the support of a majority of voters, and controlled the executive branch, in all but 16 of those 72 years. When the Democrats did gain control of the presidency, they held office for only short periods. The two elections of Democrat Woodrow Wilson in 1912 and 1916, for example, were caused by temporary voter shifts in party support and by splits within the Republican party.

The social and economic earthquake called the Great Depression of the 1930s destroyed the Republicans' majority support, and contributed to a realignment in the two-party system. Under Franklin Delano Roosevelt, the Democrats became the majority party, representing labor, the poor, minorities, the cities, immigrants, eastern liberals, and the white South. This *"New Deal Coalition"* kept majority support in the country at least through the Democratic administrations of John Kennedy and Lyndon Johnson in the 1960s. Democrats dominated Congress through most of the period until 1994. During this time the party gradually weakened in the face of growing Republican voting strength in the South and the West and among the suburban middle class.

Beginning in 1968 and continuing through the two elections of Ronald Reagan in 1980 and 1984 and beyond, a rolling Republican realignment occurred. The social disruptions of the 1960s led to divisions within the Democrats' New Deal Coalition, which the Republicans took advantage of. The 1968 independent presidential candidacy of segregationist Alabama Governor George Wallace exposed a traditionally Democratic white working class alienated from a party they felt to be too pro–civil rights and too anti–Vietnam War. Wallace's conservative populism claimed that pointy-headed bureaucrats and ivory-tower liberals were promoting government programs that helped minorities by taxing the white majority. Rising crime and taxes symbolized this alienation. Republicans saw the chance to steer blue-collar voters away from blaming the country's problems on their traditional New Deal enemy of Wall Street's Big Business to the new liberal targets found in Georgetown, Hollywood, and Harvard.

Riding this wave of conservative populism, with a smattering of racism, Republicans were elected president in five of the six elections before 1992. The southern and western states were consistently voting for Republican presidential nominees, the youth vote shifted to the GOP, and polls of party identification showed almost as many Republicans as Democrats. Despite dominating the presidency the GOP marketed themselves as the antigovernment party.

Political crosscurrents allowed the Democrats to capture the presidency in the Bill Clinton elections of 1992 and 1996. Having a gifted southern politician who could run as a middle-of-the-road "New" Democrat helped; as did a certain public weariness over Republican presidents for the previous 12 years. A changing electorate increasingly refused to identify with either party, with almost one-third of voters declaring themselves Independents. The emergence of Ross Perot as a nonparty presidential alternative in 1992 exposed the weakness of the two major parties. The Texas billionaire for a short time that summer outpolled both Democratic and Republican candidates. Perot's 19 percent of the vote in 1992 helped Clinton defeat the incumbent George H. W. Bush.

2004 and 2008: Whose Realignment?

The two elections of Bush's eldest son, George W. Bush in 2000 and 2004, convinced many that a Republican realignment had indeed arrived. After all, by 2004 Republicans were in control of all three branches of the federal government. Democrats, who had dominated the Congress for almost all of the 62 years up to 1994, had failed to win a majority in the House of Representatives for six straight elections, 1994–2004. They had been a minority in the Senate for most of these 10 years. While equal numbers of voters declared themselves Democrats and Republicans, and independents leaned Democrats, it did not seem to matter. The country might be divided; the government was not.

Much of the explanation for this lay in one region: The South had switched parties. Since 1980 the South had consistently voted for Republican presidential nominees. The only Democrats to win the presidency after 1960 and until 2008 were from the South—Johnson, Carter, and Clinton. The 1994 election marked the first time that a majority of southerners voted Republican for Congress. It was this realignment in the South as well as an effective national party organization that led to a GOP majority in both houses of Congress in1994. Bringing together small-town religious believers with Wall Street financial clout, conservatives shifted the party to the Right. Republican leaders delivered cultural populist speeches on the values of faith and family, while more concretely delivering pro-business economic and tax legislation. After 9/11 in 2001 the Republican president could add to his clout by stressing the dangers of terrorism, especially if "cut and run" Democrats were put in power.

None of this seemed to matter in the 2008 elections. The Democrats in 2006 had recaptured control of both houses of Congress and a majority of governors, and made substantial gains in state legislatures. Popular opinion had turned bitter toward the war in Iraq, the Bush administration's ineptness after Hurricane Katrina, and the corruption on display among lobbyists and members of congress. More voters declared themselves Democrats than Republicans (39 percent to 32 percent in exit polls), and the quarter of the population that called themselves Independents voted Democratic by better than 3 to 2. And then there was Barack Obama.

Paralleling Obama's 2008 victory, students of realignment discovered a more politically liberal America. Ruy Teixeira and John Judis wrote about the rise of an "emerging Democratic majority" produced by a post-industrial economy devoted to ideas and employed in professional occupations, like teachers and IT workers. This new majority was made up of those with college degrees; minorities—African Americans, Latinos, Asian Americans, women—particularly working, single, and college educated; and young people. All these groups lined up behind Obama.

Meanwhile the Republicans were divided and demoralized. The culture wars that conservatives waged for decades (against homosexuality, pornography, abortion, etc.) no longer found a place on the agenda of these rising liberal groups. Much like their new president, they were progressive and pragmatic on civil rights and liberties, lifestyle choices, religion, regulation of business, the environment, immigration, and trade. Bonded by the economic crisis, they were willing to support ambitious government initiatives to correct a damaged, unfair economy. And these groups were not only shifting to the Democrats they were also growing in numbers, especially among Hispanics and young professionals. They will, happy Democrats predict, make up the backbone of a new Democratic majority for the coming generation. Unfortunately for Democrats just one year after Obama took office, in early 2010, the party unexpectedly lost a Senate election in heavily Democratic Massachusetts at the same time that public support for both the President and his health care reform seemed to erode. A reminder that predictions of realignment are more common than actual realignments.

Polarizing the Parties: The Growth of Partisans

The differences between the two major parties lie in both image and reality. The image of the parties is usually based on a stereotype of people who support the parties. Typical Republicans are white, middle and

TABLE 7.1 HOW TO TELL A LIBERAL FROM A CONSERVATIVE		
Here are some of the political beliefs likely to be preferred by liberals and conservatives.		
	LIBERALS	CONSERVATIVES
On Social Policy:		
Abortion	Support "freedom of choice"	Support "right to life"
School prayer	Opposed	Supportive
Affirmative action	Favor	Oppose
On Economic Policy:		
Role of the government	Government can be a regulator in the public interest	Government messes up free-market solutions
Taxes	Want to tax the rich more	Want to keep taxes low
Spending	View government as offering solutions to national issues	View government as expanding and spending too much
On Crime:		
How to cut crime	Believe we should solve the problems that cause crime	Believe we should support the police
Defendants' rights	Believe we should respect everyone's civil liberties	Believe we should not let criminals escape justice

upper-middle class, and Protestant; they are educated and, with the rise of the "gender gap," are less often women. They support business, organized religion, law and order, a hardline policy in foreign affairs, and limited government intervention in the economy but more involvement in enforcing moral values in people's lives. They call themselves "conservatives." (See Table 7.1.)

Typical Democrats are members of a minority, ethnic, or racial group; belong to a labor union; and are working-class, non-Protestant, and urban residents, or professionals with liberal views. They support social welfare measures to help the poor at home, government regulation of big business, more equal distribution of wealth, and more internationalist, less aggressive foreign policies, except perhaps in favoring trade restrictions to protect jobs. The majority of Democrats are female (55 percent). Blacks, Latinos, Asian Americans, and Native Americans make up 46 percent of the party. While labeled liberals, they prefer to be called "progressives."

Not surprisingly the reality is more complex than the image. Leaders of the Democratic and Republican parties do disagree on major issues, more often than party members. Party *followers*, not actively involved with the party, tend to be more moderate (or indifferent) than *leaders* on issues. A number of voters straddle the positions of their parties; for example, Democratic union members who favor expanded liberal social programs at home but stronger military actions abroad. Democratic and Republican party members often agree more with each other than with their own leaders, though the numbers of strong partisans have grown in both parties.

Another complicating factor in party differences is that each party is a coalition of often differing groups. The Democrats include liberal, black, urban, working-class supporters from the northern industrial cities, and moderate, white, wealthy, educated suburbanites from the West. The GOP includes moderate business and skilled working people from the East, and small-town religious fundamentalists or conservative farmers from the South and Midwest.

Because of their conservative cultural and religious beliefs white, working-class southerners and westerners have increasingly voted for Republicans. (If only whites had voted in 2006, the Republicans would have won a majority of seats in Congress.) Despite what seems like the white working class's economic self-interest in government programs—job training, money for education, and expanded health care—identification with conservative positions on abortion, school prayer, and gay marriages have outweighed liberal concerns for increased public services funded by higher taxes on the wealthy. Cultural populism and anger at government elites has been more important than economic populism and resentment of corporate elites. This conservative populism has been used by Republican strategists to polarize the electorate and win elections.

The 2008 election revived the counter argument—that voters remain moderate. Because the party elites were so ideological and angry with each other, they had in the past forced voters to make extreme choices. Bush Republicans in their winning presidential campaigns had pursued a "base" strategy of mobilizing their core voters and adopting emotionally polarizing positions to get their partisans to vote. But in 2008 both Barack Obama and John McCain had run in opposition to the partisan voices in their parties. They preached reaching across the red-state (Republican) and blue-state (Democratic) divisions. As Obama said in his stump speech, "We can't afford four more years of the same divisive food fight in Washington that's about scoring political points instead of solving problems; that's about tearing your opponents down instead of lifting this country up . . . we have the chance to build a new majority of not just Democrats, but Independents and Republicans."

Ultimately the ability to win elections is the key measure by which parties judge the strategies and policies they adopt.

View from the Inside: Party Organizations

Historically American parties have been weak national organizations. Traditionally there have been few ties knitting various local parties together, and fewer still binding them into a coherent countrywide organization. The late twentieth century saw the rise of candidate-centered campaigns, media dominance over political communications, and the importance of interest group money for advertising—all three undermined the classic functions of parties.

The current national parties seem to have made a comeback. They have centralized their organizations by controlling campaign technology, strategy, and fundraising. American parties may appear weak and locally based when compared with the strong centrally run parties of Europe and Asia. But the two national parties are far from powerless, and they now appear to be gaining strength.

Machines—Old and New

Particularly in the last half of the nineteenth century, many local American parties were so tightly organized that they were called *political machines*. Party machines have a party *boss* (leader) who directly controlled the political party workers at the city or district levels. Local leaders obeyed the boss because he handpicked party nominees, and distributed patronage jobs, political favors, and party finances to loyal supporters. While an effective instrument for managing a precinct or city government and giving support to needy immigrants, machines had a well-deserved reputation for corruption. Until his death in 1976, Richard Daley Sr., mayor of Chicago for more than 20 years, kept firm control of a strong Democratic party machine. Daley's machine acted as an informal government and social service agency, meeting the immediate needs of urban citizens. Chicago's party organization has declined (despite Mayor Daley's son, also Richard Daley, now serving as mayor) and political machines, in general, have gone the way of the dinosaur. (See "Machine Politics.")

Political machines lost much of their leverage early in the twentieth century when three things happened: (1) local, state, and federal agencies took over distributing benefits (like welfare) to the poor; (2) civil service reforms made most city jobs require competitive examinations; and (3) direct primaries turned the party's nomination into an election contest anyone could enter and win.

Modern machines have appeared that allow political leaders to use the new technologies of fundraising and direct-mail campaigns to raise and give away money to party colleagues. These *leadership PACs* can cement loyalty to their creators and promote their ambitions for higher office. While they have been around since the 1970s, former Speaker Newt Gingrich is credited for starting the model for this fundraising machine. GOPAC was Gingrich's political action committee that raised millions for Republicans and aided his rise to House Speaker. Congressional leaders in both parties are now expected to have a leadership PAC to raise money. Typically, committee chairs raise funds from

Machine Politics

During Richard Daley Sr.'s long reign as mayor of Chicago and boss of the "machine," he was seldom seriously challenged in an election. One who did run against him was a lawyer named Benjamin Adamowski. Mike Royko, a Chicago columnist, illustrates why he and other Daley opponents did not get very far.

The owner of a small restaurant at Division and Ashland, the heart of the city's Polish neighborhood, put up a big Adamowski sign. The day it went up the precinct captain came around and said, "How come the sign, Harry?"

"Ben's a friend of mine," the restaurant owner said.

"Ben's a nice guy, Harry, but that's a pretty big sign. I'd appreciate it if you'd take it down."

"No, it's staying up."

The next day the captain came back. "Look, I'm the precinct captain. Is there anything wrong, any problem, anything I can help you with?" Harry said no. "Then why don't you take it down. You know how this looks in my job." Harry wouldn't budge. The sign stayed up. On the third day, the city building inspectors came. The plumbing improvements alone cost Harry $2,100.

Source: From *Boss: Richard J. Daley of Chicago* by Mike Royko, Copyright © 1971 by Mike Royko. Used by permission of Sutton Signet, an imprint of New American Library, a division of Penguin Books USA Inc.

---

interest groups with issues before their committees. They then spread the wealth to more junior party members of their committees.

Recent White Houses have been accused of using their young campaign staff to form modern political machines. Labeled a *permanent campaign,* many of the media advisers and organizers who shaped the president's march to the White House found jobs in the party's national committee. But now they pushed for the president's budget and legislative packages and, ultimately, his reelection. Obama added a new wrinkle to this model in forming Organizing for America (OFA) within the Democratic National Committee. OFA relies on a 13 million-strong e-mail list, calls volunteers to go door to door, and mobilizes grassroots support through the Internet,—all techniques that are used because they worked in the election. (See "Triple O: Obama's Online Operation".)

American Party Structure

Picture the American party structure as a pyramid. Local political organizations or clubs are at the bottom, county committees are above them, and state committees are above the county. (See Figure 7.3.) The

FIGURE 7.3
Typical State Party Organization.

national committee of each party is over them all with the national conventions the ultimate elected authority. The strength of the party, which had traditionally been at the bottom, has now gravitated toward the top.

As a result of the welfare, civil service, and primary election reforms, most local parties have few resources with which to maintain a strong organization. Local parties range from virtual disorganization to still-powerful operations, with most parties falling closer to the pole of disarray. In much of the United States, a handful of officials meet occasionally to carry out the essential affairs needed to keep the party going. The party revives only around elections to support candidates selected by their own efforts.

What do the party's officers do in nonelection years? Their duties primarily depend on whether they are the *in-party* or the *out-party*. The party that is out of office tries to show that it is still alive by operating booths at fairs and issuing press releases. However, political activity takes money, which out-parties have difficulty raising without the "clout" of a member in a powerful public office. Systems for collecting regular contributions have been only modestly successful. State parties typically sponsor "Jefferson-Jackson Day" dinners (Democrats) or "Lincoln Day" dinners (Republicans). The current Republican National Committee chairman, Michael Steele, has emphasized decentralizing the party and putting funds into grassroots activities. But as the minority party the RNC's $300 million annual budget was going largely to just keeping staff hired and party offices operational.

One would guess that the in-party—the party with more of its own members in important government positions—has more power than the out-party. This ain't necessarily so. It is the public official, rather than the party, who actually exercises the power of the office. The official uses the party organization, rather than vice versa. For example, a governor usually names the state party chairperson, who serves as a voice of the governor. When George W. Bush was president the national Republican party became centralized under White House control and used as an instrument for promoting his policies.

State parties are generally stronger than local parties because of their connection to the national party. They have a professional staff of several people hired from funds supplied by the national party. Paralleling the national structure, there is a state committee and a chairperson, all chosen by election or state convention. The committee's ability to select party nominees for state or national offices is severely limited by primaries. The state party may channel funds from the wealthy campaigns of incumbents into those of new, promising candidates. This builds party loyalty. Patronage, ranging from placing a traffic light to awarding a building contract, helps grease the wheels of state party activities.

National Party Organization

Historically the local party was the closest link to the voter. Party workers in the community would turn out the vote and deliver needed services, like that traffic light, to supporters. In recent years the increased reliance on modern campaign technology (such as direct mail, phone banks, the Internet, and media ads) has blended with the use of local volunteers going door-to-door, often with handheld computers. The management of these canvassers and other party functions have been centralized and placed in the hands of professionals in the national organization and outside consultants, known as "hired guns." These efforts have complemented the campaigns run by the staffs of well-financed candidates.

Each party is officially governed by its *national committee.* The national committee consists of representatives chosen from each state party organization and various other party groups. The committee is led by the *chairperson,* who is often unofficially chosen by the party's presidential nominee every four years, but is formally elected by the national committee. The selection of the current chairmen of the two parties illustrates the difference that control of the White House makes. The chair of the Democratic National Committee (DNC), Virginia Governor Tim Kaine was picked by President Obama in January 2009. The chair of the Republican National Committee (RNC), Michael Steele, ran for the office against four other men, and after six rounds of balloting was elected by 168 members of the central committee.

Under these authorities is the party's *professional staff.* These professionals have gained power through their understanding of the modern technology of campaigning and the complicated laws overseeing how money is raised and spent. The Republican staff has been larger than the Democrats because the Democrats contract out much of their work, such as direct-mail fundraising, to campaign consultants. In both fundraising and organization—until the Democrats' recent electoral successes—the Republicans had done a better job of strengthening their party than the Democrats.

Fundraising

There are two things that are important in politics. The first is money and I can't remember what the second one is.

—*Mark Hanna, Republican boss, 1895*

In the 2008 elections the two parties and their committees raised record amounts of money, nearly a billion dollars each. Democratic party committees raised $961 million, and for the first time in memory had more than the Republicans, who were credited with $920 million. These amounts showed a considerable increase over 2004, when Democrats raised $731 million and Republicans outpaced them with $892 million. Both parties' totals reflected their large pool of small donors and their increasing use of online technology. The Democrats could more than match the GOP in the money race because of their control of Congress, their revitalized organization, and the popularity of their presidential candidate.

These funds were used to support the party's candidates through expensive campaign technology and, most importantly, advertising. Besides increasing party loyalty among their candidates, the funds were spent on media and mail campaigns to reach and register potential voters. Throughout most of the last decade the Democrats have been the majority party, but the Republicans have had the advantage in money and technology. That seems to have changed with Democrats now dominating across the board. The power of both national committees is likely to increase as the formerly weak parties use these funds to strengthen their central organizations. (See "Money Talks, Nobody Walks.")

Money Talks, Nobody Walks

By providing a back door for wealthy interests, campaign money has been involved in many political scandals. One that emerged a few years ago involved an aggressive businessman, Charles H. Keating Jr., and five senators of both parties.

These "Keating Five" had attempted to intervene with the Federal Home Loan Bank Board to protect Lincoln Savings and Loan from regulatory penalties. Mr. Keating was the bank's owner and, not accidentally, had contributed over $1.3 million to the five senators' campaigns. Each of the senators claimed the intervention amounted to constituent service because Lincoln S&L had assets in their states. The S&L failed anyway, costing taxpayers some $2 billion in deposit insurance costs. Mr. Keating ended up in jail.

Afterward Keating himself raised and answered the question "whether my financial support in any way influenced several political figures to take up my cause. I want to say in the most forceful way I can, I certainly hope so."

President Obama's election victory was aided by his own campaign's fundraising operation. Apart from his party's efforts, Obama broke the record for most money raised by a presidential candidate—some $745 million versus John McCain's $368 million. Obama's campaign relied on both bigger donors and smaller donors nearly equally, and pulled in donations largely over the Internet. (See Case study: "Triple O: Obama's Online Operation.") After becoming his party's nominee Obama declined public financing in the general election and the spending limits that came with it. He became the first major-party candidate since the system was created to reject public money in the general election. Obama also didn't accept government *matching funds* for the primaries, which give qualifying presidential candidates a dollar for dollar match as long as they obey spending limits. Other candidates for their party's nomination (including Bush and Kerry in 2004) had rejected these matching funds. But Obama's rejection of general election funds may mean the end of the reforms that attempted to restrict private money in electing a president. (See Table 7.2.)

The National Convention

Much of the public attention the party receives comes at its *national convention.* Held during the summer before the presidential election, the national convention is attended by delegates chosen by the

TABLE 7.2 A CONTINUING CLIMB		

PARTY FUNDRAISING FOR ELECTION CYCLES (IN MILLIONS)

	2000	2004	2008
Democrats	$520	$731	$961
Republicans	$716	$893	$920

PRESIDENTIAL CANDIDATES' FUNDRAISING

SEPARATE FROM THE PARTIES, THE CANDIDATES THEMSELVES HAVE INCREASED THEIR
FUNDRAISING OVER THE PAST THREE PRESIDENTIAL CYCLES (IN MILLIONS):

	2000 (GORE V. BUSH)	2004 (KERRY V. BUSH)	2008 (OBAMA V. MCCAIN)
Democrats	$133	$328	$745
Republicans	$193	$367	$368

Source: http://www.opensecrets.org/pres08/index.php; http://www.opensecrets.org/parties/
index.php?cmte=&cycle=2008;

state parties. In late summer of 2008, the Republican convention in
Minneapolis had 2,380 delegates, while the earlier Democratic convention in Denver had 4,419. The delegates to the convention adopt
a platform, elect the party's presidential nominee, and act as the
party's highest governing body assembled every four years.

The *party platform* actually is written by a platform committee and
then approved by the convention. In the document, the party declares
its—or more to the point its presidential candidate's—views and promises on many issues. If the party is in power, the platform will boast of
the party's achievements. If the party is out of power, the platform will
criticize the policies of the incumbent. The platform will emphasize
the party's differences with the other major party and minimize the divisions within the party. Since the goal of the platform is to win elections, it may fudge on controversial issues.

Frequently, groups of convention delegates will organize into factions in order to press for statements to be included in the platform
representing their minority political views. In 2000 a group of women
at the Republican national convention pressed unsuccessfully for
planks (parts of the platform) supporting abortion rights. Platforms are
important in reaching compromises among groups within the party before the election. Party platforms are surprisingly accurate in predicting what a president will actually try to do when in office.

Early in the 1970s—beginning with the Democrats trying to recover
popularity from their disastrous 1968 convention in Chicago—party

reforms led to greater popular participation in the nominating process. Until these reforms, about 40 percent of convention delegates were chosen in states with *presidential primaries*—elections usually limited to registered voters from that one party. The rest were chosen by *caucuses*—party meetings dominated by party leaders and active members. Since then, 70 percent of delegates have been chosen by voters supporting candidates in primary elections.

The names of the candidates for president are placed in nomination toward the end of the convention. A roll-call vote of the delegates is then taken. The final party nominee for the office of president is elected by a simple majority vote. In 1924, the Democratic convention took 103 ballots before it was able to reach a majority decision. In recent decades the presidential nominee has been named on the first ballot, reflecting the votes in the state primaries and caucuses. Conventions today can be described as *approving* or *ratifying* the candidate selected by the party voters. The delegates, who are mostly pledged to a candidate, do not make the choice themselves.

The presidential nominee chooses a vice presidential running mate who is then formally approved by the convention. A main goal has been to *balance the ticket*. Dick Cheney's long public service was seen in 2000 as compensating for George W. Bush's lack of government experience. The vice presidential choice may be a popular competitor of the nominee from the primaries, as was John Edwards when John Kerry chose him in 2004. Arkansan Bill Clinton's 1992 choice of Senator Al Gore from the neighboring state of Tennessee was unusual in putting two southerners on the ticket, but reinforced the campaign's image of youth and change. The 2008 vice presidential choices of both parties were attempts to bolster the nominees. Joe Biden was seen as a party regular with long service in the Senate, a somewhat reassuring contrast to the younger, less experienced nominee. Sarah Palin, on the other hand, was a young, first-term female governor of Alaska who, it was hoped, could light a fire among the GOP's social conservative base notably indifferent to John McCain's campaign.

The national convention is the exciting starting gate for the fall presidential campaign. That is why Barack Obama gave his acceptance speech outdoors in front of a cheering crowd of 84,000 people in an NFL stadium, on a stage built to resemble the White House. Stevie Wonder sang as 24 American flags provided a patriotic backdrop. The nominee's speech set a convention record by attracting 38 million viewers watching on 10 networks, marking a successful media launch of his general election campaign.

View from the Outside: The Two-Party System

Despite the occasional calls for a third political party, the United States retains a *two-party system,* in which two parties dominate national politics. In a *one-party system,* a single party monopolizes the organization of power and the positions of authority. In a *multiparty system,* more than two political parties compete for power and elected offices.

From the Civil War until at least the election of Dwight D. Eisenhower to the presidency in 1952, the 11 southern states of the Civil War Confederacy had virtual one-party systems. These states were so heavily Democratic that the Republicans were a permanent minority. The important electoral contests took place in the primaries, where blacks were excluded, and where factions within the party competed like separate parties. Multiparty systems also have existed in the United States. When former wrestler Jesse Ventura (loosely connected to the Reform party) was elected governor in 1998, Minnesota was said to have a three-party system, or did until he left his party and office in 2003.

Causes of the Two-Party System

There are four main reasons for the continued dominance of two parties in the United States. One is the *historic dualism* of American political conflicts. The first major political division among Americans was dual, or two sided, between Federalists and Anti-Federalists over adopting the constitution. It is said that this original two-sided battle established the two-party tradition in this country. This dominance is more than just tradition. It has been reinforced by state laws passed by legislators from these two parties that confront third parties with high barriers to qualify for a place on the ballot.

The second reason is the *moderate views of the American voter.* Even with the recent rise of strong partisanship in both political parties, American politics tends toward the center. Socialist parties on the left or conservative ones on the right have had a difficult time winning support. Americans may be moderate because their party system forces them to choose between two traditionally moderate parties, or American parties may be moderate because Americans do not want to make more extreme political choices. As with the chicken and the egg, it is tough to know which came first.

Third, the *structure of the electoral system* encourages two-party dominance. We elect one representative at a time from each district (or state) to Congress, which is called election by *single-member districts.* The winning candidate is the one who gets the most votes, or a *plurality.* (A majority of votes means more than 50 percent of the votes cast; as mentioned earlier, a plurality simply means more votes than anyone else.) Similarly, in the fall presidential elections, the party with a plurality in a state gets all the electoral votes of that state. This system makes it difficult for minor-party candidates to win elections, and without election victories, parties fade fast.

Many European countries with multiparty systems elect representatives by *proportional representation.* Each district has more than one representative, and each party that receives a certain number of votes gets to send a proportionate number of representatives to the legislature. For example, in a single-member district a minor party that received 10 percent of the vote would not be able to send its candidate to Congress. In a multimember district the size of 10 congressional districts, however, that 10 percent of the vote would mean that 1 out of 10 representatives sent from the district would be a minor-party member. In Europe and elsewhere, this has preserved radical parties holding views challenging mainstream opinion.

Finally, the Democratic and Republican parties continue to dominate national politics because they are flexible enough to *adopt some of the programs proposed by third parties,* and thus win over third-party supporters. The Socialist party in America, even during its strongest period, always had difficulty achieving national support partly because the Democrats were able to *co-opt,* or win over, most organized unions with pro-labor economic programs. The Republican party lured voters away from Alabama Governor George Wallace's American Independent Party by stressing law and order and ignoring civil rights in its 1968 presidential campaign. After seeing the disastrous results for Democrats of Ralph Nader running in 2000, the 2004 Democratic presidential candidate John Kerry made clear his support for at least the populist themes of Nader's positions.

For all these historical and structural reasons, the odds are against either the emergence of a stable third party or an independent candidate being elected president. Operating as an umbrella over the broad political center, the two-party system has kept radical factions from winning power. This has meant that dissenting opinions traditionally received little consideration from voters, and kept the two parties from taking extreme positions. It also meant that there was little room for third parties, except at the fringe of the political arena.

But do the Two Parties Have a Future?

And yet neither party can claim to be beloved by public opinion. Before Obama no Democratic presidential candidate had won a majority of the votes since 1976. The rise of conservatism led to the popular

rejection of the Democratic party's core ideology—that government could be an effective instrument to improve the lives of working people. As seen in the harsh debate over health care reform, large parts of the public remain more worried about big government's flaws than hopeful of its solutions.

The new president benefited from simply being new. Barack Obama was praised as the nation's first twenty-first-century president, the first post-partisan, Independent, post-American, post-racial president; and therefore the new Lincoln, the new Kennedy, even a new, if inside-out, Reagan. He spoke about building a grand coalition that could lead a future majority-minority country. Yet as centrist as his words were, Obama still had to retain the backing of his party's liberal base while keeping their expectations realistic. If those political tasks weren't daunting enough there were inherited messes to deal with such as the global economic meltdown, wars in Afghanistan and Iraq, record deficits, climate warming, energy dependence, millions without health care, immigration, and so on. Even those unwilling to support the president might feel some sympathy.

Republicans faced their own dilemmas. A Bush administration widely regarded as long on arrogance and short on competence left behind a shell-shocked party. The Republicans' conservative base seemed to be shrinking, and the appeal to national security fears was no longer shrewd enough to help in regaining power. An internal tug of war focused over which direction the party should head. The traditionalists saw GOP setbacks as just desserts for having betrayed bedrock conservative principles and called for more faith, more commitment, and more orthodoxy in a stronger, if narrower, party. The reformers spoke of building a moderate "Big Tent" of ideas that would welcome growing groups like the young, the suburban, the minorities, and the college-educated, to which social conservatism no longer appealed. The party's leadership vacuum deferred any agreement on strategies, other than a unified opposition to Democratic proposals.

Actually the two parties remain close in popular support. The pragmatic voters whose decisions swing elections are neither extreme nor particularly partisan in their political beliefs. The Democrats have revived less because of their own agenda than because of a moderate consensus that the incumbent Republicans had stretched their partisanship and competence, as well as America's military, about as far as they could reach. These voters are still holding the two parties to account. Whatever may be new about the current party in power—new generation, new ideas, new technologies—it will still be judged by a decisive band of voters in the old way: on its performance in office.

CASE STUDY

Triple O—Obama's Online Operation

No part of Barack Obama's successful campaign for election got more praise than his use of the Internet. Some called it decisive in his primary victory over Hillary Clinton, and it certainly helped beat John McCain in the general election. Others thought that his use of the Internet changed American politics in the same way John Kennedy's use of television did in 1960. Joe Trippi, one of the pioneers of the Internet in Governor Howard Dean's 2004 campaign, said that they were the Wright brothers at Kitty Hawk, while Obama's team was the Apollo project putting a man on the moon.

The campaign's online achievements are real enough.

THE BIG MO: INTERNET MOBILIZING

Remember that the Obama campaign started from scratch in early 2007 with few resources and little name recognition. The Internet offered low-cost tools to find core supporters and put them on the ground before any other campaign. Using his

CHANGE WE BELIEVE IN...

oratory, his compelling personal history, and his opposition to the war in Iraq, Obama attracted young people to his campaign. By organizing early in states ignored by his rivals, Obama would win key caucus states where relatively few people turned out to vote in these meetings. And the Internet helped.

In February 2007 a networking site, MyBarackObama.com, was launched. It eventually created 2 million profiles, 35,000 volunteer groups, and 200,000 offline events. Obama sites were started on other social networks, and Obama fan groups grew to 3.2 million supporters. Obamaniacs could create their own blogs, get call lists and scripts, and organize events. These contacts became data about supporters, allowing the campaign to use "cookies" to identify which other sites the user visited, and to shape specific pitches to the individual voter.

Texting proved critical in growing the campaign's database. Texts were sent collecting names and e-mail addresses, asking users to help. One breakthrough event occurred in December 2007 at a rally of 30,000 people in South Carolina, when the crowd was asked to take out their cell phones and text "SC" to 62262, a code that spells "Obama." In the following weeks the campaign used these numbers to send texts asking people to make phone calls, to volunteer, and to vote in the January primary. Obama won the state primary by 28 points.

BYPASSING THE MEDIA

"I got a crush on Obama" sang the seductive "Obama Girl" in June 2007. Her YouTube video was a sensation, eventually getting 12 million views. It was also the first example of the campaign taking advantage of the Web for free advertising. By election day the campaign's YouTube channel had produced 1,800 videos. Joe Trippi, by then working for the campaign, estimated that these had been watched for 14.5 million hours, which if broadcast on TV would have cost $47 million. The Obama campaign paid almost nothing.

The Web allowed the campaign to leapfrog the traditional media. Whether it was rebutting his opponents' attacks or explaining why he wasn't taking public financing in the general election, Obama used his own videos on YouTube to reach millions of supporters, unfiltered by the news media. For months the campaign's most popular video was Obama's 37-minute speech on race following the public controversy over the fiery remarks of his former pastor Reverend Wright. The video was seen by 7 million people—a striking example of how the Internet let people listen immediately, completely and repeatedly, to the candidate's own words in response to attacks.

INTERNET FUNDRAISING

Obama raised more money than any presidential candidate in history. Of the $750 million he raised some $500 million came online, 12 times as much as the last Democratic candidate John Kerry raised through the Internet. The immediacy of the Internet allowed the campaign access to money in times of crisis, such as the $10 million collected after Governor Sarah Palin spoke at the Republican convention. While small donors were an important part of Obama's fundraising—about 26 percent contributed $200 or less—almost half were sending in $1,000 or more. Some 3 million donors contributed, with many repeats.

An important change these online donations brought is that they bypassed the lobbyists and special interests whose organized fundraisers usually provided the bulk of funds for presidential candidates. They allowed the candidate to (over)state during the campaign, "I don't take a dime of their [lobbyist] money, and when I am president they won't find a job in my White House."

A WIRED PRESIDENCY?

The Internet followed the president to Washington. In living up to his pledge to conduct the most accessible and transparent administration ever, Obama launched a new website, Change.gov. Soon his staff posted a short video posing the question: "What worries you most about the health care system in our country?" It then rated the popularity of the responses. In March 2009 Obama held an "online town hall" streamed live with a 36-hour window for submitting questions and voting on preferences. Some 104,000 questions were submitted with 3.6 million votes for a favorite. A surprising number were about legalizing marijuana, part of an organized campaign. Before answering "no" to legalization, Obama joked, "I don't know what this says about the online audience."

Whether the president could maintain the intense support of his online supporters wasn't clear. An August 15, 2009, headline in The New York Times read "Health Debate Fails to Ignite Obama's Web" and quoted an Iowa member of Organizing for America—the Democrats' grass roots organization—saying that the enthusiasm of the election year wasn't there. This may reveal a longer term problem of keeping supporters mobilized.

CONCLUSION

There is no denying the success of Barack Obama's campaign in using the Internet. As an articulate candidate with an attractive message of change, he skillfully merged decentralized volunteer groups under a centralized campaign. But his victory was not the same as a victory for the Internet as an independent political force. In fact "netroot" bloggers and activists—like MoveOn.org and Daily Kos—with their in-your-face partisanship and anti-establishment style were mostly ignored by the campaign. These bloggers, on issues like wiretapping and prosecuting Bush officials for using torture, were unable to shape the direction of the election. The Obama campaign used the techniques of the Internet but had no interest in working with independent bloggers who might challenge their control over messages.

The Obama campaign showed how the Internet could change politics, but it also showed how politics could change the Internet.

Source: From Steven Hill, "The World Wide Webbed: The Obama Campaign's Masterful Use of the Internet," New America Foundation, April 8, 2009; Jose Antonio Vargas, "Obama's Wide Web," The Washington Post, August 20, 2008. Henry Farrell, "Do the Netroots Matter?" The American Prospect, July/August 2009.

WRAP-UP

Voters are the most numerous and most representative players in the political game. Through elections voters choose who is to run the government, and legitimate that choice. Many factors, like political socialization, party membership, religion, race, and class, influence how people vote or even *if* they vote. While participation in politics takes place outside of voting, nonvoting and mistrust of Washington have in the past posed serious questions about the representative nature of a democracy. Recent elections have brought more people to the polls, especially the young.

The political parties provide a major link between voters and elected officials. Historically the parties have evolved into a two-party system, with the Democrats and Republicans dominating elections for 150 years. Though the national parties in the past have been weakly organized, recent reforms have strengthened the national organizations. Candidates organize their own campaigns to compete for their party's presidential nomination. They jump into a lengthy process of state caucuses and primaries, media debates, fundraising, and finally nominating conventions, where the two major parties put their labels on candidates to run in the general election in the fall. These candidates may also make creative use of the Internet as seen in Barack Obama's successful 2008 campaign.

The major parties have been subjected to internal polarizing forces pushing them to extremes. At the same time, nonparty public opinion seemed largely indifferent to the ideas dominating the parties' agendas. However, both parties still have a few cards left to play, as seen in the excitement generated around the 2008 elections. This flexibility has always been critical to the survival of the two-party system. American parties have adapted to the demands of newly mobilized groups, whether feminists or fundamentalists, blacks or bloggers. A willingness to honestly grapple with the pressing national issues of the day, both at home and abroad, will allow them to continue as vital links between people and their government. Not to do so will lead to questioning their role in the political game, and to the continuing apathy of citizens turned off by partisan battles.

THOUGHT QUESTIONS

1. If you voted in the last election, what influenced the way you voted? Can you relate your political views to your family, religion, or class background?
2. If you did not vote, what led you not to vote? What would motivate you to vote in the future? Do you participate in politics even if you do not vote?
3. How have the Internet and modern technology connected people to the campaigns of elected officials? What has been gained and what has been lost, compared to traditional methods?
4. How important is money in elections? Would you do anything to change the role of money in campaigns?
5. Have recent election campaigns become nastier and more partisan? Did anything you learn from a recent campaign change your vote?

SUGGESTED READINGS

Douthat, Ross, and Reihan Salam. *Grand New Party*. New York: Doubleday, 2008.
    An effort to reform and rescue the Republican party from the despair following Bush and election disasters.
Frank, Thomas. *What's the Matter with Kansas?* New York: Metropolitan Books, 2004.
    Subtitled, "How Conservatives Won the Heart of America," this book by a liberal Kansan, describes in personal terms how his state journeyed from economic populism to social conservatism.
Judis, John B., and Ruy Teixeira. *The Emerging Democratic Majority*. New York: Simon & Schuster, 2004. Pb.
    A prophecy with hard data predicts the dawn of a new era of "progressive centrism" fueled by the fastest-growing areas of the country.

Lakoff, George. *Don't Think of an Elephant: Know Your Values and Frame the Debate*. Vermont: Chelsea Green Publishing, 2004. Pb.

> A Berkeley professor advises liberals on how to talk to plain folks and why conservatives are so good at it.

Overton, Spencer. *Stealing Democracy: The New Politics of Voter Suppression*. New York: W. W. Norton, 2006. Pb.

> Approachable stories of how the right to vote doesn't always overcome the obstacles put in the way of fair elections.

Schudson, Michael. *The Good Citizen*. Cambridge, MA: Harvard University Press, 1998. Pb.

> A well-written history of Americans' participation in public affairs with some surprisingly positive conclusions about the state of modern citizenship.

Stimson, James A. *Tides of Consent: How Public Opinion Shapes American Politics*. Cambridge, United Kingdom: Cambridge University, 2004. Pb.

> How a very small part of public opinion democratically and pragmatically decides elections in America.

Todd, Chuck, and Sheldon Gawiser. *How Barack Obama Won*. New York: Knopf, 2009. Pb.

> A state-by-state guide by the NBC TV journalist that breezes through the facts and figures of the most recent presidential election.

CHAPTER 8

Interest Groups
and the Media

Our last two players—interest groups and the media—are blamed for much of what is wrong in the American political game. "Special interests" are viewed as the rich and powerful pulling the strings of public officials behind the scenes. Media, more visibly, are seen distorting politics by being too simplistic, too negative, too liberal, or too conservative, depending on one's leanings. On the other hand, political scientists often conclude that these two players are popular scapegoats: the power they have is overrated, the evil they do overstated. Whatever conclusions we reach, both are central to understanding today's politics.

The Constitution has little to say about either. The First Amendment guarantees freedom of the press and the right "to petition the Government for a redress of grievances," which protects these players briefly if profoundly. The profound part is that both interest groups and media provide legitimate access to the government. Interest groups offer tools for people with common concerns to bring their views to the attention of those in power. The media are two-way communications links (and participants as well) by which people keep informed about government, and vice versa. As instruments of power, the two change the political game they play. Who they are, what they do, and how interest groups and media are shaped by politics are central to what follows.

Interest Groups

In his famous study *Democracy in America* in 1835, Alexis de Tocqueville, was impressed that Americans constantly joined all kinds of groups. The Frenchman thought these "associations" were essential to why democracy worked in the United States. The groups kept a balance between the state and the individual, offering a buffer between a large powerful government and small powerless individuals. By doing this they preserved individuals' rights. As he put it,

> An association for political, commercial or manufacturing purposes, or even for those of science and literature, is a powerful and enlightened member of the community . . . which, by defending its own rights against the encroachments of government, saves the common liberties of the country.

Tocqueville's endorsement of the political importance of diverse group interests made him the father of what would later be called pluralism (see Chapter 9).

Though Tocqueville included local government when he wrote about associations, today we speak of *interest groups* as people organized to pursue a common interest by applying pressure on the political process. In the last chapter, we saw that American parties are not structured very well for representing specific interests. Interest groups help fill this gap.

Our parties and the electoral system are organized by geography. Senators and representatives represent us on the basis of the state or the district in which we live. But within one region there are different group interests. Members of various religions, races, incomes, or economic associations may have important political concerns. Interest groups give Americans with common causes a way to express their views to decision makers. While interest groups may try to influence elections, unlike parties they do not compete for public office. Candidates may be sympathetic to a certain interest, or even be a member of that group, but they will not run for election representing that group.

Interest groups usually are more tightly organized than political parties. They are financed through contributions and/or dues paid by members. Organizers communicate with members through newsletters, e-mails, and conferences. Union members, for example, are in regular contact with their leadership, who inform them about political activities, policies, and candidates they are expected to support.

Types of Interest Groups

The most important groupings are economic interests, including business, professional, labor, and agricultural. James Madison, in *The Federalist Papers* No. 10, expressed the fear that if people united on the basis of economic interests, all the have-nots in society would take control of the government. This clearly has not happened. The most influential groups generally, though not always, spend the most money. *Business groups* have a common interest in making profits, which also involves supporting the markets that makes profits possible. The Chamber of Commerce, the National Association of Manufacturers, and the National Small Business Association are well-known business groups. Powerful companies, like Exxon and General Electric, often act as interest groups by themselves.

Business groups are not always united on one side of an issue. Competitors within an industry extend their rivalries to the political arena. Just recently Microsoft lobbied the Justice Department to look into Google's Book Search project and was reported to hold "screw Google" meetings in Washington to plot strategy for getting regulators to look at their competitor's business. Railroads and truckers regularly battle over transportation policies. Even when a political conflict is viewed as business opposing, say, environmentalists, a closer look will reveal business groups on both sides of the issue. The battle over health care reform saw Wal-Mart favoring the requirement that businesses must provide health insurance to employees, while the National Federation of Independent Business opposed this coverage. Most contested major issues show splits in the business community.

Professional groups include the American Medical Association, the National Association of Realtors, and the American Bar Association, all of which have powerful lobbies in Washington. *Labor unions,* like the International Brotherhood of Teamsters and the unions that make up the American Federation of Labor and the Congress of Industrial Organizations (AFL-CIO), are the most important financial supporters of the Democratic party. In many urban Democratic districts, election day will find the local labor unions and the local party practically merging to turn out voters. Labor leaders, who tend to stay in power longer than most politicians, are powerful political figures in their own right. Although there have been recent signs of revival, the influence of organized labor has declined, along with its membership, over the last 50 years.

Agricultural interests have a long history of influential lobbying. The American Farm Bureau Federation, the National Farmers Union, and the National Grange are powerful groups in Washington. Specialized groups, like the Associated Milk Producers, Inc. (AMP), strongly lobby farm legislation.

Some interest groups are organized around ethnic, social, or political concerns. Groups like the National Association for the Advancement of Colored People (NAACP) and the Urban League represent constituencies within the black community in national forums. The American Israel Public Affairs Committee (AIPAC) is a strong advocate of close ties with Israel and attempts to influence American foreign policies in the Middle East. The American Association of Retired Persons (AARP) may be the most powerful lobby in Washington; it represents 40 million dues-paying members over the age of 50 on the many issues of interest to them.

Interest groups may organize people sharing similar social or political ideas. The Sierra Club lobbies in Washington to protect the environment but is considered more moderate than Greenpeace, a group of activists who take direct action to oppose issues like the clear-cutting of old-growth forests. People for the Ethical Treatment of Animals (PETA) has 2 million members who fund the nonprofit corporation that fights factory farming and animal testing. The National Taxpayers Union (NTU) advocates for taxpayers by favoring a Flat Tax and opposing the current income tax system.

Lobbying

Lobbying is when individuals or interest groups pressure the government to act in their favor. Interest groups today maintain professional staffs of lobbyists or hire consulting firms in Washington, D.C., to promote their concerns. These lobbyists include former members of Congress or the executive branch who are knowledgeable in a particular area and personally connected to decision makers. When Senator Phil Gramm of Texas retired from the Senate in 2003, he joined the Wall Street firm of UBS Warburg for an annual salary of over $1 million. The former chairman of the Senate Banking committee had coauthored a bill in 1999 that permitted banks to merge with securities firms, a law

that allowed UBS to purchase a brokerage for $12 billion. Gramm's transition to Wall Street barely caused a ripple in Washington, where getting a job from firms that once lobbied you is a common practice. (See "Is There Life After Congress?")

Almost 15,000 lobbyists spent $3.3 billion lobbying Congress and federal agencies in 2008. While lobbyists are required to register and

Is There Life After Congress?

Lobbyists had no bigger fight in the 111th Congress than Health Care Reform. Leading the battle to make sure that reform didn't hurt their business were the nation's largest insurers, hospitals and medical groups who spent $1.4 million A DAY lobbying Congress. Working for them as lobbyists were 350 former members of Congress and government staff members. Many of them had worked on the committees that now had to write a new health care law for the country. These former colleagues were there to make sure that Congress didn't endanger health care interests, which make up one-sixth of the U.S. economy.

Despite various reforms large numbers of congressmen and staff use their government positions as a stepping stone to higher paying jobs as lobbyists. The non-partisan Public Citizen found that half the senators and 42% of House members became lobbyists when they left Congress. Some feared that public service had become not a goal, but a revolving door to riches in the private sector.

Source: The Washington Post, July 6, 2009.

are limited to a $100 cap in gifts to public officials, the disclosure rules governing lobbying are not considered strict. The Center for Public Integrity took a survey of state lobbying laws and found that only three states had lobby disclosure rules that were as weak as those applying to lobbying Congress. The new Democratic majority promised that their ethics reforms would bring real transparency to lobbying money in Washington.

During his presidential campaign, Barack Obama vowed that lobbyists "won't find a job in my White House." After the election this prohibition moderated a bit. In November 2008 Obama announced that he would allow lobbyists on his transition team as long as they worked on issues unrelated to their lobbying. The transition staff was barred from lobbying the administration for one year afterward, a harsher restriction than the usual transition rules. Ultimately Obama appointed several lobbyists to his administration. According to the *National Journal* about 11 percent of the president's top staff has lobbied within the past five years for organizations ranging from Goldman Sachs to Mothers Against Drunk Driving (MADD).

Direct lobbying usually takes place quietly in congressional committees and executive bureaucracies. Although lobbying the legislature gets most of the publicity, lobbyists devote more attention to executive agencies in influencing their regulations. It is said that the real decisions of government are made among lobbyists, executive bureaucrats, and congressional committees staff—forming flexible, often temporary *issue networks.* Lobbyists provide information about their clients to committees and bureaucracies. They argue their position with congressional staffers, or have their powerful industries or influential grassroots supporters speak directly with decision makers. Knowledge of the issues, personal contacts, and frequent attendance at campaign fundraisers place lobbyists in a position to be heard. (See "The Five Commandments of Lobbying.")

Indirect lobbying may involve massive letter-writing that looks as if each letter has been individually written. Modern phone technologies allow lobbying firms to contact sympathetic voters and connect them directly to their member's office. The Internet can produce a flood of e-mails. Fax attacks can clog a congressional office's lines. More subtle lobbying efforts involve "nonpolitical" public relations campaigns. Oil companies respond to criticism about oil spills with advertising showing their concern for the environment. Lumber companies do not discuss clear-cutting but instead show commercials of their employees planting trees. Op-eds, letters

The Five Commandments of Lobbying

In meeting with elected officials, lobbyists follow a set of "informal rules" helpful to anyone lobbying Congress:

1. *Demonstrate a constituent interest.* One of the best ways to ensure attention is to show the impact on the representative's voters.
2. *Be well informed.* Officials want information in return for the time and attention they give.
3. *Be balanced.* Compromise is inevitable in legislation. Lobbyists who present both sides leave the official with the impression that they have looked at all sides of the question and then arrived at a conclusion.
4. *Keep it short and sweet.* The challenge is to present the relevant information in the shortest time and in the most memorable way.
5. *Leave a written summary of the case.* It relieves officials of the necessity of taking notes and ensures that the correct information stays behind.

to the editor, and even columnists are sometimes funded by private interests.

Interest groups try to persuade other groups to join them in a *grassroots campaign.* They will form a *coalition* of different groups, often using a letterhead name, such as Americans for Free Trade, invented for the campaign. Using money from private interests, such as Japanese corporations opposing trade restrictions, the lobbyists managing the campaign try to give Congress the impression that much of the voting public supports their position. These campaigns mobilize local leaders from a member of congress's district, employees to write their member of Congress, and allied businesses to join the coalition. At other times, these efforts merely produce Washington's famed "smoke and mirrors"—the illusion of broad popular support for what is, in fact, a narrow interest group spending lots of money. Congress and the press seem to be getting better at telling the difference. (See Chart 8.1, "Lobbyists and their Spending.")

The essence of grassroots lobbying is voters contacting their representative or senator. This demonstrates intensity and broad popular support, reflects the issue's local impact in the member's home region, and reminds elected officials of the electoral pain that awaits a wrong decision. Personal lobbying of this kind often is applied to members of Congress while they are visiting their districts. Organizations with a

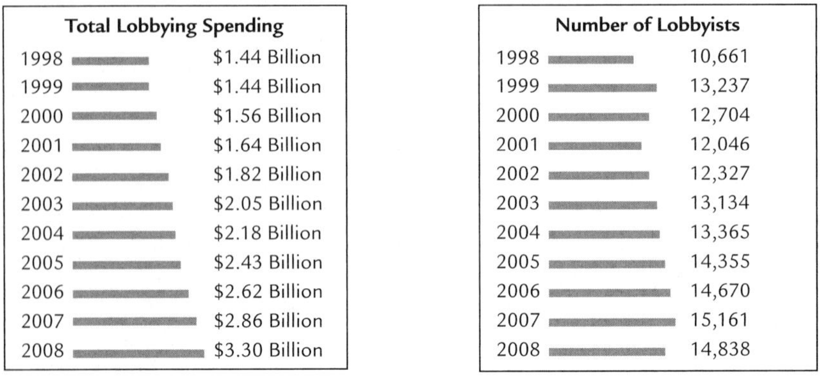

Total Lobbying Spending	
1998	$1.44 Billion
1999	$1.44 Billion
2000	$1.56 Billion
2001	$1.64 Billion
2002	$1.82 Billion
2003	$2.05 Billion
2004	$2.18 Billion
2005	$2.43 Billion
2006	$2.62 Billion
2007	$2.86 Billion
2008	$3.30 Billion

Number of Lobbyists	
1998	10,661
1999	13,237
2000	12,704
2001	12,046
2002	12,327
2003	13,134
2004	13,365
2005	14,355
2006	14,670
2007	15,161
2008	14,838

CHART 8.1
Money Spent on Lobbying (Does not include money spent on campaign contributions)
Source: http://www.opensecrets.org/lobby/index.php.

national membership, such as AARP and the National Rifle Association (NRA), can effectively lobby Congress just by contacting their association members. Single-issue groups like AIPAC and pro- and anti-abortion groups can use their members' intense feelings on narrow issues to influence legislators. These "passionate minorities" are usually the only voices members hear on a policy. Elected officials know that their position on one of these hot-button issues will directly affect these activists' votes, and their money.

Lobbying scandals are recurring Washington events that throw the usually quiet system of lobbying into a harsh public light. Much of the critical commentary about Washington's "business as usual" is well deserved. But the overwhelming number of lobbyists are not the fly-by-night wheeler-dealers that editorial cartoonists present in the newspapers. They are experts skilled in both substantive areas of public policy and the process of passing legislation. They often represent big business, but they also work for unions, environmentalists, local governments, human rights groups, and universities. They bring issues to the attention of busy legislators and their staffs, they publicize overlooked national problems, and they help outsiders navigate a complex, often unresponsive government. In a modern world of specialists, lobbyists specialize in influencing government decisions for their clients' benefit. They are neither the cause of most of our country's political problems nor the solution. Perhaps regrettably, they have become in twenty-first-century America, a needed tool of governing. (See "Lobbying, Corruption and Jack Abramoff.")

Lobbying, Corruption, and Jack Abramoff

On Friday the 13th of October 2006 Congressman Robert Ney, Republican of Ohio, pleaded guilty to performing official acts in exchange for campaign contributions, luxury vacations, and skybox sports tickets. Many of these gifts had come from Jack Abramoff, a lobbyist who had pleaded guilty earlier in the year to a host of illegal activities.

An ambitious dealmaker and former college Republican leader, Abramoff had used his friendships on the Hill to trample the norms of doing business in Washington. He gained notoriety by winning Native American tribes as clients at outrageous fees of $150,000 a month, and then getting state lawmakers to introduce laws that would scare these tribes into paying him even more to protect them. It also led other lobbyists to blow the whistle on him.

In the 2006 midterm elections, corruption by lobbyists became an issue. One Democratic ad ran: "When Washington special interests wine and dine [Congresswoman] Nancy Johnson, what do you think they talk about?" The punch line: "It probably isn't you." Lobbyists complained that such attacks were hypocritical. One wrote a letter to both parties saying, "If you think we're the biggest problem in the system, return our money." No one took up his offer.

Campaign Contributions

Money has been called the mother's milk of politics. Unlike milk, however, money in elections is combustible and controversial. By contributing money to a political campaign, interest groups can reward a politician who has supported them in the past and encourage support in the future. In the 2008 presidential election, financial support went overwhelmingly to the winning candidate, largely from law firms, universities, and investment bankers. The Democrats, despite  pleading poverty in the past, received millions in funding from labor unions and special-interest groups like trial lawyers. The Republicans were the recipients of money from corporations. However one should note that the organizations themselves did not donate. The money came from individuals and their families, as well as Political Action Committees (PACs). Money is hardly playing a reduced role in American elections. (See Table 8.1.)

TABLE 8.1 OBAMA'S TOP DONORS IN 2008	

The organizations themselves did not donate; rather the money came from the organization's PAC(s), its individual members or employees or owners, and those individuals' immediate families.

University of California	$1,564,490
Goldman Sachs	$ 994,795
Harvard University	$ 854,017
Microsoft Corp.	$ 833,617
Google Inc.	$ 803,436
Citigroup Inc.	$ 699,790
JPMorgan Chase & Co.	$ 695,132
Time Warner	$ 589,334
Sidley Austin LLP	$ 588,598
Stanford University	$ 586,557
National Amusements Inc.	$ 550,683
UBS AG	$ 543,219
Wilmerhale Llp.	$ 542,618
Skadden, Arps et. al	$ 530,839
IBM Corp.	$ 527,572

Source: http://www.opensecrets.org/pres08/contrib.php?cycle=2008&cid=N00009638; http://www.opensecrets.org/lobby/index.php.

What does this money buy? At the least, it buys *access*, or the right to talk to the elected official. A campaign contributor may say: "I don't want any special promise from you; all I want is the right to come and talk to you when I need to." This seemingly modest request is critical. Access is power. A former congressman offered this perspective:

> You have to make a choice. Who are you going to let in the door first? You get back from lunch. You've got fourteen phone messages on your desk. Thirteen of them are from constituents you've never heard of, and one of them is from a guy who just came to your fundraiser two weeks earlier and gave you $2,000. Which phone call are you going to return first?

As we saw in the last chapter, the money raised and spent in political campaigning has increased. Clearly this increase in funds has affected Congress. One representative remarked, "It is a simple fact of life that when big money enters the political arena, big obligations are entertained." There also may be relatively little that can be done to block the impact of money and the creative ways that campaigning politicians use to get it. As one lobbyist skeptically concluded, "Trying to cleanse the political system from the evils of money is like writing a law ordering teenagers not to think about sex. . . . You don't need a law, you need a lobotomy."

There is another side to the Washington money game. Most money is donated at the request of an elected official. With this comes the implicit, and sometimes explicit, threat that without the contribution, the donor will not get much help from the member of Congress or from the White House. Shortly before a recent election, a Republican leader met with lobbyists and told them to give to GOP candidates or they could expect their "two coldest years in Washington." One senator bluntly put it: "I've had people who contribute to my campaign, and they get access; the others get good government." Of course, giving money does not guarantee that the representative will vote the right way. A lobbyist who had just seen his bill voted down and was shortly thereafter approached for another contribution said, "It's almost like blackmail. They ask for money from you as they're screwing you to the wall."

One important change in the role of interest groups in elections has been the rise of *PACs (political action committees)*. PACs are organizations set up by private groups such as businesses or labor unions to influence the political process by raising funds from their members. These organizations are not new in American politics. Their model was created in 1955 when the newly formed AFL-CIO started the Committee on Political Education (COPE). Through its national and local units, COPE not only contributed money to pro-union candidates but also organized Get Out the Vote drives (GOTV) and sought to politically educate its members.

The big expansion in business PACs occurred in the late 1970s as an unexpected result of campaign finance reforms. These laws, backed by labor, put strict limits on individual donations and provided for public disclosure. Before this legislation, money could legally go into campaigns in large amounts as individual donations from wealthy corporate leaders. There was thus little need for business PACs.

The reforms backfired. Instead of reducing the influence of large contributors, the reforms increased them. Corporations and trade associations organized PACs that more effectively channeled their money and influence into campaigns than individuals had been able to do. The number of PACs mushroomed from 608 in 1975 to 4,611 by 2009. Although there are many more corporate and trade association PACs, and they give more money, labor unions have been closing the spending gap. (See Table 8.2.)

The amounts of money skyrocketed. In 1974 interest group donations to congressional candidates totaled $12 million. By the 2008 elections, PAC contributions reached $408 million for the two-year election cycle. Incumbents collect most of the PAC money. In the same 2008 election cycle, incumbents received $305 million, which was almost 80 percent of PAC contributions. Money also followed the majority party. In 1994 when Republicans won majorities in Congress, money from PACs started to flow toward them and away from the Democrats. In 2006 when the Democrats unexpectedly won a majority in

TABLE 8.2 TOP 12 PAC CONTRIBUTORS TO CANDIDATES, 2007–2008			
PAC Name	Total Amount	Dem. Pct.	Repub. Pct.
National Assn of Realtors	$4,020,900	58%	42%
Intl Brotherhood of Electrical Workers	$3,344,650	98%	2%
AT&T Inc	$3,108,200	47%	52%
American Bankers Assn	$2,918,143	43%	57%
National Beer Wholesalers Assn	$2,869,000	53%	47%
National Auto Dealers Assn	$2,860,000	34%	66%
International Assn of Fire Fighters	$2,734,900	77%	22%
Operating Engineers Union	$2,704,067	87%	13%
American Assn for Justice	$2,700,500	95%	4%
Laborers Union	$2,555,350	92%	8%
Honeywell International	$2,515,616	52%	48%
National Assn of Home Builders	$2,480,000	46%	54%

Source: www.opensecrets.org/pacs/toppacs.php?=C&cycle=2008&Pty=A.

both houses, PAC money still went to Republicans 57 percent to 43 percent. But by 2008 the PAC flows reversed, with 57 percent going to the majority Democrats and 43 percent to the GOP. PACs like winners.

The cost of winning has continued to increase. The average spent in winning a House seat in 2008 was $1.1 million. A Senate seat cost $6.5 million—47 percent more than it cost in 2002. These figures included safe seats where little money had to be spent by incumbents. Spending more money than an opponent did not guarantee victory. In 28 House seats, a candidate won despite spending less than their opponent. This happened twice in the Senate including in North Carolina, where the incumbent Elizabeth Dole spent $15.7 million but lost to Kay Hagan, who spent $6 million. The most expensive race in 2008 was the Minnesota Senate race, where Norm Coleman lost to Democrat Al Franken. Each of them spent a bit over $21 million.

Congressional efforts to reform overall campaign spending have proven unsuccessful. Members of congress simply refused to restrain their campaign spending to keep their jobs. The limits placed on contributions have also been overcome. PACs, restricted in what they can give to a candidate, have *bundled* contributions from their members. This means that 50 corporate executives from the same industry can give $3,000 each, which the PAC then bundles and gives to the candidate. Presto, there appears to be a $150,000 contribution from a single industry.

Nonprofit 527 groups, which are not allowed to coordinate with campaigns, were established to accept large, unregulated amounts to help presidential campaigns. In 2004 this allowed one man, billionaire George Soros, to contribute $27 million to try to defeat George W. Bush. These 527s played a smaller role in the 2008 presidential campaign than they did in 2004, with contributions totaling $202 million in 2008 and $426 million in 2004. (Soros only spent $5 million to defeat John McCain.) This was in part due to the fines some 527s received for campaign finance violations, and in part because candidates like Obama wanted to control the message of his campaign without interference from these independent supporters.

Early in 2010 a divided Supreme Court threw out limits on corporations' spending during election campaigns. In *Citizens United vs. Federal Election Commission* the Court ruled that reforms limiting independent spending on attack ads violated the First Amendment protections for political speech. Direct contributions to candidates and parties were still regulated and any group paying for a campaign commercial would have to publicly disclose its spending. Democrats were alarmed that the decision would increase the influence of wealthy interest groups who could now spend unlimited amounts of corporate money supporting or opposing candidates. Other analysts worried that parties and politicians would lose control over the messages dominating the election.

Do Group Interests Overwhelm the Public Interest?

"Politics: The conduct of public affairs for private advantage."

—*Ambrose Bierce*

The idea that interest groups and their lobbyists dominate American politics is widely accepted today. What the framers of the Constitution saw as many voices harmonized by the institutions of government has become to some a haggling marketplace where special interests negotiate laws, regulations, and the use of public money. Political power, especially that of corporations, has become a tool for avoiding laws you do not like and passing laws you do like. Whatever the public purposes proclaimed in the laws, just below the surface lies the real spirit of lobbying—"universalized ticket fixing."

Despite newspaper headlines to the contrary, political scientists have generally downplayed the influence of lobbyists. Many studies have found that lobbyists have little success in persuading members of Congress to change their minds. Even money, in the form of campaign contributions, can seldom be tracked down as motivating congressional votes. Lobbyists for their part have a human tendency to overstate their influence, to boast of their successes in order to attract more paying clients. But members' support for a major corporate employer in their state or for a tax break for senior citizens or for foreign aid to an ally may have little to do with the activities of lobbyists.

For lobbying influence to be effective on major policies, it needs to have public opinion on its side. Lobbyists gain support by presenting their narrow cause as consistent with a national concern. This link to public policies is very influential when it is done over a long period of time in hearings, personal contacts, and through constructing an attractive narrative. Its impact can be seen when gun owners make gun control a violation of civil liberties, or environmentalists make forest clear-cutting an issue of global warming, or opponents of health care expansion make the issue government intrusion into family life. At least as important, members of Congress must see the lobbyists' cause as helping their own career prospects, especially their chances for reelection.

There is little argument that the resources devoted to lobbying have rocketed. Just between 1961 and 1982, corporations with Washington, D.C., offices rose tenfold; between 1998 and 2008, spending on lobbying more than doubled, from $1.4 billion to $3.3 billion. With thousands of lobbyists now working in Washington, it would seem foolish to argue that they do not have an impact on American politics. They are mainly hired by wealthy interests to influence how public officials treat those interests. The leaders of these interest groups are not people who throw away their money on activities that produce no benefits for their corporations, unions, or trade associations. When compared to the relative decline in political parties, it seems fair to conclude that the major channel through which private interests influence American politics are lobbyists.

This rise in lobbying has increased demands on government. Corporate executives, veterans, farmers, realtors, doctors, retirees, and university administrators push their claims for the resources of government. As the benefits provided by government increase, more groups organize to protect what they have or to get more. This results in what has been called *hyperpluralism,* too many groups making too many demands on government. Groups demand benefits. These subsidies preserve the groups, which work to expand the resource flows, until at last government begins to choke. Government is paralyzed. There are too many special interests—and their lobbyists/lawyers/PR consultants—to overcome. Programs serving a general interest, such as the climate, get less support, whereas those helping narrow interests keep their hold on public resources—almost forever.

Average Washington deal making is not available to average American citizens. Reforms to reduce the influence of powerful interest groups have failed. We might quickly conclude that government is held hostage by narrow groups resisting all changes not benefiting them. Nonetheless, lobbyists have not yet rigged the entire game.

As seen in recent elections politicians still get elected on their political parties' platforms calling for broad changes. To win power political parties need the votes of a national coalition more influential in elections than Washington lobbyists. When Barack Obama told a campaign rally in December 2007, "I am running to tell the lobbyists in Washington that their days of setting the agenda are over," he knew he would be held to that promise and would have to explain the inevitable fudging that came when he took power. The president knows that when incumbents' explanations are not believed, a lot of them lose their jobs. His position was also helped by the fact that he could be elected without a great deal of lobbyists' money.

Other players beside political parties and elected officials limit lobbyists as well. The press investigates and exposes their cozy backroom deals; the civil service is generally competent and committed to their agencies' programs; and public interest groups can often elbow their issues onto the policy agenda. And as we will see shortly, new forms of communications from radio talk shows to Internet blogs can upset Washington's business as usual.

The outcomes of the political game remain unpredictable. Lobbyists' ability to defang reforms depends on their success in convincing the public, press, and politicians that what they want these audiences should also want. Their influence ultimately depends on the resistance, acceptance, or indifference by other players as well as public opinion. Any explanation of the political game based on the dominance of a few wealthy interests is unlikely to understand the surprising directions that American politics has taken, and will take in the future. Some of these unexpected turns will involve our last player—the media.

Media

The media are the only private business that the Constitution singles out for protection. The First Amendment prohibits any law "abridging the freedom of speech, or of the press." But like any business the media are subject to the ups and downs of the private marketplace. And since the turn of the new century, they have been in crisis mainly because of the rise of the Internet. Advertisements that once provided four-fifths of the money for newspapers and magazines and almost all the money for TV and radio are now going to the Internet.

The question then is whether this "fourth branch of government" will continue to fulfill its vital roles in the political game. What are these roles?

First, media are the channels through which those in power talk to the public. Whether a new policy is being launched, a crisis responded to, or announcements made, political leaders depend on the media to relay the information to the rest of us. Second, if less apparent, media are often the way those in power talk to each other. If an official in the Department of Agriculture thinks the subsidy for corn-based ethanol is being poorly run (and the White House disagrees) he or she might communicate that to Congress by leaks to a reporter that become an article in the *Washington Post*.

Third, news media are a watchdog. Media investigate whether elected officials and others are abusing their privileges, showing favoritism to cronies, or not keeping their campaign promises. Media try to hold those in power to legal and ethical *standards* such as honesty, consistency, and transparency. Fourth, news media provide feedback so officials can learn whether their policies are working. While the full impact of a complex program may not be clear for a long time, news stories allow a more immediate response. For example, in the mid-1990s Congress required single mothers to get jobs in order to continue welfare support for their children. If these mothers or their children are suffering it will be journalists who will see that officials know.

Finally, news media provide channels through which the general public can bring its needs, demands, and views to the attention of officials. This "voice of the people" function can be seen in reporting on the full destruction left by Hurricane Katrina in 2006, or the despair created by the economic recession of 2008–2009. The news media furnish the street-level observations that enable authorities to assess the situation, get some idea of what the public expects them to do, and respond accordingly.

In this part of the chapter, we will answer the following questions: What are the media? What do the media do? Who controls the media? How do the media influence politics, and how do other players influence media content?

What Are the Media?

Media are those means of communication that permit messages to be made public. Media such as television, radio, newspapers, and, now, the Internet provide important links connecting people to one another. But these are links with an important quality: They have the ability to communicate messages to a great many people at roughly the same time. We will concentrate on television, newspapers, and the Internet. (See Figure 8.1.)

Ninety-nine percent of American households own at least one TV. Actually, the average TV-owning household has 2.8 TV sets (for only 2.5 people!). The abundance of TVs and the powerful impact of pictures are why television dominates the mass media—as well as dominating American kids, who watch some three hours of TV a day. TV's political influence varies greatly. There is the exceptional event, like the Sarah Palin–Joe Biden vice presidential debate in October 2008, watched by almost 70 million Americans—considerably more than the

Audience for Media News, 2008

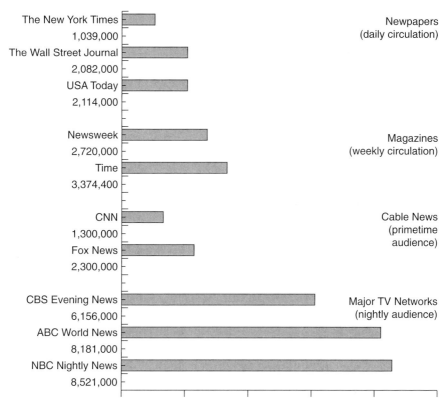

FIGURE 8.1
Sources: *Magazine Publishers of America*; *Audit Bureau of Circulations*, *Nielsen Media Research*, 2008.

57 million average for the three presidential candidate debates that year (though still way down from the record 80-plus million who saw the Carter–Reagan debate in 1980).

Just how closely people follow presidential campaigns, even hotly contested ones, is inconsistent. One poll during the 2000 campaign found that only half of voting-age Americans thought about the election or could recall even one news story about it. The 2008 election, on the other hand, offered the first African-American presidential candidate, and the first serious female presidential candidate (Hillary Clinton), set against the backdrop of two wars and a looming economic crisis, and propelled by record campaign spending. The results were dramatically higher levels of political awareness. In one 2009 poll nearly 85 percent of college freshmen said they had discussed politics "frequently or occasionally".

Thanks to the growth of cable and satellite systems—which have much more capacity than the over-the-air signals of traditional TV broadcasting—the average household now gets 104 channels, including round-the-clock news and talk on CNN, MSNBC, and Fox News. However the most-watched TV newscasts remain the half-hour evening programs produced by the three traditional broadcast networks—CBS, NBC, and ABC. These networks rely on local stations to relay their signals to households. Some of these stations they own. Some local stations the networks don't own but contract with; they are called *affiliates*. Each of the broadcast networks has over 200 affiliates that enable them to reach a truly national audience with their programming, and in turn sell national advertising. This arrangement with local affiliates allows the networks to sell time at stratospheric rates—the record, set during the 2009 pro football Super Bowl, was $3 million for a 30-second ad.

In recent years, the dominance of the three networks over TV news has been reduced, as has the overall importance of TV news. Traditional national network newscasts still outdraw cable for audiences: The 23 million people who watch the three evening network newscasts are several times the number who watch any cable news network during prime time (8 to 11 at night). Fox News' *top-rated* news program, *The O'Reilly Factor*, draws a measly one-third of the viewers of the *least* popular evening network news program—*CBS Evening News* with Katie Couric. (See Figure 8.1.)

Americans are increasingly relying on news available round-the-clock. And in the 2008 election cable replaced traditional TV for the first time as the most often cited source of political news. Online news sites also surfaced. It was Web-based sites that first reported—again and again—the angry sermon of candidate Barack Obama's minister, the Reverend Jeremiah Wright, in which he denounced U.S. actions abroad in fierce terms that offended many voters. When Obama responded with a widely praised speech on race, his comments reached 4 million people via cable TV, but even more viewers—5.5 million— watched the speech later when they downloaded it from YouTube.

Whatever problems the TV industry has, *newspapers* have made the most dramatic decline in American media. Circulation of daily papers has been declining for decades—and that decline has been accelerating. By late 2008 newspaper circulation was falling nearly 5 percent a year. The money picture was even worse. Advertisers shifted their spending to cheaper targeted sites on the Internet that promised better results than scattershot advertising in the general media. Newspaper revenue fell dramatically, reaching $38 billion in 2008, a plunge of 23 percent in less than two years.

The results: Fewer newspapers. Metro papers in Denver, Seattle, Philadelphia, San Francisco, and Minneapolis closed. Those newspapers that remain are employing fewer journalists and are spending less on covering political news. Some 600 newspapers had their own D.C.

bureaus in 1985. *Half had been shut down by 2008.* The three main TV networks had 110 journalists covering Washington in 1985; by 2009 they had 46. From city commissions to county councils to state legislatures, governments have fewer journalists keeping an eye on them.

Newspapers that remain vary in size and quality, from the prestigious The *New York Times,* carrying world news collected by its own reporters, to small-town dailies that relay crop reports and cover local fires but provide sketchy coverage of national events reprinted from the wire services. (*Wire services* are specialized agencies like the Associated Press [AP], Bloomberg News, and Reuters that gather, write, and sell news to media that subscribe to them.) Historically much of the news reaching us through TV and radio originated in stories done by the reporters of major newspapers.

This decline in the number of newspapers and their competitiveness is nothing new. In 1900, there were 2,226 daily papers in the United States. A century later, while the population had more than tripled, there were only 1,647. The same period has seen a decline in the cities with competing newspapers. In 1920, there were 700 cities with competing daily papers. Currently there are fewer than a dozen. Of major American cities, only New York has three separately owned dailies, all of them in financial trouble.

Then there is the *Internet.* While the Internet—which started life in the late 1960s as a U.S. military project to create a computer network that could survive a nuclear attack—is still young, large numbers of people already rely on it as a news source. More than a third of Americans say they got most of their campaign news online in 2008, three times the percentage who said that in 2004. When it comes to national and international news, 40 percent of people say they get most of it from the Internet—up from 24 percent four years ago. The percentage still isn't as high as television (70 percent), but it's higher than newspapers (35 percent.)

Online news is exploding in importance. Numerous sites offer national news reported by their own staffs (Politico.com, TalkingPointsMemo, CNN.com, Slate) or offer commentary about news they select from elsewhere (Huntington Post, InstaPundit). There is a wave of local citizen-run sites that track city and neighborhood news. All of this has been made possible because the number of U.S. Internet users hit 194 million in 2008 (85 percent of families), each averaging 15 hours a week online.

In 1998 the scandal involving White House intern Monica Lewinsky showed the Internet in the first full bloom of its political role. President Bill Clinton's sexual affair with the young woman first surfaced that January on a website run by a freelance reporter named Matt Drudge. Throughout the controversy, tens of thousands of people were debating impeachment and more sordid aspects of the scandal in newsgroups and chat rooms. The customary news cycle for newspapers or evening news—geared to the hours of the working day—was replaced by a non-stop flow of information and rumors surfacing 24/7 on the Internet. The mainstream press struggled to catch up. Whether the Internet allowed a positive expansion of public debate or whether it was the cyberbabble of an electronic mob talking to themselves was less certain.

More recently the spread of mobile telephones that can transmit images and the growing popularity of social networks such as Twitter, which enables people to share short messages with thousands of others, have begun to impact news coverage. The earliest eyewitness reports and pictures on the 2008 terrorist attacks in Mumbai, India, came from non-journalists at the scene. And the street demonstrations in Tehran that shook the regime in Iran following the disputed 2009 elections was covered extensively by people relying on Twitter to communicate with each other and the outside world. When pictures of a dying young woman shot in the streets spread around the world, Tehran became viral. News was becoming participatory—more people than ever have their hands on the tools of media.

What Do the Media Do?

The media provide three major types of messages. Through their *news reports, entertainment programs,* and *advertising,* the media help shape public opinion on many things—including politics. In news reports, the media supply up-to-date accounts of what journalists believe to be the most important, interesting, and newsworthy events, issues, and developments. But the influence of news reports goes well beyond relaying facts. The key to this power is *selectivity.* By reporting certain items (President Obama's daily workout) and ignoring others (President Roosevelt's crippled legs), the media suggests what is important. Media coverage gives status to people and events—a national television interview or a *Time* magazine cover creates a "national figure."

There are limits. Few people pay attention to political news. Most people reading the newspapers are interested in the sports, comics, and local events. Those under 30 are unlikely to follow political news. What they find out about politics comes when it is relayed to them by friends or downloaded as video reports—or sketches from *The Daily Show* that they get from YouTube. This is not because they do not have enough time. Young people spend more time watching sports, celebrity news, and entertainment programming on television than do adults over 30. The more young viewers ignore coverage of politics, the less they know about their government. (See "The Daily Show Shapes Political Journalism.")

The Daily Show Shapes Political Journalism

While the popularity of television news has declined in recent years, late night comedy, especially Comedy Central's *The Daily Show,* has doubled its audience (to 2 million) since the 2004 presidential campaign. *The Daily Show* uses factual content, making its humor understandable only if the viewer knows the news. Host Jon Stewart weaves his satiric commentary around footage of news events. He also conducts live interviews with political figures. As a result, *The Daily Show* is a serious source of political information for its audience.

Admirers of the program point to its willingness to confront the hypocrisy of political figures as evidence of its commitment to journalism. The program's producers are at their best when combing the Internet for historical materials that expose politicians as liars. On one memorable program, immediately after footage of Vice President Dick Cheney insisting that he "absolutely never said" that a meeting between one of the 9/11 hijackers and Iraqi agents had been "pretty well confirmed," the program aired video of Cheney appearing on *Meet the Press* and saying precisely that, word for word. Stewart then comments, "Mr. Vice President, your pants are on fire."

News reports perform two important informational functions: agenda-setting and framing. *Agenda-setting* means presenting national priorities—what should be taken seriously, what should be taken lightly, and what can be ignored altogether. "The media can't tell people what to think," one expert put it, "but they can tell people what to think *about.*" The attention the media give to health care reform, climate change, or genocide in Darfur will affect how important people think these issues are. What is in the front-page headlines of the morning newspaper or what leads the evening news makes some events, issues, or people seem more significant than others.

Framing defines problems, suggesting *how* we should understand issues. Media coverage can present, or frame, an issue in many ways. Is crime linked to unemployment, to lax immigration laws, or to poor police training? How the problem is understood may influence whether the solution is a jobs program, barriers on the border, or more cops. Linguistics professor George Lakoff points out that when President Bush arrived in the White House he began speaking about *tax relief,* which meant tax cuts. "Relief," of course, implies that taxes are a headache or illness and that someone needs to relieve the pain. That such cuts might increase the deficit or slash social programs was not part of this frame. Media scholar Kathleen Hall Jamieson has written, "Frames tell us what is important, what the range of acceptable debate on a topic is, and when an issue has been resolved."

Entertainment programs offer amusement while giving people images of "normal" behavior. That doesn't mean behavior on television always offers socially acceptable models. Some fictional characters, such as Tony Soprano of *The Sopranos,* engage in immoral business practices that bring wealth and power. Such media programs may substitute for learning from life's more complex experiences, and they sometimes become as important as real life. As one analyst of television observed: "If you can write a nation's stories, you needn't worry about who makes its laws. Today, television tells most of the stories to most of the people most of the time."

Finally, most programs and news that media present are built around a flow of *advertisements.* Television programs are constructed to reach emotional high points just before the commercials so that the audience will stay put during the advertisement. Newspapers devote almost two-thirds of their space to ads rather than to news, which led one English author to define a journalist as "someone who writes on the back of advertisements." Ads, especially television commercials, present images of what the audience finds pleasing about themselves. Presented with compelling symbols, commercials offer viewers comfort, good looks, and amusement. They may change what we expect in other arenas, including politics. TV's emphasis on entertaining visuals may alter how we look at our political leaders and how they present themselves: Instead of a public discussion of issues, we find a competition between reassuring visual images. In this case, the medium has changed the message of politics.

Reliance on advertising means that the media must attract the right audiences—not only people who are *interested* in what's being presented but also people who are *interesting* to advertisers. TV network news has found that its audience is too old for the advertisers it wants to sell to. Hoping to appeal to a younger demographic—especially women of child-bearing age, who are avid consumers of many goods and services—news programs in the late 1990s expanded their coverage of education, crime, marriage, health care, and other concerns to growing families. In that way the agenda of newsworthy topics shifted, and critics accused the networks of a liberal bias when in fact the change had more to do with marketing.

Media and the Marketplace of Ideas

The framers of the Constitution believed that a free flow of information from many voices was basic to democratic government. Opinions would compete with one another without restraint in a "marketplace of ideas."

That phrase has since been expanded to include radio and television. The principle remains the same, as Judge Learned Hand wrote:

> Right conclusions are more likely to be gathered out of a multitude of tongues than through any kind of authoritative selection. To many this is, and always will be folly; but we have staked upon it our all.

The ability of media to fulfill this goal of presenting a variety of opinion representing the widest range of political ideas has, to no one's surprise, been limited in practice. It is limited by (1) *the media themselves*, (2) *the government*, and (3) *the public*.

As businesses media are operated, bought, and sold to make money for their owners. Profitability, not public service, has led to the increasing concentration of media ownership; owners sought to operate more cheaply and reach larger audiences by controlling larger markets. That has encouraged an increase in control by *chains*, which are companies that combine different media in different cities under a single owner. More than 80 percent of U.S. newspapers are owned by chains, and the country's 10 largest ownership groups control 179 magazines. Clear Channel Communications, the largest U.S. radio broadcaster, owns 900 local stations.

Mergers have left major media in fewer corporate hands than ever. In the 1990s, Disney purchased ABC for $19 billion, Westinghouse paid $5.4 billion for CBS and Time Warner bought Turner Broadcasting, including CNN, for $7.5 billion. General Electric acquired NBC (later sold to the nation's largest cable company, Comcast, in 2009). In May 2000, the combination of Viacom (which owned Paramount Pictures, Blockbuster, MTV, Nickelodeon, and Simon & Schuster, among others) with CBS created the second-largest media company in the world. But this was soon surpassed. In 2001 Internet pioneer America OnLine acquired Time Warner, the largest media corporation. Consolidation continued with the 2007 purchase of Dow Jones & Co., publisher of the *Wall Street Journal*, by Rupert Murdoch's News Corp.—which owns Fox News, the *New York Post*, many other newspapers including the *Times* of London, and satellite systems throughout the world. The *Christian Science Monitor* concluded: "The bulk of what we see, hear, learn, sing, play, rent and consume will shortly be controlled by a dozen corporate entities." (See "Rupert Murdoch's Politics.")

In the past, federal regulators discouraged such mergers, arguing that monopolies over information did not serve the public interest. But with increasing bankruptcies and declining profitability, regulators are inclined to permit mergers to help media survive. Still, news might be influenced by corporate interests. An example of this a few years ago involved *NBC Nightly News*, which ran three segments, totaling

Rupert Murdoch's Politics

Rupert Murdoch is the Australian-born media baron whose U.S. holdings include the *Wall Street Journal*, the *New York Post*, and the Fox Network. Fox News, a 24-hour cable news network created in 1996, has appealed to an audience that considers other U.S. news sources as tainted by a liberal bias. Its most popular commentators—Bill O'Reilly and Sean Hannity—are strongly conservative, and its slogan, "Fair and balanced," is seen as backhanded criticisms of its competitors, especially CNN.

But Murdoch's political leanings throughout his career have followed his corporate interests. In Great Britain, where he bought the *Times* in 1981, he backed the Conservative Party under Prime Minister Margaret Thatcher until its popularity declined. Then he moved his support to the Labor Party. In the United States, Fox News strongly favored the George W. Bush administration; all 175 Murdoch-owned newspapers worldwide came out in favor of the Iraq war. But as Bush's popularity declined, Murdoch's enthusiasm waned. By 2006 he hosted a fundraiser for liberal Democratic Senator Hillary Clinton, and in 2008 Murdoch declared himself a fan of Barack Obama.

Moderating his political image may have helped Murdoch in his 2007 takeover of Dow Jones, the Bancroft family–owned company that publishes the *Wall Street Journal*—the second-biggest U.S. newspaper. Some members of the family were apprehensive about Murdoch. His emergence as a pragmatic centrist—rather than a right-wing ideologue—may have helped overcome their resistance, close the $5 billion deal, and make him America's most powerful media owner.

14 minutes, about a new device to detect breast cancer without mentioning that its parent corporation, General Electric, manufactured the machine.

There is no question that the *quantity* of information available to the public has increased. One innovation was CNN (Cable Network News), with 24-hour coverage. Started in 1980 by Ted Turner, few people believed there would be enough demand for such a station, and it was jokingly called "Chicken Noodle News." CNN went on to become a success, and in times of crisis it has become the channel of choice for the public, political leaders, and news junkies. Less popular C-SPAN provides continuous coverage of both houses of Congress, and many community cable stations provide similar coverage of state and local governments. National Public Radio, a noncommercial broadcast network that relies chiefly on cash contributions from its listeners now has one of the industry's most extensive news operations. The popularity of talk and call-in shows has made radio an important political force with a huge following, especially among conservatives. Here the market leader is Rush Limbaugh, one of the few commentators to defend the abuse of Iraqi prisoners of war, arguing that the U.S. guards "need to blow some steam off."

Media and Government

Government and media in the United States have long danced an unsteady waltz. In the early years of the Republic the press was consciously partisan. Newspapers were sponsored by parties to appeal to their voters. They were also grateful for fat printing contracts once their party got into power. By the 1830s, printing by machine allowed mass circulation newspapers to be sold for a fraction of the price papers had cost until then. These new "penny papers" now depended on advertising for most of their revenues. Advertisers wanted to reach customers, no matter what their political views. The Civil War increased the demand for human interest stories and up-to-date news unaffected by party loyalties. By the end of the nineteenth century, advertisers and publishers, not politicians, bankrolled newspapers.

Still, the media continued to benefit from government help, but now government supported the press through subsidies and support for new technology, notably the telegraph and later the radio—developed initially under the supervision of the U.S. Navy—and still later microwave, satellite communications, and the Internet. In the twentieth century, federal regulation under the Federal Communications Commission (FCC), created in 1934, generally took a pro-industry stance in restricting entry to broadcasting competitors. Regulators steadily weakened the public service requirements broadcasters had to meet, until now license renewals—which come every six years—are usually a formality. The media have long been exempted from a host of government laws and antitrust regulations, including making sure that minimum wage and child labor laws did not apply to newspaper delivery boys. Plus, the media benefit from an important subsidy from all government agencies—free information for the press through public affairs offices.

For campaigning politicians, the media are both opportunity and adversary. Two-thirds of the money in presidential races goes to advertising. Politicians—as seen in the case study at the end of this chapter—live and die by media coverage. Some of their activities have been called *pseudoevents*—not real news at all, but happenings that are staged solely to be reported. One example, seen in 2006, was when President Bush took campaigning Republicans for rides on Air Force One with television cameras aboard. While coverage has been increased by the rise in media outlets such as cable, the quality of political news has not necessarily risen with the coverage. One study showed that the average *sound bite*—a video clip of a candidate speaking—had declined from 42 seconds in 1968 to just over 7 seconds currently. Newscasts emphasize the quick and the dramatic in covering politics.

Examples of government leaders pressuring media are numerous. Presidents try to get on the good side of the media by giving favored reporters exclusive "leaks" of information and by controlling information going to the public. Press conferences have been used by presidents since Theodore Roosevelt to give the media direct contact with the chief executive. Though disliked by both Clinton and George W. Bush, such conferences, when broadcast, can allow presidents to present their views directly to the public. Franklin Roosevelt's radio "fireside chats" were a brilliant way of personally reassuring people during the Great Depression. Television and politicians can also make uneasy partners. In 1960, presidential candidate Richard Nixon's streaky makeup, dull suit, and unshaven looks made a poor impression—and may have cost him the election—in the first-ever televised debate with his opponent, John F. Kennedy.

Presidents work on perfecting their public images. As a former movie actor and television personality, the late Ronald Reagan was known as "the Great Communicator" due to his unrivaled skill of looking and sounding absolutely forthright. (See "Mixed Media Messages.") President Clinton was an intelligent, articulate media celebrity. But Clinton's press relations came to a screeching halt at the feet of Monica Lewinsky where the scandal displayed the president's negatives—questionable honesty, and womanizing. George W. Bush was not as good as Clinton in public performances, but he didn't have to defend his private life, and he usually followed the message of the day. He avoided unscripted press conferences, favored less critical reporters from outside Washington, and frequently garbled his few question-and-answer media sessions.

Barack Obama developed a reputation as a gifted orator and a thoughtful writer even before he became a presidential candidate, thanks to his keynote address at the 2004 Democratic convention and his autobiography, *Dreams from My Father.* As a campaigner, he was widely admired for his verbal skills, to the point where his adversaries tried to use his "glibness" against him, with mixed results. Labeled the "commenter-in-chief " he is his administration's most capable communicator. (See "Obama: The Prime Time Prez.")

Media and the Public

The "definition of alternatives is the supreme instrument of power," wrote political scientist E. E. Schattschneider. "Definition of alternatives" means the ability to set limits on political debates, to define what

Mixed Media Messages

During the 1984 presidential campaign, Lesley Stahl, a CBS reporter, prepared a critical commentary on how President Reagan used television. Her blunt report charged the president with manipulation, if not hypocrisy. She reported that he would appear at the Special Olympics or the opening of a senior housing facility, but no hint was given that he cut the budgets for subsidized housing for the elderly. He also distanced himself from bad news, Stahl reported. After he pulled the U.S. Marines out of Lebanon, in the aftermath of a disastrous October 1983 bombing of their barracks in Beirut—which killed 241 U.S. soldiers—he flew off to his California ranch, leaving others to make the announcement.

To illustrate her piece, Stahl put together Reagan's video clips: Reagan greeting handicapped athletes, cutting the ribbon at a home for the elderly, and relaxing on his ranch in jeans.

"I thought it was the single toughest piece I had ever done on Reagan," Stahl said. She worried about the White House reaction.

After the piece aired, the phone rang. It was a senior White House official.

"And the voice said, 'Great piece.'"

"I said, 'What?'"

"And he said, 'Great piece!'"

"I said, 'Did you listen to what I said?'"

He said, "Lesley, when you're showing four and a half minutes of great pictures of Ronald Reagan, no one listens to what you say. Don't you know that the pictures are overriding your message because they conflict with your message? The public sees those pictures and they block your message . . . it was a four-and-a-half-minute free ad for the Ronald Reagan campaign for re-election."

I sat here numb. . . . None of us had figured that out.

She broke into laughter. "They loved it. They really did love it."

Source: Hedrick Smith, *The Power Game* (New York: Random House, 1988), pp. 413–14.

---

is politically important and what is not, and to make certain solutions reasonable and acceptable, and others not. Media, to a great extent, have this power. Who influences the exercise of this power is another question.

Certainly media managers (editors, newscasters, producers, reporters) have a vital role in shaping political views. Advertisers, by buying space in some programs or papers and not in others, affect the messages sent out to the public. The owners of media, whether television networks, cable operators, or newspaper chains, play a part in

Obama: The Prime Time Prez

There was never any guarantee that Barack Obama would have four hour-long evening press conferences televised in prime time by the three main TV networks in his first half-year in office. When Bill Clinton held his first evening news conference as president two of the networks refused to carry it. George W. Bush held only four of them during his entire eight years. The difficulty is commercial: It costs the networks millions of dollars in lost advertising to broadcast the president. As one Republican press secretary put it, "If it's not a big night for the networks they put civic duty and pride first. But you don't go up against 'American Idol'—not even Barack Obama."

Part of the explanation for the networks' agreement to televise his press conferences was old-fashioned Chicago arm-twisting. Rahm Emmanuel, the White House chief of staff, phoned the heads of the networks' parent companies—General Electric, Disney, and CBS—to pressure them to cover the president. While that worked, the audiences for the press conferences gradually declined, and it seemed that the arguably over-exposed president would have to make real news (or speak before Congress, which he did on health care) to guarantee this coverage in the future.

Source: From Howard Kurtz, "The Prez, The Press, The Pressure," *Washington Post*, August 3, 2009.

selecting who runs the day-to-day operations and the general "slant" of the media they own. Owners may take a more direct involvement, as illustrated in late 2003 when Viacom's corporate leaders took a CBS drama on Ronald Reagan off the network after it aroused criticism from Republican party leaders.

People have a right to expect that the press will fulfill the major political functions described at the beginning of this section, particularly (1) telling the public what their leaders are doing and (2) serving as a watchdog to hold leaders accountable. The demands of the marketplace, by turning newscasts into entertainment and undermining the financial viability of many newspapers, have limited the media's ability to fulfill either political function.

The public does not have to be passive. By watching or not watching certain programs, by buying or not buying publications, and by demanding or not demanding that dissenting voices be heard, the public can help shape the output of the media. The rise of talk radio, the Internet, and community-based programs on public access channels shows that flexibility and diversity are still possible in today's media.

CASE STUDY

The Candidate: A Day in the Life . . .

Elections allow interest groups and media to influence who will gain power in the political game. In this fictional account of a day in the life of a candidate we see, through her eyes, the importance of these players.

MORNING

The phone jars her awake. It is still dark outside. But months ago, she started leaving the light on in the bathroom of each motel she stayed in so that she could quickly get her bearings when, like this morning, she woke up disoriented.

"Yes?" she asks rasping into the mouthpiece, her voice slightly hoarse from too many speeches.

"Time to get moving, boss," an aide's voice says. There is an important breakfast meeting this morning with the state teachers' union. They have already given her the maximum allowable contribution, but she hopes they will get their national PAC to contribute and that they will encourage their members to volunteer for her campaign.

She has learned to travel light and dress quickly. Her short functional haircut is ready as soon as it dries. As she settles into the backseat of her midsize American-made car, she tries to recall what brought her to the southeast part of the state for two days of campaigning.

Her schedule is done by regions. To save travel time and money, she does events in neighboring communities. The two good-sized towns she will be in today offer her enough voters to make her stay worthwhile. More importantly, they offer opportunities for money and media. Every day must include a money event in the community being visited. And, of course, if you do not get media on a trip, you were not there.

She works the crowd, prodded by an aide's earlier reminders of the key names, spouses, and previous times she has met them. As she eases into her seat at the head table, she turns to the aide for her purse, which reminds her of an argument at the beginning of the campaign.

Should she carry a purse? Her campaign manager said no. Why should a candidate for the U.S. Senate carry a purse? That was not even the worst of the special problems facing a woman running for office. How feminine should she look? Does she wear dresses or suits? Jewelry? Do heels make her look too tall, or do people want to look up at their next senator?

At the breakfast, she tries to eat the by-now-cold eggs because she has been losing weight and her face is looking haggard on television. Her major campaign promise is a cut in income taxes for the middle class, but she assures the teachers that savings in program management will still allow for a cost-of-living increase in educational salaries. She thanks them for their contributions and makes a pitch that teachers are the best volunteers—bright, but used to drudge work.

There is a ten o'clock news conference at the local press club. A reporter rides with her. He is doing a story about her family life. "But don't you feel bad about having to be away from your children so much?" he asks. It is a question she has fielded a hundred times before. "My husband is very good with them," she says, "and then Betsy, who's eleven, and Henry, who's fourteen, are very much involved in the campaign themselves, and they feel that what we are all doing together is very important."

The press conference goes smoothly. She reads the prepared statement, which explains how much her proposed income tax cut will mean for an average family. During the last two weeks of the campaign, she will issue two such statements each day, one for the morning newspapers and one for the afternoon papers. But the main hope is that she will get a segment on the nightly news. Television news is the key to a successful statewide campaign, and she has planned her campaign accordingly. In this case, she is well under the 2:00 P.M. deadline for the 6:00 P.M. local news.

Afternoon

At noon, she visits a senior citizen's center where hot lunches are served to about 60 retirees each day. Unfortunately, the local college student serving as her driver gets lost. She is late. This happens at least once a week.

After lunch, she goes back to her motel room for some urgent fundraising. She learns that she could lose some vital last-week television advertising spots unless she can come up with $30,000 before the day ends. At the motel, two wealthy supporters are waiting. She has another cup of coffee, pours them a beer, and makes the pitch. "I know you've given more than you should be asked to give, but we've got to raise the money for these spots." She always finds this a little demeaning. One of the men heads the state Bankers' Association. The other is a homebuilder. She wonders what they will want when she becomes senator.

Since they've already contributed the maximum $3,000 from each member of their family, the two commit to raising from friends another $20,000 and leave. She talks to other prospective contributors on the telephone, as each is dialed in turn by an aide. A number of these are directors of PACs in Washington, D.C. "Did you see the *Tribune* poll?" she asks. "We're really coming up, but these spots are crucial." With all but $4,000 of the needed money raised (which will probably be picked up through an aide's follow-up calls), she changes clothes and heads for a working-class café to film a television spot.

The café is crammed with television lights, reflectors, cameras, technicians, and spectators anxious to get into the picture. The candidate briefly studies a script, which will take 45 seconds to recite. With the café and its customers as backdrops, she looks into the camera on cue and begins. "In the closing days of this campaign, ordinary people have increasingly been joining with me in demanding a cut in income taxes . . . "

"Hold it!" the producer says. "We're getting a buzzing on the sound track from the ice machine."

She starts again. "In the closing days of this campaign . . . "

"Wait a minute," the producer interrupts. "There's some kind of funny shadow on her face."

The lights are adjusted, and she begins again—and again. A minute spot takes two hours to film.

After filming the television spot she hurries to two "coffees," one at the home of a wealthy friend active in environmental groups, the other sponsored by the sisterhood of a local synagogue. She makes a brief opening statement at each coffee, and then answers questions. At the end of each session, she asks for volunteers willing to help with email, door-to-door canvassing, or other campaign chores to sign a pledge sheet. After she leaves, her hosts make a pitch for money. Almost $15,000 is promised at the two coffees.

EVENING

Back at the motel, she takes the phone from an aide and responds to a prearranged, live radio interview for 15 minutes. She spends 20 minutes with her campaign manager going over the latest poll results. "We're cutting down the general," her chief opponent in the race, "but I'm worried about the increase in your 'negatives'; maybe we should soften our attack a little," the manager says. Knowing that her attacks on an opponent will also increase voters' negative feelings toward her, she agrees.

"Then there's the contribution by Sleaze. We've really got the state party steamed at us for telling them to wait on this one." She nods. She knows that money is given to the state party to fund their Get Out the Vote efforts to help candidates like her, without having to worry about campaign laws or disclosure. Now, Ben A. Sleaze, the owner of Jefferson S&L, wants to give $100,000 to the state party for GOTV activities aimed indirectly at supporting her campaign. The S&L has some regulatory problems, and Sleaze is going to expect help from her if she wins.

Besides the fact that her campaign desperately needs the money, the party also wants the funds to build up their voter contact program. The party chairman, who says he is amazed Sleaze would even offer help to a nonincumbent, is leaning on her to OK the money. It is all perfectly legal, he tells her. Yet she worries about the bad press when it leaks out, and she does not trust or like Sleaze. But, as her manager said, "It's only a press problem. You need the money now; you can deal with the media later, when you're senator." She decides to talk with her husband about it and tells her manager she will let him know her decision in the morning.

Her stomach tightens as she begins to think ahead to the last of the day's activities, a televised "debate" with the other senatorial candidates before a League of Women Voters' audience. Too tense to eat, she turns down a sandwich and goes over her notes. "Should I be rough with the general or not?" she asks nobody in particular.

Riding back to the motel after the debate, she feels good. She is sure that the local news tomorrow evening will make a "sound bite" out of her statement, "The general may have served honorably protecting our government, but I want to be a senator because I feel our people now need protection *from* that same government."

She talks to her husband and one of the children by telephone; the younger child is already asleep. Her husband is enthusiastic about the debate, and that is a good note to end the day on. Maybe that is why she does not raise the issue of Sleaze's contribution, or maybe she is just too tired to remember. She gets into bed and calls the motel desk. "Would you ring me in the morning at five?"

WRAP-UP

Both interest groups and media are bridges over which people and players can reach the political game. Interest groups provide the means for business, labor, professional, or citizens' organizations to make their views known to government officials. They unify people with common concerns to bring pressure on decision makers through grassroots campaigns, fundraising, lobbying, or publicity. Those interest groups with the most resources tend to be the most effective. Reforms to limit the influence of powerful interests have been notably unsuccessful.

Media seem to be everywhere. As both a communications tool and an economic asset, media affect politics. Through news reports, entertainment, and advertisements, media shape the national agenda and frame the nation's issues and personalities. What is broadcast and printed establishes political figures, sets priorities, focuses attention on issues, and largely makes politics understandable to most people. The media in turn are affected by the corporations that own them, the advertisers that pay for their messages, the managers who run them, and the public that looks, reads, and listens to what they offer. Technology has increased the variety of media outlets and led to the merger of many of them under giant corporate banners. With the rise of the Internet new forms of communications have flourished while older media now seem endangered.

Political leaders influence—and are influenced by—media in numerous ways. They grant them licenses if they are television and radio stations, provide a large part of the news about government and its policies that media reports, and "spin" information in ways favorable to their interests. Media give government feedback on programs, act as a watchdog exposing their foibles and provide a voice for people to express their opinions. Campaigning candidates—including our Senate candidate—spend much of their days seeking free access to media or raising the money for ads. As a player and a communications link, the media are among the political game's most powerful, complex, and controversial forces.

Interest groups and media offer the potential for wide public participation. The rise in interest groups and the explosion of media outlets provide linkages that could be used by a broader public. But it is the public that is more likely to be used—by players enhancing their own political positions. Interest groups, through lobbying campaigns, mobilize parts of the public to support their own policies. Media offer the public news-as-entertainment for the commercial and political benefits that come from claiming a larger share of the audience. The public is the object of the efforts, not the creator. These instruments of power remain in the hands of the powerful.

THOUGHT QUESTIONS

1. Which interests are represented best by American interest groups? How would you reform interest groups so that groups that are now poorly represented would have a greater voice?

2. Do you think that President Obama's ban on lobbyists in government is a good idea? Would you include nonprofits?

3. By making news entertaining, are media putting their commercial needs ahead of the goal of an informed public? Are public education and media entertainment contradictory goals?

4. How would you "save" newspapers? Some have suggested running them as nonprofit foundations. Or are they just economic dinosaurs that should be allowed to go extinct?

5. Do you think our candidate for the Senate (See Case Study: "The Candidate: A Day in the Life . . .") will accept Sleaze's money? If you were her aide, what would you recommend? How should she "spin" her responses to press questions about the contribution?

SUGGESTED READINGS

Interest Groups

Berry, Jeffrey M., and Clyde Wilcox. *The Interest Group Society.* 5th ed. New York: Longman, 2009. Pb.
> A concise overview of how, and how much, interest groups influence American politics.

Buckley, Christopher. *Thank You for Smoking.* New York: Random House, 1994. Pb.
> A funny, smart novel (and a popular movie) of a tobacco lobbyist and his uphill struggle to preserve truth, justice, and the American smoker.

Graetz, Michael J., and Ian Shapiro. *Death By Thousand Cuts.* Princeton, NJ: Princeton University Press, 2005.
> An insightful case study of the campaign that turned the estate tax on multimillionaires' properties into an issue of fairness for ordinary people.

Kaiser, Robert G. *So Damn Much Money.* New York: Alfred A. Knopf, 2009.
> Tracks the career of a liberal do-gooder becoming Washington's leading lobbyist doing-well. You can find out how universities were first in line for congressional pork.

Rauch, Jonathan. *Demosclerosis: The Silent Killer of American Government.* New York: Times Books, 1995. Pb.
> Argues that what ails the body politic is too many interest groups clogging the arteries of government.

Media

Cook, Timothy E. *Governing with the News.* 2nd ed. Chicago: University of Chicago Press, 2005. Pb.
> Traces the history of the media as a political institution joined at the hip with the government which it negotiates with and serves.

Gabler, Neal. *Life: The Movie.* New York: Vintage Books, 2000. Pb.
> How the media have turned everything of importance, including the news, into entertainment.

Goldberg, Bernard. *Bias: A CBS Insider Exposes How the Media Distort the News.* New York: Harper Perennial, 2003. Pb.
> Takes aim at the liberal bias in the news while also describing how events become "news."

Jamieson, Kathleen Hall, and Joseph N. Cappella. *Echo Chamber: Rush Limbaugh and the Conservative Media Establishment,* New York: Oxford, 2008.
> A critical look at the rise and influence of the networks of conservative media.

CHAPTER 9

Who Wins, Who Loses:
Pluralism versus Elitism

U nderstanding American politics isn't just describing the players and rules of the game. In this last chapter, we will step back to analyze the game as a whole. Are there general conclusions to be drawn about how the game is played and with what results? Put another way, we will ask our basic questions: Who (if anyone) is running the game? Who wins, who loses?

It should be no surprise that there is no single accepted conclusion to these questions. Rather, there are two competing approaches to an answer. The traditional one, supported with reservations by most political scientists and most of the players in the political game, is *pluralism*. Its competitor, the *elite* school of thought, has attracted dissenters on both the right and left who are critical of the American political game. More recent views have modified and attempted to close the gap between the differing ideas.

Pluralism

Pluralism is a group theory of democracy. Pluralism states that society contains many competing groups with political power, and that the competition and cooperation of these organizations shape government decisions. Although most individuals do not have much power in society, they can gain influence through their membership in what de Tocqueville called "associations." These groups bargain among themselves and with government institutions. The compromises that result become public policy.

Several key concepts make up the pluralist argument: *fragmentation of power, bargaining, compromise,* and *consensus. Fragmentation of power* is the pluralists' way of saying that no one group dominates the political game. Power is divided, though not equally, among a number of groups— labor unions, businesses, nonprofits, religions, ethnics, and many others. To gain their goals, the groups must *bargain* with each other. Within this bargaining process, the government, though it may have its own interests, acts essentially as a referee and scorekeeper. The government will make sure the rules of the game are followed and may intervene to help groups that consistently have less power than their opponents. Ultimately the government will respond to the winners. It is to the advantage of all the groups to follow the "rules of the game," for the bargaining-compromise method is the most effective way to gain changes.

The results of this bargaining process lead inevitably to *compromises.* Because no single group dominates, each must take a little less than it wants in order to achieve the support of the others. This accommodation is made easier because both the interests and the membership of the groups overlap. Groups disagreeing on one issue know that they may need each other's support in the future on another issue on which they agree. Individuals may be a member of two groups with different views on an issue. Their membership in both will tend to reduce the conflict between them. A black doctor who is a member of the American Medical Association (AMA), which opposes some expansions of government-sponsored health care, may also be a member of the National Association for the Advancement of Colored People (NAACP), which supports these reforms. As a member of both groups, this doctor may influence them to compromise with each other.

Underlying this bargaining-compromise process is a *consensus*—an agreement on basic political questions that reasonably satisfies most groups. This agreement on the rules of the game, and also on most of its results, is the cooperative cement that holds society together. Aspects of this consensus in American society are the general agreement on the importance of civil liberties, on equal opportunity for all citizens, on the duty of citizens to participate in politics, and on the necessity for compromise. The pluralists maintain not only that there is widespread participation (open to all who wish to organize) in political decisions but also that the decisions and the decision-making process, have a consensus behind them. Government decisions, in the pluralist universe, essentially reflect the compromises reached by the major groups orbiting the political system.

Pluralism presents a picture of complex bargaining among organized groups, and between these groups and various parts of the government. The bargaining results in a series of compromises that become public policy and determine who gets what, when, and how. A widespread consensus on the rules, and results, of this process keeps the political game from descending into an unruly conflict.

Examples of Pluralism

Pluralists have no difficulty pointing to examples of the bargaining-compromise process. When major environmental groups decided that a new law regulating air pollution was needed, they formed a Clean Air Coalition to lead the fight. Helped by environmental lobbyists, the coalition raised funds from wealthy groups like the Environmental Defense Fund and the Sierra Club. Chemical and oil companies, tired of fighting lawsuits brought under what they considered unrealistic regulations, reluctantly supported compromise proposals. They worried about public opinion, which strongly supported the environmentalists' health arguments over business' cost objections. The press weighed in with editorials and generally favorable coverage. Democrats were enthusiastic; Republicans, less so. The government's Environmental Protection Agency (EPA) supported the bill with studies and testimony. The appropriate committees of the House and Senate, reacting to competing substantive arguments, political pressures, and, yes, fundraising, approved a bill that became the Clean Air Act. Pluralists would say the law reflected the relative power of the various groups as well as the compromises they reached.

A classic study supporting the pluralist model is Robert Dahl's book on politics in New Haven, Connecticut, *Who Governs?* Dahl examined several important issues, such as urban development and public education, to see who made the key decisions. He concluded that the people influential in education policy were not the same as those involved in urban development or political nominations. Dahl concluded there were a number of different economic and social groups wielding political power in New Haven. In his 1998 book, *On Democracy,* Dahl updates and argues the virtues of democracy, and discusses under what conditions it exists in modern societies. (See "The Pluralist View.")

Criticisms of Pluralist Theory

Pluralism has run into numerous criticisms. One argument condemns pluralism for emphasizing *how* the political game is played rather than the results. Critics say that the pluralists do not give enough importance to how benefits really are distributed. A consensus supporting equal participation is not the same as actually having equality. A system of democratic procedures may simply conceal the powerful getting their way. Critics of pluralism ask: What good are the rules of the game to the majority of people who never get a chance to play?

Other critics point out that pluralists believe that groups will balance off each other, producing a self-regulating stable system. But what if powerful groups are better at forming groups to gain or protect their benefits. Their needs become paramount in political decisions by government leaders. Elected officials then have neither the incentives nor the resources to take care of the real needs in society. Some saw this more pessimistic portrait of current politics in the debate over health care reform, where the medical industry of insurers, drug companies, and hospitals could preserve their privileges at the expense of the public.

Elite

Many of those disagreeing with pluralism believe that an *elite* approach more realistically describes American politics. Supporters of this approach see society as dominated by unified and nonrepresentative

The Pluralist View

The fact is that the Economic Notables operate within that vague political consensus, the prevailing system of beliefs, to which all the major groups in the community subscribe. . . . Within limits, they can influence the content of that belief system; but they cannot determine it wholly (p. 84).

In the United States the political stratum does not constitute a homogeneous class with well-defined class interests (p. 91).

Thus the distribution of resources and the ways in which they are or are not used in a pluralistic political system like New Haven's constitute an important source of both political change and political stability. If the distribution and use of resources gives aspiring leaders great opportunities for gaining influences, these very features also provide a built-in throttle that makes it difficult for any leader, no matter how skillful, to run away with the system (p. 310).

Source: Robert A. Dahl, *Who Governs?* New Haven, CT: Yale University Press, 1961.

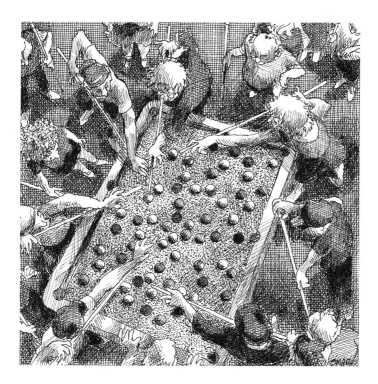

leaders called the *power elite*. This elite occupies the important decision-making positions while encouraging powerlessness below. Those in power do not reflect the varied interests in society. Instead, they look after their own interests and prevent dissenting views from surfacing. American politics is not a collection of pluralist groups maintaining a balance of power among themselves, but an elite of economic, political, and military leaders in unresponsive control of the political game.

This elite rules the country through the positions that its members occupy. Power does not come from individuals but from *institutions*. Thus, to have power you need a role of leadership in a key organization—you have to be the chief executive of a large corporation, a cabinet secretary, or a full admiral in the U.S. Navy. The broader society's social classes limit who can climb up to these leadership positions. They are open only to the rich and the powerful, the *ruling class* of the country, whose names can be found in newspapers' society columns and whose children go to the "right" private schools. This dominant class manages the country's economy and uses power to preserve the status quo and its own privileges.

The results of this elite control, needless to say, are different from the pluralist outcome. Political decisions, rather than representing a consensus in society, represent the *conflict* within it. Society is held together not by widespread agreement but by force and control: the control the elite has over the majority. The only consensus that exists is that some have power and others do not. From this pessimistic viewpoint, politics is a constant conflict between those with power (who seek to keep it) and those without power (who seek to gain it). The policies that result from this political game reflect the conflict between the elite and the majority, and the domination by the elite.

Elite Examples

One of the best-known, and denounced, elite policy organizations is the *Council on Foreign Relations*. It was founded after World War I by what would loosely be called the Eastern Establishment—socially connected, New York-based bankers, lawyers, and academics. One study found that 23 of the country's largest banks and corporations had four or more directors who were members of the council. Its members played key roles after World War II in creating the International Monetary Fund, the World Bank, and the United Nations. Its journal, *Foreign Affairs*, is a must-read by foreign policy decision makers, many of whom are members of the council. Its meetings bring together leaders from business, government, universities, and the military. To those in the council, it is a policy-oriented group analyzing issues and producing broad agreements on American foreign policies. To critics of the elite, it looks more like an Old Boy network deciding on jobs and issues among themselves.

The best known study of elite control in the United States, *The Power Elite*, was written by sociologist C. Wright Mills, who maintained that American politics was dominated by a unified group of leaders from corporations, the military, and politics. More recently, David Rothkopf continues the Mills tradition but expands it to the world in *Superclass: The Global Power Elite and the World They are Making*. Rothkopf identifies roughly 6,000 individuals (mostly men, but Angelina Jolie is in) who have "the ability to regularly influence the lives of millions of people in multiple countries worldwide." Through their membership on boards of corporations, universities, think tanks, and foundations, they network with each other. Their loyalties are more to each other than to any particular nation. (See "The Elite View.")

Criticisms of the Elite View

Critics have joined the fight with the elite view. Although they may agree that only a few people participate in politics, they argue that this minority of activists is much less unified than elite theory assumes.

 ## The Elite View

Of all the powers the superclass possesses, one of the clearest and most important is the ability to set agendas for the rest of us (p. 303).

Today, the most powerful elites are global citizens tied more to international finance than national politics (p. 320).

Conspiracy theory is the comfort food of politics . . . it fills a fundamental desire to balance perceived causes with perceived consequences and thus satisfies our sense that big outcomes are not the product of happenstance (p. 254).

Source: David Rothkopf, *Superclass,* New York: Farrar Straus and Giroux, 2008.

They point to conflicts over taxes or the environment or the war or any presidential election as examples of how elites check each other. These elites compete, and democracy consists of people choosing among them. Besides, some critics argue, the ideals of democracy are probably in better, if fewer, hands than they would be in the grip of an uninformed majority. Public surveys have shown intolerance for dissent among the less educated classes. Hence greater participation might mean fewer liberties, not more.

Another criticism aimed at careless power elite supporters is that they are *conspiracy theorists.* Ideologues of both the right and left may veer close to blaming specific racial, religious, or economic groups for secret conspiracies that are then "covered up." Conspiracies are responsible for President Kennedy's assassination or the World Trade Center bombings, or the AIDS epidemic or the Iraq war. There is an old American tradition pointing to Freemasons or the Papacy or Jews or "government" as the cause of society's ills. Believers in conspiracies find them psychologically reassuring because they mean nothing happens by accident; there is at least some order in the world.

The Debate

The debate between supporters of the pluralist and elite theories does not boil down to *whether* a small number of people dominate the political game. Even in the pluralist model, the bargaining among the groups is carried on by relatively few leaders. Clearly only a minority of people directly participates in politics, and this small group has more influence than the majority. The key questions are how *competitive* and *representative* these elites are.

To what degree do elites compete rather than cooperate with one another over who gets what, when, and how? How much conflict is there between, say, heads of government agencies and corporations over regulations and taxes? Or how much do they share views on major questions of policy and cooperate among themselves regardless of the "public good"? Certainly anyone reading the newspaper can point to numerous examples of conflicts over policy among political groups. Are these conflicts to be dismissed as mere bickering among a small, tight clique on the top? Or are vital issues being resolved in fairly open free-for-all contests?

Next is the question of how representative these elites are of the broader public. Do powerful groups reflect, however imperfectly, the wishes of the majority? In recent years, elite circles in America have opened their doors, not always voluntarily, to minorities and women.

Has this made these institutions more representative of formerly excluded groups? Is this just tokenism, or do the leaders of these associations, businesses, political parties, or government agencies reflect a broader public?

Take the question of what we watch from Hollywood. After America witnessed a series of shootings in its public schools, critics charged that popular movies, television programs, and video games were undermining traditional family values. But do we know why? Some say it is because an elite seeking profits controls what we see. Others argue that abundant violence, casual sex, and silly commercials reflect what the majority wants, as shown by opinion polls. Do elites, including elected officials, follow public opinion? Or do they use control of the media to shape the public to follow their own preferences?

A glance back at the chapters' case studies is a reminder of how difficult it is to put the political game under a single umbrella of ideas. The use of the Internet in Barack Obama's 2008 campaign was an encouraging sign of grassroots participation using modern technology in the service of a political campaign. The case study of the decline and fall of racial segregation seems even more clear-cut—widespread pluralist participation resolving a difficult political conflict, but requiring enormous effort.

The other cases are not as clear. The president's response to 9/11 was both timely and popular, but it hardly reflected broad debate among a diversity of voices. The Bush administration's reaction to Hurricane Katrina was neither timely nor adequate, and the broad input of voices unfortunately dissolved into a confusion of noise. Even in calmer times, the courts had difficulty getting the executive arm of the government to obey constitutional liberties in the war on terrorism. The House passing a bill that confronts climate change shows political leaders reacting to a global problem, yet only in a limited way because of powerful groups' objections. In "The Candidate: A Day in the Life? . . ." a woman running for the Senate aims to win a popular vote, but her immediate targets are narrowed to interest groups and media. Both in process and results, the pluralist and elite frameworks highlight certain parts of America's politics, but ignore others.

Newer Views

The pluralist and elite approaches are two ends of a range of ideas about American politics. Recent modifications have attempted to bridge the gap between the two. One has discussed a *plural elitism.* This stresses that politics is divided into separate policy arenas where narrow elites dominate, usually at the expense of the public interest.

So, for example, when it comes to deciding on government spending levels for the Army, a trio of military leaders, defense contractors, and key congressional committees dominate the decisions—making sure they all benefit, usually at the public expense. The general public is confused by ideology and patriotic symbols from clearly seeing the elite dominance that occurs in these issue areas.

Underlying this approach is the view that whether pluralists or the power elite school is right depends on which political conflict we are talking about. Sometimes, as in town meetings held in many New England towns, we can see a number of views being expressed and a democratic decision being reached by the community. In other policy arenas, such as the making of antiterrorism policies, national security officials meet behind closed doors to decide issues that will affect the lives of millions. Thus, the issue being decided affects how decisions will be made and who participates. Pluralism may be most appropriate in describing a small community's politics, but the elite approach may help us understand the making of national security policy.

Other students of American politics have emphasized how the *government* itself acts. In both pluralism and elitism, government actions are basically viewed as the result of outside forces: in one case, compromises among different groups; in the other, the goals and wishes of a unified elite. But clearly government—its elected branches and agencies—is more than a passive mirror of dominant outside groups. Government has interests of its own and may even, at times, act to represent a broad national interest.

The concept of power may need to be more broadly defined to understand who is influential in politics, and how. "Power" may not be just the ability to influence political decisions; it may also involve preventing issues from even reaching decision makers. Having power may explain what does not happen, not just how behavior is changed. People may not voice grievances that, looking back, historians conclude they may have felt. Just because air pollution is poisoning children doesn't make it a political issue; women in other countries may be much more oppressed than in America, and yet they may be prevented from finding this out. Power in this case is not changing behavior, but preventing that change. Whether general discontent becomes a political demand may first require enlightened political leaders.

The concepts we adopt as most accurately reflecting political reality are bound also to reflect our own ideals. The pluralists and elitists (and those in between) are asking not only what *is* but also what *should be*. The pluralists state that politics in America is democratic, with widespread participation in decisions to which most people agree. The elitists say that politics is dominated by an elite that controls and keeps the rest of us in the dark. The elitists contend that basic changes in the American system are needed to create a pluralist democracy, while the pluralists argue that we have one and that the means for change are available.

What do you think? The position you take will reflect not only your understanding and study of politics but also your ideals, interests, and experience. Further, the position you take will guide your future political choices.

WRAP-UP

This book has presented American politics as a game. We have discussed the nature of the game and how the competition takes place. We talked about the rules of the conflict, many of them in the Constitution, and how they have changed. Most of the book has covered the major governmental and non-governmental players, their history, organization, and influence. This last chapter has looked at two schools of thought that try to analyze how the game is really played and for whom. But we are not quite finished.

What we have called this "game" of politics is more than that. It is a contest that defines who we are as a people: whether we are selfish or generous, arrogant or compassionate, brave or fearful. Like any country, America is a mix of conflicting values and interests, amplified by great wealth and power. Which America will win out? Will it reflect an America of pioneers who expanded on the democratic principles they inherited, offering them to those who had been excluded while defending them at great cost in blood and treasure? Or will it be a self-righteous America so lulled by material comfort that it can refuse to listen to voices seeking justice at home and abroad? The answers lie in the political game.

We said that most of us are spectators of the game—nonparticipants. But just as politics is a special kind of game, so too are we a special kind of audience. We *can* participate in the game and, by participating, change the way the game is played and its outcome. As a respected scholar of politics wrote:

> Political conflict is not like a football game, played on a measured field by a fixed number of players in the presence of an audience scrupulously excluded from the playing field. Politics is much more like the original primitive game of football in which everybody was free to join, a game in which the whole population of one town might play the entire population of another town moving freely back and forth across the countryside.
>
> Many conflicts are narrowly confined by a variety of devices, but the distinctive quality of political conflicts is that the relations between the players and the audience have not been well defined and there is usually nothing to keep the audience from getting into the game.

Someone said that war is too important to be left to the generals. In a similar spirit, American politics may be too important to be left to the politicians. In whatever way you think best, get in the game.

THOUGHT QUESTIONS

1. Give examples from throughout the book that support the pluralist approach. Give other examples that lean toward the power elite.
2. Pluralism has been described as essentially "liberal," whereas elitism can be either "radical" or "conservative." Do you agree?
3. Which approach, pluralism or elitism, do you feel best describes the political game in your own community? Give examples.
4. Do you think interest in politics is growing among students? Why? How is political participation by students encouraged or discouraged?

SUGGESTED READINGS

Dahl, Robert A. *Who Governs?* New Haven, CT: Yale University Press, 1961. Pb.
   A case study showing pluralism operating in New Haven's city government.
———. *On Democracy.* New Haven, CT: Yale University Press, 1998.
   Intelligently reviews and argues the merits of democracy.
D'Souza, Dinesh. *What's So Great About America?* New York: Regnery Publishing, 2002.
   An articulate conservative immigrant fires away at critics of the United States of America.
Greider, William. *Who Will Tell the People?* New York: Simon & Schuster, 1992.
   This *Rolling Stone* editor gives a muckraking view of how issues are wheeled and dealed in Washington with little regard for the American people.
Lukes, Steven. *Power: A Radical View*, 2nd ed. New York: Palgrave Macmillan, 2005. Pb.
   An English theorist examines the "least observable" aspects of power.
Mills, C. Wright. *The Power Elite.* New York: Oxford University Press, 1959. Pb.
   A well-known sociologist's attempt to show that an elite governs America in its own interest.
Rothkopf, David. *Superclass: The Global Power Elite and the World they Are Making.* New York: Farrar Straus and Giroux, 2008.
   A former Kissinger Associates director dissects and then urges the global elite to reform the unequal, unstable world they're creating.
Schattschneider, E. E. *The Semisovereign People.* New York: Holt, Rinehart & Winston, 1961. Pb.
   This landmark work presents a basic explanation of how and why some people get into politics and some stay out.

APPENDIX

The Declaration of Independence

In Congress, July 4, 1776

The Unanimous Declaration of the Thirteen United States of America

When in the Course of human events, it becomes necessary for one people to dissolve the political bands, which have connected them with another, and to assume among the powers of the earth, the separate and equal station to which the Laws of Nature and of Nature's God entitle them, a decent respect to the opinions of mankind requires that they should declare the causes which impel them to the separation.—We hold these truths to be self-evident, that all men are created equal, that they are endowed by their Creator with certain unalienable Rights, that among these are Life, Liberty and the pursuit of Happiness.—That to secure these rights, Governments are instituted among Men, deriving their just powers from the consent of the governed,—That whenever any Form of Government becomes destructive of these ends, it is the Right of the People to alter or to abolish it, and to institute new Government, laying its foundation on such principles and organizing its powers in such form, as to them shall seem most likely to effect their Safety and Happiness. Prudence, indeed, will dictate that Governments long established should not be changed for light and transient causes; and accordingly all experience hath shown, that mankind are more disposed to suffer, while evils are sufferable, than to right themselves by abolishing the forms to which they are accustomed. But when a long train of abuses and usurpations, pursuing invariably the same Object evinces a design to reduce them under absolute Despotism, it is their right, it is their duty, to throw off such Government, and to provide new Guards for their future security.—Such has been the patient sufferance of these Colonies; and such is now the necessity which constrains them to alter their former Systems of Government. The history of the present King of Great Britain is a history of repeated injuries and usurpations, all having in direct object the establishment of an absolute Tyranny over these States. To prove this, let Facts be submitted to a candid world.—He has refused his Assent to Laws, the most wholesome and necessary for the public good.—He has forbidden his Governors to pass Laws of immediate and pressing importance, unless suspended in their operation till his Assent should be obtained; and when so suspended, he has utterly neglected to attend to them.—He has refused to pass other Laws for the accommodation of large districts of people, unless those people would relinquish the right of Representation in the Legislature, a right inestimable to them and formidable to tyrants only.—He has called together legislative bodies at places unusual, uncomfortable, and distant from the depository of their public Records, for the sole purpose of fatiguing them into compliance with his measures.—He has dissolved Representative Houses repeatedly, for opposing with manly firmness his invasions on the rights of the people.—He has refused for a long time, after such dissolutions, to cause others to be elected; whereby the Legislative powers, incapable of Annihilation, have returned to the People at large for their exercise; the State remaining in the meantime exposed to all the dangers of invasion from without, and convulsions within.—He has endeavored to prevent the population of these States; for that purpose obstructing the Laws for Naturalization of Foreigners; refusing to pass others to encourage their migrations hither, and raising the conditions of new Appropriations of Lands.—He has obstructed the Administration of Justice, by refusing his Assent to Laws for establishing Judiciary powers.—He has made Judges dependent on his Will alone, for the tenure of their offices, and the amount and payment of their salaries.—He has erected a multitude of New Offices, and sent hither swarms of Officers to harass our people, and eat out their substance.— He has kept among us, in times of peace, Standing Armies without the Consent of our legislatures.—He has affected to render the Military independent of and superior to the Civil power.—He has combined with others to subject us to a jurisdiction foreign to our constitution, and unacknowledged by our laws; giving his Assent to their Acts of pretended Legislation.—For quartering large bodies of armed troops among us:— For protecting them, by a mock Trial, from punishment for any Murders which they should commit on the Inhabitants of these States:—For cutting off our Trade with all parts of the world:—For imposing Taxes on us without our Consent:—For depriving us in many cases, of the benefits of Trial by Jury:—For transporting us beyond Seas to be tried for pretended offenses:—For abolishing the free System of English Laws in a neighboring Province, establishing therein an Arbitrary government, and enlarging its Boundaries so as to render it at once an example and fit instrument for introducing the same absolute rule into these Colonies:—For taking away our Charters, abolishing our most valuable Laws, and altering fundamentally the Forms of our Governments:—For suspending our own Legislatures, and declaring themselves invested with power to legislate for us in all cases whatsoever.—He has abdicated Government here, by declaring us out of his Protection and waging War against us.—He has plundered our seas, ravaged our Coasts, burnt our towns, and destroyed the lives of our people.—He is at this time transporting large armies of foreign Mercenaries to complete the works of death, desolation and tyranny, already begun with circumstances of Cruelty & perfidy, scarcely paralleled in the most barbarous ages, and totally unworthy the Head of a civilized nation.—He has constrained our fellow Citizens taken Captive on the High Seas to bear Arms against their Country, to become the executioners of their friends and Brethren, or to fall themselves by their hands.—He has excited domestic insurrections amongst us, and has endeavored to bring on the inhabitants of our frontiers, the merciless Indian Savages, whose known rule of warfare, is an undistinguished destruction of all ages, sexes and conditions. In every stage of these Oppressions We have Petitioned for Redress in the most humble terms: Our repeated Petitions have been answered only by repeated injury. A Prince whose character is thus marked by every act which may define a Tyrant, is unfit to be the ruler of a free people. Nor have We been wanting in attentions to our British brethren. We have warned them from time to time of attempts by their legislature to extend an unwarrantable jurisdiction over us. We have reminded them of the circumstances of our emigration and settlement here. We have appealed to their native justice and magnanimity, and we have conjured them by the ties of our common kindred to disavow these usurpations, which would inevitably interrupt our connections and correspondence. They too have been deaf to the voice of justice and of consanguinity. We must, therefore, acquiesce in the necessity, which denounces our Separation, and hold them, as we hold the rest of mankind, Enemies in War, in Peace Friends.—

We, therefore, the Representatives of the United States of America, in General Congress, Assembled, appealing to the Supreme Judge of the world for the rectitude of our intentions do, in the Name, and by the Authority of the good People of these Colonies, solemnly publish and declare, That these United Colonies are, and of Right ought to be Free and Independent States, that they are Absolved from all Allegiance to the British Crown, and that all political connection between them and the State of Great Britain, is and ought to be totally dissolved; and that as Free and Independent States, they have full Power to levy War, conclude Peace, contract Alliances, establish Commerce, and to do all other Acts and Things which Independent States may of right do.—And for the support of this Declaration, with a firm reliance on the protection of divine Providence, we mutually pledge to each other our Lives, our Fortunes and our sacred Honor.

The Constitution of the United States

Submitted on September 17, 1787 by the Constitutional Convention, and became effective on March 4, 1789.

We the People of the United States, in Order to form a more perfect Union, establish Justice, insure domestic Tranquility, provide for the common defense, promote the general Welfare, and secure the Blessings of Liberty to ourselves and our Posterity, do ordain and establish this CONSTITUTION for the United States of America.

Article I

Section 1. All legislative Powers herein granted shall be vested in a Congress of the United States, which shall consist of a Senate and House of Representatives.

Section 2. (1) The House of Representatives shall be composed of Members chosen every second Year by the People of the several States, and the Electors in each State shall have the Qualifications requisite for Electors of the most numerous Branch of the State Legislature.

(2) No Person shall be a Representative who shall not have attained to the Age of twenty-five Years, and been seven Years a Citizen of the United States, and who shall not, when elected, be an Inhabitant of that State in which he shall be chosen.

(3) [Representatives and direct Taxes[1] shall be apportioned among the several States which may be included within this Union, according to their respective Numbers, which shall be determined by adding to the whole Number of free Persons, including those bound to Service for a Term of Years, and excluding Indians not taxed, three fifths of all other Persons.][2] The actual Enumeration shall be made within three Years after the first Meeting of the Congress of the United States, and within every subsequent Term of ten Years, in such Manner as they shall by Law direct. The Number of Representatives shall not exceed one for every thirty Thousand, but each State shall have at Least one Representative; and until such enumeration shall be made, the State of New Hampshire shall be entitled to choose three, Massachusetts eight, Rhode-Island and Providence Plantations one, Connecticut five, New York six, New Jersey four, Pennsylvania eight, Delaware one, Maryland six, Virginia ten, North Carolina five, South Carolina five, and Georgia three.

(4) When vacancies happen in the Representation from any State, the Executive Authority thereof shall issue Writs of Election to fill such Vacancies.

(5) The House of Representatives shall choose their Speaker and other Officers; and shall have the sole Power of Impeachment.

Section 3. (1) The Senate of the United States shall be composed of two Senators from each State, [chosen by the Legislature][3] thereof, for six Years; and each Senator shall have one Vote.

(2) Immediately after they shall be assembled in Consequence of the first Election, they shall be divided as equally as may be into three Classes. The Seats of the Senators of the first Class shall be vacated at the Expiration of the second Year, of the second Class at the Expiration of the fourth Year, and of the third Class at the Expiration of the sixth Year, so that one-third may be chosen every second year; [and if Vacancies happen by Resignation, or otherwise, during the Recess of the Legislature of

---

[1]The Sixteenth Amendment replaced this with respect to income taxes.

[2]Repealed by the Fourteenth Amendment.

[3]Repealed by the Seventeenth Amendment.

any State, the Executive thereof may make temporary Appointments until the next Meeting of the Legislature, which shall then fill such Vacancies].[4]

(3) No person shall be a Senator who shall not have attained to the Age of thirty Years, and been nine Years a Citizen of the United States, and who shall not, when elected, be an Inhabitant of that State for which he shall be chosen.

(4) The Vice President of the United States shall be President of the Senate, but shall have no Vote, unless they be equally divided.

(5) The Senate shall choose their other Officers, and also a President *pro tempore,* in the Absence of the Vice President, or when he shall exercise the Office of President of the United States.

(6) The Senate shall have the sole Power to try all Impeachments. When sitting for that Purpose, they shall be on Oath or Affirmation. When the President of the United States is tried, the Chief Justice shall preside: And no Person shall be convicted without the Concurrence of two thirds of the Members present.

(7) Judgment in Cases of Impeachment shall not extend further than to removal from Office, and disqualification to hold and enjoy any Office of honor, Trust or Profit under the United States: but the Party convicted shall nevertheless be liable and subject to Indictment, Trial, Judgment and Punishment according to Law.

Section 4. (1) The Times, Places and Manner of holding Elections for Senators and Representatives, shall be prescribed in each State by the Legislature thereof; but the Congress may at any time by Law make or alter such Regulations, except as to the Places of choosing Senators.

(2) The Congress shall assemble at least once in every Year, and such Meeting shall [be on the first Monday in December,][5] unless they shall by Law appoint a different Day.

Section 5. (1) Each House shall be the Judge of the Elections, Returns and Qualifications of its own Members, and a Majority of each shall constitute a Quorum to do Business; but a smaller Number may adjourn from day to day, and may be authorized to compel the Attendance of absent Members, in such Manner, and under such Penalties as each House may provide.

(2) Each House may determine the Rules of its Proceedings, punish its Members for disorderly Behavior, and, with the Concurrence of two thirds, expel a Member.

(3) Each House shall keep a Journal of its Proceedings, and from time to time publish the same, excepting such Parts as may in their Judgment require Secrecy; and the Yeas and Nays of the Members of either House on any question shall, at the Desire of one fifth of those Present, be entered on the Journal.

(4) Neither House, during the Session of Congress, shall, without the Consent of the other, adjourn for more than three days, nor to any other Place than that in which the two Houses shall be sitting.

Section 6. (1) The Senators and Representatives shall receive a Compensation for their Services, to be ascertained by Law, and paid out of the Treasury of the United States. They shall in all Cases, except Treason, Felony and Breach of the Peace, be privileged from Arrest during their Attendance at the Session of their respective Houses, and in going to and returning from the same; and for any Speech or Debate in either House, they shall not be questioned in any other Place.

(2) No Senator or Representative shall, during the Time for which he was elected, be appointed to any civil Office under the Authority of the United States, which shall have been created, or the Emoluments whereof have been increased during such time;

---

[4]Changed by the Seventeenth Amendment.

[5]Changed by the Twentieth Amendment, Section 2.

and no Person holding any Office under the United States, shall be a Member of either House during his Continuance in Office.

Section 7. (1) All Bills for raising Revenue shall originate in the House of Representatives; but the Senate may propose or concur with Amendments as on other Bills.

(2) Every Bill which shall have passed the House of Representatives and the Senate, shall, before it becomes a Law, be presented to the President of the United States; If he approves he shall sign it, but if not he shall return it, with his Objections to that House in which it shall have originated, who shall enter the Objections at large on their Journal, and proceed to reconsider it. If after such Reconsideration two-thirds of that House shall agree to pass the Bill, it shall be sent, together with the Objections, to the other House, by which it shall likewise be reconsidered, and if approved by two thirds of that House, it shall become a Law. But in all such Cases the Votes of both Houses shall be determined by Yeas and Nays, and the Names of the Persons voting for and against the Bill shall be entered on the Journal of each House respectively. If any Bill shall not be returned by the President within ten Days (Sundays excepted) after it shall have been presented to him, the Same shall be a Law, in like Manner as if he had signed it, unless the Congress by their Adjournment prevent its Return, in which Case it shall not be a Law.

(3) Every Order, Resolution, or Vote to which the Concurrence of the Senate and House of Representatives may be necessary (except on a question of Adjournment) shall be presented to the President of the United States; and before the Same shall take Effect, shall be approved by him, or being disapproved by him, shall be repassed by two-thirds of the Senate and House of Representatives, according to the Rules and Limitations prescribed in the Case of a Bill.

Section 8. (1) The Congress shall have Power To lay and collect Taxes, Duties, Imposts and Excises, to pay the Debts and provide for the common Defense and general Welfare of the United States; but all Duties, Imposts and Excises shall be uniform throughout the United States;

(2) To borrow money on the credit of the United States;

(3) To regulate Commerce with foreign Nations, and among the several States, and with the Indian Tribes;

(4) To establish a uniform Rule of Naturalization, and uniform Laws on the subject of Bankruptcies throughout the United States;

(5) To coin Money, regulate the Value thereof, and of foreign Coin, and fix the Standard of Weights and Measures;

(6) To provide for the Punishment of counterfeiting the Securities and current Coin of the United States;

(7) To establish Post Offices and post Roads;

(8) To promote the Progress of Science and useful Arts, by securing for limited Times to Authors and Inventors the exclusive Right to their respective Writings and Discoveries;

(9) To constitute Tribunals inferior to the supreme Court;

(10) To define and punish Piracies and Felonies committed on the high Seas, and Offenses against the Law of Nations;

(11) To declare War, grant Letters of Marque and Reprisal, and make Rules concerning Captures on Land and Water;

(12) To raise and support Armies, but no Appropriation of Money to that Use shall be for a longer Term than two Years;

(13) To provide and maintain a Navy;

(14) To make Rules for the Government and Regulation of the land and naval Forces;

(15) To provide for calling forth the Militia to execute the Laws of the Union, suppress Insurrections and repel Invasions;

(16) To provide for organizing, arming, and disciplining the Militia, and for governing such Part of them as may be employed in the Service of the United States,

reserving to the States respectively, the Appointment of the Officers, and the Authority of training the Militia according to the discipline prescribed by Congress;

(17) To exercise exclusive Legislation in all Cases whatsoever, over such District (not exceeding ten Miles square) as may, by Cession of particular States, and the Acceptance of Congress, become the Seat of the Government of the United States, and to exercise like Authority over all Places purchased by the Consent of the Legislature of the State in which the Same shall be, for the Erection of Forts, Magazines, Arsenals, dock-Yards, and other needful Buildings;—And

(18) To make all Laws which shall be necessary and proper for carrying into Execution the foregoing Powers, and all other Powers vested by this Constitution in the Government of the United States, or in any Department or Officer thereof.

Section 9. (1) The Migration or Importation of such Persons as any of the States now existing shall think proper to admit, shall not be prohibited by the Congress prior to the Year one thousand eight hundred and eight, but a tax or duty may be imposed on such Importation, not exceeding ten dollars for each Person.

(2) The Privilege of the Writ of Habeas Corpus shall not be suspended, unless when in Cases of Rebellion or Invasion the public Safety may require it.

(3) No Bill of Attainder or ex post facto Law shall be passed.

(4) No Capitation, or other direct, Tax shall be laid, unless in Proportion to the Census or Enumeration herein before directed to be taken.[6]

(5) No Tax or Duty shall be laid on Articles exported from any State.

(6) No Preference shall be given by any Regulation of Commerce or Revenue to the Ports of one State over those of another; nor shall Vessels bound to, or from, one State, be obliged to enter, clear, or pay Duties in another.

(7) No Money shall be drawn from the Treasury, but in Consequence of Appropriations made by Law; and a regular Statement and Account of the Receipts and Expenditures of all public Money shall be published from time to time.

(8) No Title of Nobility shall be granted by the United States: And no Person holding any Office of Profit or Trust under them, shall, without the Consent of the Congress, accept of any present, Emolument, Office, or Title, of any kind whatever, from any King, Prince, or foreign State.

Section 10. (1) No State shall enter into any Treaty, Alliance, or Confederation; grant Letters of Marque and Reprisal; coin Money; emit Bills of Credit; make any Thing but gold and silver Coin a Tender in Payment of Debts; pass any Bill of Attainder, ex post facto Law, or Law impairing the Obligation of Contracts, or grant any Title of Nobility.

(2) No State shall, without the Consent of the Congress, lay any Imposts or Duties on Imports or Exports, except what may be absolutely necessary for executing its inspection Laws: and the net Produce of all Duties and Imposts, laid by any State on Imports or Exports, shall be for the Use of the Treasury of the United States; and all such laws shall be subject to the Revision and Control of the Congress.

(3) No State shall, without the Consent of Congress, lay any duty of Tonnage, keep Troops, or Ships of War in time of Peace, enter into any Agreement or Compact with another State, or with a foreign Power, or engage in War, unless actually invaded, or in such imminent Danger as will not admit of delay.

Article II

Section 1. (1) The executive Power shall be vested in a President of the United States of America. He shall hold his Office during the Term of four Years, and, together with the Vice-President, chosen for the same Term, be elected, as follows:

---

[6]Changed by the Sixteenth Amendment.

(2) Each State shall appoint, in such Manner as the Legislature thereof may direct, a Number of Electors, equal to the whole Number of Senators and Representatives to which the State may be entitled in the Congress; but no Senator or Representative, or Person holding an Office of Trust or Profit under the United States, shall be appointed an Elector.

(3) [The Electors shall meet in their respective States, and vote by Ballot for two persons, of whom one at least shall not be an Inhabitant of the same State with themselves. And they shall make a List of all the Persons voted for, and of the Number of Votes for each; which List they shall sign and certify, and transmit sealed to the Seat of the Government of the United States, directed to the President of the Senate. The President of the Senate shall, in the Presence of the Senate and House of Representatives, open all the Certificates, and the Votes shall then be counted. The Person having the greatest Number of Votes shall be the President, if such Number be a Majority of the whole Number of Electors appointed; and if there be more than one who have such Majority, and have an equal Number of Votes, then the House of Representatives shall immediately choose by Ballot one of them for President; and if no Person have a Majority, then from the five highest on the List the said House shall in like Manner choose the President. But in choosing the President, the Votes shall be taken by States, the Representation from each State having one Vote; A quorum for this purpose shall consist of a Member or Members from two-thirds of the States, and a Majority of all the States shall be necessary to a Choice. In every Case, after the Choice of the President, the Person having the greatest Number of Votes of the Electors shall be the Vice-President. But if there should remain two or more who have equal Votes, the Senate shall choose from them by Ballot the Vice-President.][7]

(4) (3) The Congress may determine the Time of choosing the Electors, and the Day on which they shall give their Votes; which Day shall be the same throughout the United States.

(5)(4) No person except a natural born Citizen, or a Citizen of the United States, at the time of the Adoption of this Constitution, shall be eligible to the Office of President; neither shall any Person be eligible to that Office who shall not have attained to the Age of thirty-five Years, and been fourteen Years a Resident within the United States.

(6)(5) In case of the Removal of the President from Office, or of his Death, Resignation, or Inability to discharge the Powers and Duties of the said Office, the same shall devolve on the Vice-President, and the Congress may by Law provide for the Case of Removal, Death, Resignation or Inability, both of the President and Vice-President, declaring what Officer shall then act as President, and such Officer shall act accordingly, until the Disability be removed, or a President shall be elected.[8]

(7) (6) The President shall, at stated Times, receive for his Services, a Compensation, which shall neither be increased nor diminished during the Period for which he shall have been elected, and he shall not receive within that Period any other Emolument from the United States, or any of them.

(8) (7) Before he enter on the Execution of his Office, he shall take the following Oath or Affirmation:—"I do solemnly swear (or affirm) that I will faithfully execute the Office of President of the United States, and will to the best of my Ability, preserve, protect and defend the Constitution of the United States."

Section 2. (1) The President shall be Commander in Chief of the Army and Navy of the United States, and of the Militia of the several States, when called into the actual Service of the United States; he may require the Opinion in writing, of the

---

[7]This paragraph was superseded in 1804 by the Twelfth Amendment.

[8]Changed by the Twenty-fifth Amendment.

principal Officer in each of the executive Departments, upon any subject relating to the Duties of their respective Offices, and he shall have Power to Grant Reprieves and Pardons for Offenses against the United States, except in Cases of Impeachment.

(2) He shall have Power, by and with the Advice and Consent of the Senate, to make Treaties, provided two-thirds of the Senators present concur; and he shall nominate, and by and with the Advice and Consent of the Senate, shall appoint Ambassadors, other public Ministers and Consuls, Judges of the supreme Court, and all other Officers of the United States, whose Appointments are not herein otherwise provided for, and which shall be established by Law: but the Congress may by Law vest the Appointment of such inferior Officers, as they think proper, in the President alone, in the Court of Law, or in the Heads of Departments.

(3) The President shall have Power to fill up all Vacancies that may happen during the Recess of the Senate, by granting Commissions which shall expire at the End of their next Session.

Section 3. He shall from time to time give to the Congress Information of the State of the Union, and recommend to their Consideration such Measures as he shall judge necessary and expedient; he may, on extraordinary Occasions, convene both Houses, or either of them, and in Case of Disagreement between them, with Respect to the Time of Adjournment, he may adjourn them to such Time as he shall think proper; he shall receive Ambassadors and other public Ministers; he shall take Care that the Laws be faithfully executed, and shall Commission all the Officers of the United States.

Section 4. The President, Vice President and all civil Officers of the United States, shall be removed from Office on Impeachment for, and Conviction of, Treason, Bribery, or other high Crimes and Misdemeanors.

Article III

Section 1. The judicial Power of the United States, shall be vested in one supreme Court, and in such inferior Courts as the Congress may from time to time ordain and establish. The Judges, both of the supreme and inferior Courts, shall hold their Offices during good Behavior, and shall, at stated Times, receive for their Services a Compensation which shall not be diminished during their Continuance in Office.

Section 2. (1) The judicial Power shall extend to all Cases, in Law and Equity, arising under this Constitution, the Laws of the United States, and Treaties made, or which shall be made, under their Authority;—to all Cases affecting Ambassadors, other public Ministers and Consuls;—to all Cases of admiralty and maritime Jurisdiction;—to Controversies to which the United States shall be a Party;—to Controversies between two or more states;—[between a State and Citizens of another State];[9]—between Citizens of different States;—between Citizens of the same State claiming Lands under Grants of different States, and [between a State, or the Citizens thereof, and foreign States, Citizens or Subjects].[10]

(2) In all Cases affecting Ambassadors, other public Ministers and Consuls, and those in which a State shall be Party, the supreme Court shall have original Jurisdiction. In all the other Cases before mentioned, the supreme Court shall have appellate Jurisdiction, both as to Law and Fact, with such Exceptions, and under such Regulations as the Congress shall make.

(3) The trial of all Crimes, except in Cases of Impeachment, shall be by Jury; and such Trial shall be held in the State where the said Crimes shall have been committed:

---

[9]Restricted by the Eleventh Amendment.

[10]Restricted by the Eleventh Amendment.

but when not committed within any State, the Trial shall be at such Place or Places as the Congress may by Law have directed.

Section 3. (1) Treason against the United States, shall consist only in levying War against them, or in adhering to their Enemies, giving them Aid and Comfort. No Person shall be convicted of Treason unless on the Testimony of two Witnesses to the same overt Act, or on Confession in open Court.

(2) The Congress shall have Power to declare the Punishment of Treason, but no Attainder of Treason shall work Corruption of Blood, or Forfeiture except during the Life of the Person attained.

Article IV

Section 1. Full Faith and Credit shall be given in each State to the public Acts, Records, and judicial Proceedings of every other State. And the Congress may by general Laws prescribe the Manner in which such Acts, Records and Proceedings shall be proved, and the Effect thereof.

Section 2. (1) The Citizens of each State shall be entitled to all Privileges and Immunities of Citizens in the several States.

(2) A Person charged in any State with Treason, Felony, or other Crime, who shall flee from Justice, and be found in another State, shall on demand of the executive Authority of the State from which he fled, be delivered up, to be removed to the State having Jurisdiction of the Crime.

(3) [No Person held to Service or Labor in one State, under the Laws thereof, escaping into another, shall, in Consequence of any Law or Regulation therein, be discharged from such Service or Labor, but shall be delivered up on Claim of the Party to whom such Service or Labor may be due.][11]

Section 3. (1) New States may be admitted by the Congress into this Union; but no new State shall be formed or erected within the Jurisdiction of any other State; nor any State be formed by the Junction of two or more States, or Parts of States, without the Consent of the Legislatures of the States concerned as well as of the Congress.

(2) The Congress shall have Power to dispose of and make all needful Rules and Regulations respecting the Territory or other Property belonging to the United States; and nothing in this Constitution shall be so construed as to Prejudice any Claims of the United States, or of any particular State.

Section 4. The United States shall guarantee to every State in this Union a Republican Form of Government, and shall protect each of them against Invasion; and on Application of the Legislature, or of the Executive (when the Legislature cannot be convened) against domestic Violence.

Article V

The Congress, whenever two-thirds of both Houses shall deem it necessary, shall propose Amendments to this Constitution, or, on the Application of the Legislatures of two-thirds of the several States, shall call a Convention for proposing Amendments, which, in either Case, shall be valid to all Intents and Purposes, as part of this Constitution, when ratified by the Legislature of three-fourths of the several States, or by Conventions in three-fourths thereof, as the one or the other Mode of Ratification may be proposed by the Congress; Provided that no Amendment which may be made prior to the Year One thousand eight hundred and eight shall in any Manner affect

---

[11]This paragraph was superseded by the Thirteenth Amendment.

the first and fourth Clauses in the Ninth Section of the first Article; and that no State, without its Consent, shall be deprived of its equal Suffrage in the Senate.

Article VI

(1) All Debts contracted and Engagements entered into, before the Adoption of this Constitution, shall be as valid against the United States under this Constitution, as under the Confederation.

(2) This Constitution, and the Laws of the United States which shall be made in Pursuance thereof; and all Treaties made, or which shall be made, under the Authority of the United States, shall be the supreme Law of the Land; and the Judges in every State shall be bound thereby, any Thing in the Constitution or Laws of any State to the Contrary notwithstanding.

(3) The Senators and Representatives before mentioned, and the Members of the several State Legislatures, and all executive and judicial Officers, both of the United States and of the several States, shall be bound by Oath or Affirmation, to support this Constitution; but no religious Test shall ever be required as a Qualification to any Office or public Trust under the United States.

Article VII

(1) The Ratification of the Conventions of nine States, shall be sufficient for the Establishment of this Constitution between the States so ratifying the Same.

(2) DONE in Convention by the Unanimous Consent of the States present the Seventeenth Day of September in the Year of our Lord one thousand seven hundred and Eighty seven and the Independence of the United States of America the Twelfth. In Witness whereof We have hereunto subscribed our Names.

Go. Washington
President and deputy from Virginia

Articles in Addition to, and Amendment of, the Constitution of the United States of America, Proposed by Congress, and Ratified by the Legislatures of the Several States, Pursuant to the Fifth Article of the Original Constitution.

Amendment I[12]

Congress shall make no law respecting an establishment of religion, or prohibiting the free exercise thereof; or abridging the freedom of speech, or of the press; or the right of the people peaceably to assemble, and to petition the Government for a redress of grievances.

Amendment II

A well regulated Militia, being necessary to the security of a free State, the right of the people to keep and bear Arms, shall not be infringed.

Amendment III

No Soldier shall, in time of peace be quartered in any house, without the consent of the Owner, nor in time of war, but in a manner to be prescribed by law.

---

[12]The first ten amendments were adopted in 1791.

Amendment IV

The right of the people to be secure in their persons, houses, papers, and effects, against unreasonable searches and seizures, shall not be violated, and no Warrants shall issue, but upon probable cause, supported by Oath or affirmation, and particularly describing the place to be searched, and the persons or things to be seized.

Amendment V

No person shall be held to answer for a capital, or otherwise infamous crime, unless on a presentment or indictment of a Grand Jury, except in cases arising in the land or naval forces, or in the Militia, when in actual service in time of War or public danger; nor shall any person be subject for the same offense to be twice put in jeopardy of life or limb; nor shall be compelled in any criminal case to be witness against himself, nor be deprived of life, liberty, or property, without due process of law; nor shall private property be taken for public use without just compensation.

Amendment VI

In all criminal prosecutions, the accused shall enjoy the right to a speedy and public trial, by an impartial jury of the State and district wherein the crime shall have been committed, which district shall have been previously ascertained by law, and to be informed of the nature and cause of the accusation, to be confronted with the witnesses against him; to have compulsory process for obtaining witnesses in his favor, and to have the Assistance of Counsel for his defense.

Amendment VII

In Suits at common law, where the value in controversy shall exceed twenty dollars, the right of trial by jury shall be preserved, and no fact tried by a jury, shall be otherwise reexamined in any Court of the United States, than according to the rules of the common law.

Amendment VIII

Excessive bail shall not be required, nor excessive fines imposed, nor cruel and unusual punishments inflicted.

Amendment IX

The enumeration in the Constitution, of certain rights, shall not be construed to deny or disparage others retained by the people.

Amendment X

The powers not delegated to the United States by the Constitution, nor prohibited by it to the States, are reserved to the States respectively, or to the people.

Amendment XI[13]

The Judicial power of the United States shall not be construed to extend to any suit in law or equity, commenced or prosecuted against one of the United States by Citizens of another State, or by Citizens or Subjects of any Foreign State.

Amendment XII[14]

The Electors shall meet in their respective states and vote by ballot for President and Vice-President, one of whom, at least, shall not be an inhabitant of the same state with themselves; they shall name in their ballots the person voted for as President, and in distinct ballots the person voted for as Vice-President, and they shall make distinct lists of all persons voted for as President, and of all persons voted for as Vice-President, and of the number of votes for each, which lists they shall sign and certify, and transmit sealed to the seat of the government of the United States, directed to the President of the Senate;—The President of the Senate shall, in presence of the Senate and House of Representatives, open all the certificates and the votes shall then be counted;—The person having the greatest number of votes for President, shall be the President, if such number be a majority of the whole number of Electors appointed; and if no person have such majority, then from the persons having the highest numbers not exceeding three on the list of those voted for as President, the House of Representatives shall choose immediately, by ballot, the President. But in choosing the President, the votes shall be taken by states, the representation from each state having one vote; a quorum for this purpose shall consist of a member or members from two-thirds of the states, and a majority of all the states shall be necessary to a choice. [And if the House of Representatives shall not choose a President whenever the right of choice shall devolve upon them, before the fourth day of March next following, then the Vice-President shall act as President, as in the case of the death or other constitutional disability of the President.][15]—The person having the greatest number of votes as Vice-President, shall be the Vice-President, if such number be a majority of the whole number of Electors appointed, and if no person have a majority, then from the two highest numbers on the list, the Senate shall choose the Vice-President; a quorum for the purpose shall consist of two-thirds of the whole number of Senators, and a majority of the whole number shall be necessary to a choice. But no person constitutionally ineligible to the office of President shall be eligible to that of Vice-President of the United States.

Amendment XIII[16]

Section 1. Neither slavery nor involuntary servitude, except as a punishment for crime whereof the party shall have been duly convicted, shall exist within the United States, or any place subject to their jurisdiction.

Section 2. Congress shall have power to enforce this article by appropriate legislation.

---

[13]Adopted in 1798.

[14]Adopted in 1804.

[15]Superseded by the Twentieth Amendment, Section 3.

[16]Adopted in 1865.

Amendment XIV[17]

Section 1. All persons born or naturalized in the United States, and subject to the jurisdiction thereof, are citizens of the United States and of the State wherein they reside. No state shall make or enforce any law which shall abridge the privileges or immunities of citizens of the United States; nor shall any State deprive any person of life, liberty, or property, without due process of law; nor deny to any person within its jurisdiction the equal protection of the laws.

Section 2. Representatives shall be apportioned among the several States according to their respective numbers, counting the whole number of persons in each State, excluding Indians not taxed. But when the right to vote at any election for the choice of electors for President and Vice-President of the United States, Representatives in Congress, the Executive and Judicial officers of a State, or the members of the Legislature thereof, is denied to any of the male inhabitants of such State, being twenty-one years of age, and citizens of the United States, or in any way abridged, except for participation in rebellion, or other crime, the basis of representation therein shall be reduced in the proportion which the number of such male citizens shall bear to the whole number of male citizens twenty-one years of age in such State.

Section 3. No person shall be a Senator or Representative in Congress, or elector of President and Vice-President, or hold any office, civil or military, under the United States, or under any State, who, having previously taken an oath, as a member of Congress, or as an officer of the United States, or as a member of any State legislature, or as an executive or judicial officer of any State, to support the Constitution of the United States, shall have engaged in insurrection or rebellion against the same, or given aid or comfort to the enemies thereof. But Congress may by a vote of two-thirds of each House, remove such disability.

Section 4. The validity of the public debt of the United States, authorized by law, including debts incurred for payment of pensions and bounties for services in suppressing insurrection or rebellion, shall not be questioned. But neither the United States nor any State shall assume or pay any debt or obligation incurred in aid of insurrection or rebellion against the United States, or any claim for the loss or emancipation of any slave; but all such debts, obligations and claims shall be held illegal and void.

Section 5. The Congress shall have power to enforce, by appropriate legislation, the provisions of this article.

Amendment XV[18]

Section 1. The right of citizens of the United States to vote shall not be denied or abridged by the United States or by any State on account of race, color, or previous condition of servitude.

Section 2. The Congress shall have power to enforce this article by appropriate legislation.

Amendment XVI[19]

The Congress shall have power to lay and collect taxes on incomes, from whatever source derived, without apportionment among the several States, and without regard to any census or enumeration.

---

[17]Adopted in 1868.

[18]Adopted in 1870.

[19]Adopted in 1913.

Amendment XVII[20]

(1) The Senate of the United States shall be composed of two Senators from each State, elected by the people thereof, for six years; and each Senator shall have one vote. The electors in each State shall have the qualifications requisite for electors of the most numerous branch of the State legislatures.

(2) When vacancies happen in the representation of any State in the Senate, the executive authority of such State shall issue writs of election to fill such vacancies: *Provided,* That the legislature of any State may empower the executive thereof to make temporary appointments until the people fill the vacancies by election as the legislature may direct.

(3) This amendment shall not be so construed as to affect the election or term of any Senator chosen before it becomes valid as part of the Constitution.

Amendment XVIII[21]

Section 1. After one year from the ratification of this article the manufacture, sale, or transportation of intoxicating liquors within, the importation thereof into, or the exportation thereof from the United States and all territory subject to the jurisdiction thereof for beverage purposes is hereby prohibited.

Section 2. The Congress and the several States shall have concurrent power to enforce this article by appropriate legislation.

Section 3. This article shall be inoperative unless it shall have been ratified as an amendment to the Constitution by the legislatures of the several States, as provided in the Constitution, within seven years from the date of the submission hereof to the States by the Congress.

Amendment XIX[22]

The right of citizens of the United States to vote shall not be denied or abridged by the United States or by any State on account of sex.

Congress shall have power to enforce this article by appropriate legislation.

Amendment XX[23]

Section 1. The terms of the President and Vice-President shall end at noon on the 20th day of January, and the terms of Senators and Representatives at noon on the 3rd day of January, of the years in which such terms would have ended if this article had not been ratified; and the terms of their successors shall then begin.

Section 2. The Congress shall assemble at least once in every year, and such meeting shall begin at noon on the 3rd day of January, unless they shall by law appoint a different day.

Section 3. If, at the time fixed for the beginning of the term of the President, the President elect shall have died, the Vice-President elect shall become President. If a President shall not have been chosen before the time fixed for the beginning of his term, or if the President elect shall have failed to qualify, then the Vice-President elect shall act as President until a President shall have qualified; and the Congress may by

---

[20]Adopted in 1913.

[21]Adopted in 1919. Repealed by Section 1 of the Twenty-first Amendment.

[22]Adopted in 1920.

[23]Adopted in 1933.

law provide for the case wherein neither a President elect nor a Vice-President elect shall have qualified, declaring who shall then act as President, or the manner in which one who is to act shall be selected, and such person shall act accordingly until a President or Vice-President shall have qualified.

Section 4. The Congress may by law provide for the case of the death of any of the persons from whom the House of Representatives may choose a President whenever the right of choice shall have devolved upon them, and for the case of the death of any of the persons from whom the Senate may choose a Vice-President whenever the right of choice shall have devolved upon them.

Section 5. Sections 1 and 2 shall take effect on the 15th day of October following the ratification of this article.

Section 6. This article shall be inoperative unless it shall have been ratified as an amendment to the Constitution by the legislatures of three-fourths of the several States within seven years from the date of its submission.

Amendment XXI[24]

Section 1. The eighteenth article of amendment to the Constitution of the United States is hereby repealed.

Section 2. The transportation or importation into any State, Territory, or possession of the United States for delivery or use therein of intoxicating liquors, in violation of the laws thereof, is hereby prohibited.

Section 3. This article shall be inoperative unless it shall have been ratified as an amendment to the Constitution by conventions in the several States, as provided in the Constitution, within seven years from the date of the submission hereof to the States by the Congress.

Amendment XXII[25]

Section 1. No person shall be elected to the office of the President more than twice, and no person who has held the office of President, or acted as President, for more than two years of a term to which some other person was elected President shall be elected to the office of the President more than once. But this Article shall not apply to any person holding the office of President when this Article was proposed by the Congress, and shall not prevent any person who may be holding the office of President, or acting as President, during the term within which this Article becomes operative from holding the office of President or acting as President during the remainder of such term.

Section 2. This article shall be inoperative unless it shall have been ratified as an amendment to the Constitution by the legislatures of three-fourths of the several States within seven years from the date of its submission to the States by the Congress.

Amendment XXIII[26]

Section 1. The District constituting the seat of Government of the United States shall appoint in such manner as the Congress may direct:

A number of electors of President and Vice-President equal to the whole number of Senators and Representatives in Congress to which the District would be entitled if it were a State, but in no event more than the least populous State; they shall be in

---

[24]Adopted in 1933.

[25]Adopted in 1951.

[26]Adopted in 1961.

addition to those appointed by the States, but they shall be considered, for the purposes of the election of President and Vice-President, to be electors appointed by a State, and they shall meet in the District and perform such duties as provided by the twelfth article of amendment.

Section 2. The Congress shall have power to enforce this article by appropriate legislation.

Amendment XXIV[27]

Section 1. The right of citizens of the United States to vote in any primary or other election for President or Vice-President, for electors for President or Vice-President, or for Senator or Representative in Congress, shall not be denied or abridged by the United States or any state by reasons of failure to pay any poll tax or other tax.

Section 2. The Congress shall have power to enforce this article by appropriate legislation.

Amendment XXV[28]

Section 1. In case of the removal of the President from office or of his death or resignation, the Vice-President shall become President.

Section 2. Whenever there is a vacancy in the office of the Vice-President, the President shall nominate a Vice-President who shall take office upon confirmation by a majority vote of both Houses of Congress.

Section 3. Whenever the President transmits to the President pro tempore of the Senate and the Speaker of the House of Representatives his written declaration that he is unable to discharge the powers and duties of his office, and until he transmits to them a written declaration to the contrary, such powers and duties shall be discharged by the Vice-President as Acting President.

(1) Section 4. Whenever the Vice-President and a majority of either the principal officers of the Executive departments or of such other body as Congress may by law provide, transmit to the President pro tempore of the Senate and the Speaker of the House of Representatives their written declaration that the President is unable to discharge the powers and duties of his office, The Vice-President shall immediately assume the powers and duties of the office as Acting President.

(2) Thereafter, when the President transmits to the President pro tempore of the Senate and the Speaker of the House of Representatives his written declaration that no inability exists, he shall resume the powers and duties of his office unless the Vice-President and a majority of either the principal officers of the executive departments or of such other body as Congress may by law provide, transmit within four days to the President pro tempore of the Senate and the Speaker of the House of Representatives their written declaration that the President is unable to discharge the powers and duties of his office. Thereupon Congress shall decide the issue, assembling within forty-eight hours for that purpose if not in session. If the Congress, within twenty-one days after receipt of the latter written declaration, or, if Congress is not in session, within twenty-one days after Congress is required to assemble, determines by two-thirds vote of both houses that the President is unable to discharge the powers and duties of his office, the Vice-President shall continue to discharge the same as Acting President; otherwise, the President shall resume the powers and duties of his office.

---

[27]Adopted in 1964.

[28]Adopted in 1967.

Amendment XXVI[29]

Section 1. The right of citizens of the United States, who are 18 years of age or older, to vote shall not be denied or abridged by the United States or any state on account of age.

 Section 2. The Congress shall have power to enforce this article by appropriate legislation.

Amendment XXVII

Article the Second . . . No law, varying the compensation for the services of the Senators and Representatives, shall take effect, until an election of Representatives shall have intervened.

---

[29]Adopted in 1971.

GLOSSARY

104th Congress—The Congress elected in 1994 with the first Republican majority in both houses since the 1950s.

111th Congress—The current Congress elected in 2008 with expanded Democratic party majorities in both houses.

527 Groups—Private groups usually organized to support a presidential candidate by raising unregulated money; they are a way to get around the limits on campaign fundraising.

advocacy ads—Used by interest groups to indirectly promote or defeat candidates for election; also called issue ads, they are a way of avoiding campaign spending limits.

affirmative action—An effort to remove effects of discrimination by requiring and expanding minority job, admission, and promotion opportunities.

agenda setting—A listing of national priorities; a major media function achieved by the prominence given certain news stories.

anarchy—A society without government.

Anti-Federalists—Group opposing adoption of Constitution; they preferred stronger state governments and more popular participation.

appellate jurisdiction—The authority of higher courts to review decisions by lower courts.

Articles of Confederation—A document that from 1781 to 1789 loosely unified the newly independent American states; its shortcomings led to the U.S. Constitution.

authority—Legitimate power.

"balance the ticket"—The effort by parties to represent different population groups and regions in their candidates for office.

bicameral—A legislature with two houses, such as the U.S. Congress with the House of Representatives and Senate.

Bill of Rights—The first ten amendments to the Constitution, including freedoms of speech, press, religion, due process, and jury trial.

blogs—Internet websites used to form networks of people to support a political candidate or to share views on a common issue;

bureaucrat—An administrator in a large organization, often government; may refer to someone who slows things down by enforcing too many rules and red tape.

cabinet—The major departments of the federal government such as State and Defense, of which there are now 15.

calendars—The agendas or schedules for legislation in Congress.

casework—The efforts by members of Congress to solve voters' individual problems with the government; an important part of their constituency service.

caucus—A gathering of all the members of a political party serving in either house of Congress.

chain—Corporations that combine media in different cities under one ownership.

checks and balances—The constitutional principle that mixes together separate powers to give each branch some powers of the others; protects and balances the functions of government.

chief executive—The president's role as head of the executive branch and its federal bureaucracy.

chief of state—The role of the president as the symbolic head of the nation.

civil liberties—Legal protections against government restrictions on freedoms like speech, press, and religion.

civil rights—Legal protections against discrimination because of race, religion, ethnicity, or gender.

class action suits—Cases representing a whole class of people whose rights may have been violated.

client agency—Government departments representing and promoting the economic interests for which they were established, e.g., Labor Department helping unions.

coalition—A political grouping representing diverse interests organized to represent popular opinion on a particular issue.

commander-in-chief—The president's authority over the military; the principle behind civilian supremacy.

complete incorporationists—A judicial position that the entire Bill of Rights was extended beyond the federal government by the Fourteenth Amendment, and thus applies to the individual states.

concurrent powers—Those powers shared by the states and federal government, such as the power to tax.

conference committee—A temporary body of members from the two houses of Congress set up to resolve different versions of legislation passed by both houses.

consensus—A general agreement among the population on basic political questions and "rules of the game."

conspiracy theory—An unprovable belief that governments and specific policies or events (e.g., wars and assassinations) are controlled by a unified, secret, evil elite.

czars—Slang for officials appointed by President Obama to deal with specific issues requiring swift action; named after the Russian monarchs.

dealignment—Refers to the growing lack of popular support for either major party.

democracy—A form of government in which the people effectively participate.

deviating elections—Elections that show a temporary shift in voters' support away from the majority party.

due process—A phrase in the Fourteenth Amendment used to incorporate freedoms of the Bill of Rights to cover states' actions, including the rights to procedural fairness and impartiality by government officials.

electoral barriers—Legal obstacles to voting, such as residency and registration requirements.

electoral college—An antiquated constitutional provision whereby voters on election day select electors to reflect their state's choice for president.

elites—Those who get most of society's values, especially wealth and power.

equal protection—A clause in the Fourteenth Amendment used to prevent state officials and others from engaging in racial or sex discrimination.

equity—A flexible judicial doctrine that allows judges to resolve a case based on a sense of fairness.

exclusionary rule—A judicial rule that excludes any evidence obtained by illegal means.

exclusive and concurrent jurisdiction—Refers to whether federal courts have sole authority over a case (exclusive) or whether they share that authority with state courts (concurrent).

exclusive powers—Those powers only exercised by the federal government, such as the right to coin money.

executive agencies—Major departments of the government that are not in the Cabinet—for example, the National Aeronautics and Space Administration (NASA).

executive agreements—International agreements only needing approval by the president because they are usually less important than treaties.

federalism—The distribution of political authority between the federal government and the governments of the states.

Federalists—Supporters of the Constitution in the struggle to adopt it; they wanted a strong conservative central government.

Federal Reserve Board—A unique regulatory agency that overseas Federal Reserve Banks and general monetary policy, headed by its chairman, Ben Bernanke.

filibuster—The right under Senate rules to delay action by speaking for an unlimited amount of time, only stopped by a cloture vote requiring 60 senators.

First Amendment freedoms—Freedoms of religion, speech, press, and assembly.

Fourteenth Amendment—The post–Civil War amendment that has been used to extend the protections in the Bill of Rights to actions by state and local governments and by private individuals and groups.

fragmentation of power—A key pluralist perspective that no one group dominates American politics.

gerrymandering—Designing legislative districts to favor one party's candidates over another's.

GOP—Grand Old Party; the traditional nickname of the Republican party.

government—A political association that makes rules determining the distribution of values of a society and is the ultimate regulator of legitimate force.

grassroots campaigns—The effort to bring pressure on elected officials by mobilizing voters in their own districts and states using mail, phones, the Internet, or visits.

hyperpluralism—The view that participation by too many groups demanding too many resources from the government leads to political paralysis.

identity politics—Groups that organize on the basis of their religious, ethnic, or sexual identity and intensely pursue political objectives.

impeachment—The power of Congress to remove high officials of the executive or judicial branches from office for misconduct.

incumbent—An elected official currently in office with all the advantages that confers.

independents—Voters who publicly identify with neither major political party.

injunction—A court order preventing someone from violating someone else's rights.

interest group—An association organized to pursue a common interest by bringing pressure on the political process.

Internet—A global computer network allowing near-instant communication.

issue networks—Informal groupings of experts and lobbyists in and out of government organized to influence a specific policy.

joint committees—Permanent bodies including both senators and representatives, for example, the Joint Economic Committee.

judicial activism—The concept that the courts should be an active partner with the other branches of government in shaping policy.

judicial restraint—The opposing concept that the courts should not impose their views on other branches of the government except in extreme instances; a passive role for the courts.

judicial review—The federal courts' authority to decide on the constitutionality of the acts of state, local, and federal governments.

lame duck—The negative description of a president politically weakened because he is in the last months of his final term.

landmark decision—A judicial ruling that involves major changes in the law; e.g., *Brown* v. *Board of Education* ending legal racial segregation in public schools.

leadership PACs—Modern political machines established by congressional leaders to further their ambitions by raising funds for party colleagues. See PACs.

legitimacy—A publicly recognized quality of an institution like a family or government that makes the power of people connected to that institution both legal and correct.

limited government—The constitutional principle by which the powers of government are limited by the rights and liberties of the people.

lobbying—The process of influencing government policies by interest groups.

maintaining elections—Elections that continue the parties' popular support at the same level.

malapportionment—An outlawed practice of drawing legislative districts of grossly unequal population for political advantage.

marblecake federalism—The modern mix of overlapping relations between the states and the federal government.

Mayflower compact—An early example (1620) of American settlers' (Pilgrims) desire to be governed by a publicly accepted rule of law.

media—Those means of communications, such as television, Internet, and newspapers, that permit messages to be made public.

memorandum orders—The method by which the Supreme Court decides most cases without the need for oral arguments.

national agenda—The important political issues that are the current focus of public attention; gaining control of this agenda is a major aspect of presidential power.

national convention—An assembly of party delegates usually selected by primaries who meet every four years to nominate their party's candidates for president and vice president; it is the party's highest governing body.

news management—Techniques used by public officials to control information going to the media.

order—When the court requires someone to take a specified action to ensure someone else's rights.

original jurisdiction—The authority of the court to initially try cases.

oversight—A nonlegislative power of Congress to investigate and examine the activities of executive branch agencies.

PACs (political action committees)—Legally allowed organizations set up by private groups to raise campaign funds.

partial incorporationists—Judicial position that believes only major rights, such as the First Amendment freedoms, should be included in the Fourteenth Amendment and applied to the states.

partisans—Intense supporters of a political party.

party platform—A document stating the party's positions on issues.

plural elitism—A view of American politics as being divided into different policy arenas where various special interest elites dominate.

pluralism—A group theory of democracy that positively views the competition between many different groups as resulting in compromises that produce public policies.

political conflict—A widespread dispute over society's values—for example, wealth.

political efficacy—The sense of political effectiveness, for example that efforts like voting will produce results like a change in government policies.

political machine—A traditional locally based party organization led by a boss who controlled government jobs and services through loyalty and corruption.

political party—An organization that runs candidates for public office under the party's name.

political questions—Controversial issues that the courts refuse to deal with because they feel they lack the capacity and that other branches of government are more suited to resolve.

political science—The study of those social relations involving power and authority, especially those including government.

political socialization—The process of learning political attitudes and behavior.

politics—The process of who gets what, when, and how; actions among a number of people involving influence.

populism—American protest movements that periodically arise to protest dominance by an elite of the government or economy; present-day cultural populists represent religious conservatives opposing what they see as liberal control of the government and media.

pork barrel—Congressional actions designed to produce visible local benefits.

power elite—A theory that American politics is dominated by a unified nonrepresentative elite.

power—The ability to influence another's behavior.

precedent, or *stare decisis* The judicial practice by which the courts generally follow previous court decisions involving the same issue.

presidential primaries—Party elections held by states to determine which candidate's delegates will be sent to the national convention.

realigning elections—Elections that show a long-term shift in the popular base of support of the parties.

reciprocity—The congressional practice of members looking for guidance on legislation to members of their party on committees specializing in that area.

regulatory commissions—Agencies semi-independent from the rest of government charged with regulating parts of the economy—for example, the Federal Communications Commission (FCC).

Rehnquist court—The U.S. Supreme Court, from 1986 to 2005, named after the late Chief Justice, William Rehnquist.

Roberts court—The present Supreme Court from 2005, named after the current Chief Justice, John Roberts.

representative democracy—Government in which the people rule indirectly through elected representatives.

reserved powers—Those powers not delegated to the federal government that are reserved to the states or people by the Tenth Amendment.

residual powers—Those powers not spelled out in the Constitution but necessary for the president to carry out other responsibilities; used to expand the duties of the president.

ruling class—The economically privileged group that controls the major institutions of society according to the power elite view.

select or special committees—Temporary congressional panels established to do specific tasks, usually investigations; an example was the Select Bipartisan Committee to Investigate Hurricane Katrina.

Senate majority leader—Leader of the Senate majority party and the Senate equivalent to the House Speaker, currently Democrat Harry Reid of Nevada.

senatorial courtesy—The practice of the Senate to only approve judicial nominees who are acceptable to the senator from that state.

seniority—An informal congressional rule by which the chairman of a committee is automatically the member from the majority party who has served the longest on the committee; also refers to positions of power within the committee being assigned on the basis of longest service.

separation of powers—A constitutional principle that the powers of government should be separated into three branches of government—legislative, executive, and judicial.

single-member district—An electoral system of electing one member of Congress from each district; considered an obstacle to the rise of minor parties.

social class—A major social division based on occupation and income and the awareness this produces of relations toward other classes.

social sciences—The academic disciplines, such as history, economics, or political science, that study relationships among people.

sound bite—A brief video clip of a candidate or political official speaking.

Speaker of the House—The head of the House of Representatives and the leader of the majority party, currently Democrat Nancy Pelosi of California.

specialization—A congressional custom that members will remain on the same committee and become experts in its issues.

spin—Slang for putting a self-serving, favorable interpretation or slant on the news given to the media and public by government officials.

spoils system—Widespread practice of filling government positions with supporters of the winning politicians; largely replaced by the civil service.

standing committees—The permanent specialized units of both houses that draft legislation in subject areas like taxes and agriculture.

State of the Union address—Major presidential speech before Congress at the beginning of the year outlining the administration's legislative program.

strict constructionism—A judicial philosophy used by modern conservatives to limit the power of the courts to the original intentions of the framers of the U.S. Constitution.

Supreme Court of the United States—The head of the federal court system, composed of a chief justice and eight associate justices.

suspect classifications—A judicial doctrine that laws involving race, religion, or ethnicity will be subject to close scrutiny by the courts because they are presumed invalid.

term limits—Popular effort to limit the number of times that state legislators or members of Congress can run for reelection.

test case—Brought by interested groups seeking to establish a favorable precedent by the courts concerning a major violation of civil rights or liberties affecting a large number of people.

TV networks—Corporations owning nationwide local television outlets to whom they produce and sell programs.

U.S. courts of appeals—Thirteen federal courts above the district courts, which mainly hear appeals from those courts.

U.S. district courts—The federal courts where most cases involving federal law are first tried.

veto—A president's constitutional power to refuse to sign legislation, thus preventing it from becoming law unless overridden by a two-thirds vote of both houses of Congress.

Warren Court—Activist Supreme Court from 1953 to 1969 under Chief Justice Earl Warren; noted for landmark liberal decisions applying to civil rights and liberties and legislative reapportionment.

whips—Floor leaders in Congress who work to coordinate votes and assist the heads of the parties in both houses.

writ of certiorari—Order of a higher court to a lower court to send the record of a case for review.

INDEX